The Wonders of Language

Ian Roberts offers a stimulating introduction to our greatest gift as a species: our capacity for articulate language. We are mostly as blissfully unaware of the intricacies of the structure of language as fish are of the water they swim in. We live in a mental ocean of nouns, verbs, quantifiers, morphemes, vowels and other rich, strange and deeply fascinating linguistic objects. This book introduces the reader to this amazing world.

Offering a thought-provoking and accessible introduction to the main discoveries and theories about language, the book is aimed at general readers and undergraduates who are curious about linguistics and language. Written in a lively and direct style, technical terms are carefully introduced and explained and the book includes a full glossary. The book covers all the central areas of linguistics, including phonetics, phonology, morphology, syntax, semantics and pragmatics, as well as historical linguistics, sociolinguistics and psycholinguistics.

Ian Roberts has taught in Switzerland, Wales and Germany, and is currently Professor of Linguistics at the University of Cambridge. He has published six monographs and two textbooks, and has edited several collections of articles.

GW00645537

The Wonders of Language

Or How to Make Noises and Influence People

IAN ROBERTS
University of Cambridge

 CAMBRIDGE
UNIVERSITY PRESS

CAMBRIDGE
UNIVERSITY PRESS

University Printing House, Cambridge CB2 8BS, United Kingdom

One Liberty Plaza, 20th Floor, New York, NY 10006, USA

477 Williamstown Road, Port Melbourne, VIC 3207, Australia

4843/24, 2nd Floor, Ansari Road, Daryaganj, Delhi - 110002, India

79 Anson Road, #06-04/06, Singapore 079906

Cambridge University Press is part of the University of Cambridge.

It furthers the University's mission by disseminating knowledge in the pursuit of education, learning and research at the highest international levels of excellence.

www.cambridge.org
Information on this title: www.cambridge.org/9781316604410

© Ian Roberts 2017

First published 2017

A catalogue record for this publication is available from the British Library

Library of Congress Cataloging in Publication data
Names: Roberts, Ian G., author.
Title: The wonders of language : or how to make noises and influence people / Ian Roberts.
Other titles: How to make noises and influence people
Description: Cambridge : Cambridge University Press, [2016] | Includes bibliographical references and index.
Identifiers: LCCN 2016023663| ISBN 9781107149939 (hardback) | ISBN 9781316604410 (paperback)
Subjects: LCSH: Language awareness. | Speech acts (Linguistics) | Applied linguistics. | Language acquisition. | Linguistics–Study and teaching.
Classification: LCC P53.454 .R63 2016 | DDC 410–dc23 LC record available at https://lccn.loc.gov/2016023663

ISBN 978-1-107-14993-9 Hardback
ISBN 978-1-316-60441-0 Paperback

This book is dedicated to Miss Arabella Poulson, Consultant Vitreoretinal Surgeon at Addenbrooke's Hospital, Cambridge, who, in the summer of 2013, saved my sight.

Contents

List of Figures   viii
List of Tables   ix
Acknowledgements   x

Introduction   1

1   How to Make Noises: Phonetics   6
2   How to Organise Noises: Phonology   27
3   How to Build a Word: Morphology   45
4   How to Say Absolutely Anything You Want To: Syntax   63
5   How to Build a World: Semantics   81
6   How to Influence People: Pragmatics   105
7   How to Find Lost Languages: Historical Linguistics   118
8   How to Influence the Right People: Sociolinguistics   139
9   How to Lose a Language and How to Learn a Language: Psycholinguistics   151
10   How to Build a Language: Language Typology and Universals   169

Epilogue: More about Cats and Extra-terrestrials   181
Further Reading   183
Glossary   186
Index   221

Figures

1.1 The Organs of Speech   [7]

1.2 Spectrogram of *a pea* [ə pʰiː]   [12]

1.3 Short Vowels of Standard Southern British English   [20]

1.4 Some British English Diphthongs Plotted on the Equilateral   [22]

1.5 British English Closing Diphthongs   [23]

2.1 Spectrograms of Normal British English Pronunciation of *pie* and *spy*   [29]

7.1 Indo-European Family Tree   [126]

8.1 Isogloss for the /ʊ/ vs /ʌ/ variants in *sun*, etc.   [141]

9.1 Left Hemisphere of the Brain, Showing Broca's and Wernicke's Areas   [155]

Tables

1.1 English Fricatives   [11]

1.2 English Stops and Nasals   [15]

1.3 English Consonants   [16]

1.4 Centring Diphthongs and Their Counterparts   [23]

2.1 Vowel Phonemes of Standard British English (A Conservative Variety)   [32]

2.2 Distinctive Features for Simple Vowels of English (Non-Diphthongs)   [36]

2.3 Distinctive Features for Non-Obstruent Consonants and Semi-Vowels   [36]

2.4 Distinctive Features for English Obstruents (No Affricates)   [37]

3.1 Present-Tense Forms Italian *cantare*   [55]

3.2 Other Tenses of Italian *cantare*   [56]

3.3 Case and Number Forms of Latin *discipulus*   [59]

7.1 Systematic Correspondences among Modern Romance Languages   [123]

7.2 Latin-Greek-Sanskrit Correspondences   [125]

7.3 English-Latin Consonant Correspondences   [127]

7.4 Indo-European Numerals   [130]

7.5 An Old English Case Paradigm   [136]

Acknowledgements

This book was written at the suggestion of my son, Julian. I responded to his suggestion by saying that there was no way I could write an introductory book like this, even if I had the time. So here it is.

I'd like to thank Andrew Winnard of Cambridge University Press for excellent proposals for improving the first draft (which was too funny; as you'll see, this draft isn't), three anonymous reviewers for Cambridge University Press for correcting one or two embarrassing factual slips among many other things, Francis Nolan for help with spectrograms, and Jeffrey Watumull for helping me to keep my faith in aliens. And, of course, Clover for reasons that will become obvious.

Every effort has been made to trace or contact all copyright-holders. The publisher will be pleased to make good any omissions or rectify any mistakes brought to their attention at the earliest opportunity. Apologies are expressed for any omission.

Introduction

Spaceships are hard to build. After all, that really *is* rocket science. As far as anyone knows, spaceships have been successfully built by exactly one civilisation in the entire history of the universe: by post-1957 humans (the Space Age actually happens to coincide exactly with my lifetime, although I had nothing to do with it). We're pretty justified in thinking ourselves rather clever to build machines that can get us off our own planet.

Coming closer to home for a moment, my cat Clover (who will pop up here and there in the chapters to follow) is extremely clever, too, in his feline way. But the idea of him and his furry friends building a spaceship is completely absurd, of course. Chimps, who allegedly share around 98 percent of their genes with us, also show no interplanetary ambitions. What's in the other 2 percent of our genes that makes this vast difference?

Think about space travel for a minute: what depth and breadth of knowledge made those journeys possible? It requires knowledge of physics, maths, the human body, the cosmos and so much more. Where does all of this knowledge reside and how is it transmitted? It's mostly in the heads of scientists, and they transmit it by teaching each other. Our 2 percent extra special non-chimp genome must make all of that knowledge, and its successful trans-mission, possible. Moreover, a great deal of that knowledge is quite new; it didn't really exist before the mid-twentieth century. Where did it come from? Ideas in people's heads, obviously. Clever people, these rocket scientists, but people nonetheless; not (as far as we know) extra-terrestrials, Gods or computers and certainly not chimps.

Our extra 2 percent makes us extremely good – by the standards of everything else in the known universe, unbelievably,

extraordinarily, *cosmically* good – at generating, storing and transmitting knowledge. How do we do it? With *language*, mostly. In fact,
almost everything we do – and everything that makes us different
from chimps – we do with language. Try to imagine the world
without language. Try to imagine the chimps' language-less world,
or Clover's: no names, no descriptions, no way to store, transmit or
receive ideas. No wonder they're so hopeless at space travel.

It's a reasonable assumption that whatever gives us the
biological capacity for language is in the chimp-free 2 percent of
the human genome, although I'm not going to speculate here
about 'language genes' or 'grammar chromosomes' and whatnot.
Neither am I going to say anything about the evolution of language,
as far too little is known about that topic.

Instead, I want to introduce you to what I think is our greatest
gift as a species: our ability to make noises and influence people.
We are mostly as blissfully unaware of the intricacies of the
structure of language as fish are of the water they swim in. We
live in a mental ocean of nouns, verbs, quantifiers, morphemes,
vowels and other rich, strange and deeply fascinating linguistic
objects. I want to introduce you to this amazing world and help
you to reflect on it. That way, you reflect on what you really are –
the 2 percent of you that isn't chimp, that is.

∿

The book's ten chapters each deal with an area of linguistics where
there is by now a reasonable body of knowledge. Of course, all
scientific knowledge is a work in progress, and there are as many
loose ends, false trails, blind alleys and leaps in the dark as there
are metaphors to mix. But my goal here is not to set a received
body of knowledge about language in stone but to try to impart
the fascination, wonder and, at times, the mystery of the worlds of
language.

So we begin with the noises themselves: the study of the
sounds of language, or **phonetics** (I present the main technical

terms in **bold** when I first introduce them; the Glossary at the end of the book gives brief definitions of them). Then we move on to the ways in which those sounds are organised in languages; in language, what you hear isn't always what you get. Moreover, some people can't hear: deaf communities the world over use **sign languages**, and one of the big discoveries of recent linguistics is that sign languages are full languages in all respects, even having phonetics and phonology (see the note at the end of this section for more discussion). This study of sound patterns in languages is known as **phonology**. After this, we go on to word structure, or **morphology**. Here we'll see how to divide words up into little packets of meaning and form known as **morphemes**. We'll also see the different ways morphemes can combine to form words of varying complexity. Then we come to the big two: **syntax** and **semantics**. Syntax is the real engine of language, at once the most abstract and the most central piece of the whole picture. Syntax tells us how to match sounds and meanings over a limitless range of possible sentences. Semantics is where the tyre hits the road: it's about how we actually express ourselves, how language and non-language hook up and how the infinite forms created by syntax can be given meaning. Syntax and semantics are hard, possibly the hardest parts of this book.

In language, what you get is often more than what you hear (or see, in the case of writing or sign language). **Pragmatics** tells us how even very simple utterances can be given a much richer meaning in context than what they appear to really wear on their sleeve. The interaction of pragmatics with semantics is very intricate and subtle, as we'll see.

Then we move on to the wider fields. Next is **historical linguistics**, the study of how languages change over time and how language families can be established. Here we'll see how we can re-invent, or reconstruct, lost languages.

Socio- and **psycholinguistics** take up the next two chapters. As their names suggest, these are hybrid fields where linguistics meets sociology and psychology respectively. In the sociolinguistics chapter, I'll concentrate on how a person's language can reveal much about their social class, age or gender and how people's acute intuitive awareness of these issues can be investigated. Psycholinguistics is a huge subject, dealing as it does with all of the questions relating language, mind and brain. One really important and absolutely compelling question comes up here: how do very young children learn their first language? We'll see that this simple and innocent-looking question makes contact with centuries-old philosophical debates. Finally, we'll look at **language typology**, the study of ways to classify the world's languages. Here we'll look at some of the ways in which the languages of the world vary, and we'll touch on the question of whether and how they may all in some way be the same: the vexed question of language universals.

As I mentioned above, some of the chapters are a bit more difficult than others. I haven't shied away from presenting some rather technical material here and there, and I hope it won't seem too dull. The thing to remember if and when the going gets a bit tough is that we're trying to understand something truly amazing: our ability to invent, store and transmit new thoughts – what makes it possible for us to build spaceships (after all, you've got to be able to think about them first). But if you find certain passages a bit off-putting, skip them. You can always come back to them later. My goal here is above all to try to show you how we can approach an understanding of the wonders of language and to pique your curiosity about the ideas that linguists have been developing about those wonders. Inevitably, some chapters are a bit more technical than others, but feel free to dip in and out. This isn't a whodunit, so you won't miss out on any crucial plot details if you don't read everything in sequence.

I truly hope you'll enjoy reading this book. Fish will never understand the water they swim in; but, precisely because you have language, you can begin to understand your linguistic habitat. You are smart enough to be able to be a fish out of water.

A note on noise: language is mostly expressed through speech, or more precisely through the oral/aural channel. Hence my talk of noises here and below. But of course language doesn't have to be expressed this way. One of its amazing properties is that it can be transmitted in several different ways, through quite different channels, and yet it is fundamentally the same in all of them. So, right now, you're probably reading this silently (and I'm writing silently except for the occasional sotto-voce imprecation aimed at my laptop). It's fairly clear that writing is parasitic on speech: it's learned later (or not at all), and it's a much more recent invention, being about 5,000 years old as far as we know (while speech is estimated to be anywhere from 50,000 to over 100,000 years old).

But there's another channel for language that has assumed increasing importance in linguistics in recent years: sign. Sign involves transmission of language through the gestural-visual channel. As mentioned above, one of the more significant discoveries in linguistics in recent decades has been that sign languages (of which there are very many, all over the world) are languages in every sense of the word. They show all the structural features of oral-aural languages, including, strikingly, phonetics and phonology. Ineptitude and lack of space combine to mean that I won't say anything more about sign here, but if you're interested, see the suggestions in the Further Reading section at the end of the book.

1 How to Make Noises
Phonetics

Read this sentence aloud slowly and carefully, feeling what your tongue, lips and other **speech organs** are up to. Then pronounce it at normal speed, which takes about five seconds. The sentence contains sixty-eight sounds. As far as we know, no other species on earth has this degree of fine control over their counterparts of the human speech organs, whose primary role – and what they mainly evolved for – was something else: chewing, swallowing and breathing mainly.

But of course language isn't just pyrotechnics; we're not just making noises for fun. Our five-second, sixty-eight-sound burst of intricate activity by the tongue, lips and so on results in noises that *mean something*. If you produce that five-second, sixty-eight-sound gyration, I can understand what the words mean (which of course means finding the words in there, and then putting them together somehow). And I can do it *in real time*. You don't have to wait, not even for a few seconds, after finishing your cleverly modulated exhalation for me to register it, process it and come up with an answer; I can do it (almost) instantaneously. This, the simplest everyday currency of human interaction, is a staggeringly complex physical and neurological feat, so complex that there remains much that we don't understand. But we do know a fair bit, and over the next few chapters we'll look at some aspects of what is going on in these banal everyday speech interactions. We begin by looking at the noises themselves.

The main topics of this chapter are:

- **Consonants** and how to classify them
- **Vowels** and how to classify them
- **The International Phonetic Alphabet**
- A sketch of the phonetics of English

Normally we speak by modulating air exhaled from the lungs. This is the only way we do it in normal English although some languages make partial use of other **air-streams** (as they are called). The passage from the **larynx** through to the lips (as well as the alternative exit through the nose) is known as the **vocal tract**. The various organs that the airstream encounters on its way out from the lungs are the **organs of speech**. A diagram of the organs of speech is given in Figure 1.1.

Consonants modulate the airflow by creating an obstacle that creates a noise in one way or another. Vowels modulate it by altering the shape of the vocal tract so that it resonates in different ways. Now let's look at these two basic types of speech sound in turn. I'll limit the discussion and illustrations largely to (Standard British) English, although of course other languages have other sounds, one or two of which I'll briefly mention.

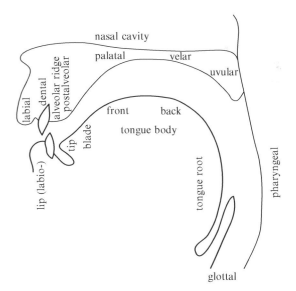

Figure 1.1 The Organs of Speech.
(Source: http://photos1.blogger.com/blogger/6995/1840/320/speech.jpg)

Consonants

Let's start with consonants, as they're easier to feel, in a way. Actually, it's a good idea to practice making the various noises that I'll be talking about as we go along; I promise you'll be able to do them all. It might be a good idea to do your phonetics practice somewhere private, as your friends, relatives and possibly your pets may be alarmed by some of the noises you start to emit.

So, start with an *s*-sound. Pretend you're a snake and just say the longest '*s*' you can: [sssssssssssssssss].

Notation: phonetic symbols are given in square brackets []. Phonetic [s] corresponds to the English spelling <s>, and spellings, as you can see, are given in angled brackets <>.

Now stop hissing and make the longest '*z*' sound you can: [zzzzzzzzzzzzzzzzz] (a bee rather than a snake). Now (and this is where you really should be somewhere private), put your finger on your Adam's Apple and repeat the long '*s*', followed immediately by the '*z*', followed again by the '*s*': [sssszzzzsssszzzz]. Do that a few times. You should be able to feel vibration in your larynx when you're saying the *z*'s, which is turned off when you say the *s*'s. Everything else, notably the position of your tongue, is the same. You should in fact be able to feel that the sides of your tongue are touching an area just above and behind your top teeth (this is called the **alveolar ridge**, see Figure 1.1), while there's a little groove down the middle of your tongue, right to the tip, through which the air is passing. The [s] and [z] sounds both have the same **place of articulation**, i.e. the tongue and all of the other organs of speech are in the same position for both sounds. What distinguishes them is the vibration that you can feel in your larynx – this is called **voicing**. So we call [z] a **voiced, alveolar, fricative**: 'voiced' because your larynx is buzzing, 'alveolar' because of the position of your tongue and 'fricative' because the air becomes turbulent passing through that little groove in your tongue and the gap between your tongue and your top teeth, creating a high-frequency noise. Correspondingly, we call [s] a voiceless alveolar fricative. It's an alveolar fricative like [z] – same place of articulation, tongue and all other speech organs in the same place – but the larynx is switched off, so there's no voicing.

What's really going on in the larynx that makes the difference between [s] and [z]? Some aspects of voicing are quite complex – both in terms of the physics of the airstream and the very precise anatomical position of the **vocal folds** (commonly but inaccurately called the vocal cords) – so I won't go into full detail here. Suffice it to say that when there is no voicing the vocal folds are at rest and apart, as in normal breathing, so the air passes through on its way out from the lungs unimpeded; thus, there is no acoustic effect. Voicing is produced when the vocal folds are drawn together in such a way as to create turbulence in the passing airstream, giving the acoustic effect of a kind of buzzing sound (this will be lower frequency in adult males as their larynxes are somewhat bigger than women's and children's). It is also possible to close the vocal folds completely. We'll come back to the **glottal stop** – the sound that emerges when your vocal folds pop open again and air comes rushing out – later.

Let's come back to fricatives. Try saying a really long [f]-sound: [ffffffffffff] (here you might imagine wanting to use a certain swear word but feeling too polite to get beyond the first consonant). Now say a long [v]-sound: [vvvvvvvvv]. Now alternate them with your finger on your larynx again: [ffffvvvvffffvvvv]. You should notice the same effect as earlier with the [s]'s and [z]'s. That's because [f] is voiceless (no laryngeal buzz, vocal folds apart and at rest), while [v] is voiced (larynx 'switched on', vocal folds vibrating). But the place of articulation of [f] and [v] is different to that for [s] and [z]. In fact, you should be able to feel it quite easily: your top teeth are just lightly touching your lower lip, just enough to create high-ish frequency noise in the airstream (lower than the noise in [s] and [z]). For these reasons, we call them **labio-dental** fricatives; *labio* for 'lip' and *dental* for 'teeth'. So [f] is a voiceless labio-dental fricative and [v] is a voiced labio-dental fricative.

Here's another pair of fricatives: try saying a really long '*th*'-sound (imagine a lisping snake). Since English awkwardly writes this single sound with two letters, the International Phonetic Alphabet (IPA) symbol is the Greek letter theta: [θθθθθθθθθθ]. Now, putting your finger on your larynx you should feel nothing: [θ] is voiceless. Its place of articulation? You should be able to feel your tongue between your teeth, or more precisely the part just behind the tip of your tongue (called the '**blade**') pushing against your top teeth, again creating turbulence and making a high-frequency noise. So we call this an **interdental** fricative.

Now put your finger against your larynx and try to switch on the voicing. You should hear a sort of 'dddhhh' sound. This sound is also, confusingly, written <th> in English: it's the <th> of *mother, brother, father, this, that, those, these* and *the* (the other sound written <th>, the voiceless [θ], is that of *earth, birth, mirth* and *thing*, for example). The phonetic symbol for the voiced <th> sound is [ð] (an old Germanic letter, still used in Modern Icelandic, called 'eth'). So [θ] is a voiceless interdental fricative and [ð] is a voiced interdental fricative.

One final pair of English fricatives. The voiceless one is the sound usually written <sh>, as in *shop, ship* and *fish*. If you compare this with [s], for example by saying *sip* then *ship* in quick succession, you'll feel your tongue move backwards and change shape for the articulation of the <sh> sound, with the sides of the tongue curling up slightly. This sound, since it's articulated a little behind the position for the alveolar fricatives [s] and [z], is known as **post-alveolar**. Again, since it's a single sound written with two letters in English, we use the IPA symbol [ʃ]. The voiced counterpart of [ʃ] is found in the middle of words such as *measure, leisure* and *treasure*, as well as in words like *rouge*. You can tell it's the voiced counterpart of [ʃ] by applying the usual finger-on-larynx test. The IPA symbol for this sound (which doesn't have a unique or terribly consistent spelling in English) is [ʒ]. So [ʃ] is a voiceless post-alveolar fricative and [ʒ] is a voiced post-alveolar fricative.

So, now we've seen almost all of the fricatives of English, which we can put in a table as follows:

Table 1.1 *English Fricatives*

	Labio-dental	Interdental	Alveolar	Post-alveolar
Voiced	v	ð	z	ʒ
Voiceless	f	θ	s	ʃ

Standard English has one other fricative, [h] as in *hill, hair* and *hide*. This sound is made by the creation of slight turbulence – but no voicing – as the air passes through the larynx. Accordingly, it is technically a voiceless glottal fricative. English has no voiced counterpart to [h], although this sound is found in Czech, Hebrew and a few other languages.

Some varieties of English, notably Liverpudlian and some types of Scots, have another fricative, the 'guttural' sound at the end of *loch*. This sound is also found in German, as in the name of the composer, *Bach*, and in Welsh, where *bach* means 'little'. To pronounce this sound, raise the back of your tongue towards the roof of your mouth, keeping the tip and blade in their resting position behind the back teeth. The IPA symbol for this sound is [x]. Raising the tongue as just described causes turbulence as the air passes between the tongue and the **soft palate** or **velum** (see Figure 1.1). Accordingly, this is called a voiceless velar fricative. If you can switch the voicing on while pronouncing [x], you'll get the sound written in IPA as [ɣ], the voiced velar fricative. This sound is how the <g> is pronounced in a Spanish word like *avogado* ('lawyer').

Next, we come to **stop consonants**. As their name implies, stop consonants involve a complete blockage of the vocal tract. To see this, try pronouncing a [p] (as in *pea, pee* or 20*p*). You can easily tell that it involves closing your lips. If you try to 'hold' the [p], you'll feel air pressure building up behind your lips. If you then open your lips, the pressure is released with a little explosion of air, making the characteristic sound of a [p]. (In fact, you can't really hold a [p] for any length of time without going blue in the face – again, this is because your lips are completely blocking the airflow to and from your lungs). Interestingly, then, you can only really 'hear' a [p] when you finish pronouncing it; the 'hold' phase of a [p] consists of silence. This can be seen in a spectrogram, as shown in Figure 1.2.

The 'release' phase – the little explosion – is what we hear. For this reason, stops are also known as **plosives**. Since the articulation of [p] involves closing both lips, it is known as a **bilabial** stop. Furthermore, the silence during the hold phase indicates that [p] is voiceless, so the full description of [p] is voiceless bilabial stop.

The voiced counterpart of [p] is [b] (as in *bee*, *bear*, *brain*, etc). If you try to hold a [b] you'll notice the same build-up of air behind your closed lips as for [p], but you'll also notice a kind of repressed grunt coming from your larynx. This is the effect of the vocal folds vibrating while the lips are closed, so the air coming from the lungs is affected by the action of the vocal folds in the same way as for the voiced fricatives but then gets

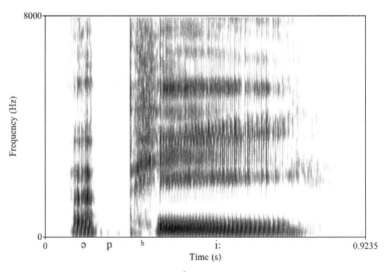

Figure 1.2 Spectrogram of *a pea* [ə pʰiː]; the moment of silence in the 'hold' phase of the articulation of [p] is clearly visible.
(Source: Phonetics Laboratory, University of Cambridge)

blocked behind the closed lips. In the release phase, there is again a small explosion as the lips part, as for [p]. So [b] is a voiced bilabial stop.

There are two other pairs of stops in English: [t, d] and [k, g]. Each of these is a voiceless-voiced pair, as for [p] and [b], and each involves blockage of a different place in the vocal tract. The [t, d] pair are alveolar stops. So here the blockage is at the alveolar ridge, the place where the fricatives [s] and [z] are articulated, as we saw. Pronounce a [t] and you should be able to feel your tongue (for most English speakers, it's the blade of the tongue) against the alveolar ridge just behind your top teeth. As you might expect by now, [d] is pronounced at the same place but with the larynx buzzing.

The [k, g] pair are pronounced by raising the back of the tongue to the velum (or soft palate), as we saw for the velar fricatives [x, ɣ]. If you pronounce *key* and *ghee*, you should be able to feel this. Again, holding the [k] produces silence while the air builds up behind the blockage, and holding [g] produces a little grunt from the larynx.

Before leaving the stops, we should come back to the glottal stop. Remember that this is produced by closing the vocal folds completely, causing air pressure to build up below the larynx and giving rise to the usual little explosion when they pop open. Glottal stops are common in English, especially British English, although there is no standard spelling for them. The glottal stop is common in the colloquial Southern British English pronunciation of <t> in between vowels, in a word like *water*; this pronunciation is sometimes written *wa'er* in an attempt to indicate the glottal stop. The IPA symbol for the glottal stop is [ʔ] (note that this symbol isn't the same as a question mark '?'). So we can write the colloquial pronunciation of *water* as [wɔːʔə] (don't worry about the vowel symbols [ɔː] and [ə] for now; we'll get to those later). The 'correct' British pronunciation of *water* can be written in IPA as [wɔːtə].

Our next little group of consonants are the **nasals**. As the name implies, their articulation involves the **nasal cavity** (see again Figure 1.1). The airstream gets access to the nasal cavity when the velum is lowered, allowing the air to pass through it. In normal, at rest, breathing the mouth is closed and the air goes in and out this way, as you notice when you get a cold and your nose is bunged up and you have to breathe through your mouth.

In speaking, of course, the mouth is mostly open (except when bilabial stops are being pronounced). And in the pronunciation of all of the consonants we've seen so far, the velum is raised, preventing the airstream from getting out through the nose – hence the silence in the hold phase of voiceless stops. Since nasals involve air going out through the nasal cavity, their articulation involves the velum being lowered to allow this. In the oral cavity, however, there is the same complete blockage as in the stops, and so the only way for the air to get out is through the nose. You can see this if you try to say a long [m]: [mmmmmmmmmmmm]. Now try saying [mmmmmmmm] while holding your nose. You'll find you can't, and you'll quickly feel the air pressure building up in your nasal cavity (you can actually pop your ears this way). This is because pronouncing [m] involves closing the lips, but lowering the velum so the air flows out through the nose. So when you block your nose, the air has no way out. The resonance in the nasal cavity gives [m] its acoustic characteristics. You'll notice that the larynx is switched on when you say [mmmmmmmmmmm]. So [m] is a voiced bilabial nasal (technically it's a stop, since the airstream is blocked in the oral cavity).

English has two other nasals. There is the alveolar [n] (as in *night, nun, noon*, etc), pronounced with blockage at the same place of articulation in the oral cavity as [t] and [d] but, again, with the velum lowered allowing the airstream to pass through the nasal cavity. For example, try saying [nnnnnnnn] and holding your nose. Then there is the velar nasal, which English writes as <ng>, as in *king, thing* and *bringing*, for example. The IPA symbol for the velar nasal is [ŋ]. This nasal is pronounced like the stops [k] and [g] but with the velum lowered so the air goes out through the nose. Try the nose-holding test again and you'll see.

The English stops and nasals are given in Table 1.2.

Table 1.2 *English Stops and Nasals*

	Bilabial	Alveolar	Velar	Glottal
Voiceless stop	p	t	k	ʔ
Voiced stop	b	d	g	
Nasal	m	n	ŋ	

English has two **affricates**, a voiced and voiceless pair again. The voiced one is usually written <j> or <dg>, as in *judge*, where it occurs twice, once in each spelling. The voiceless one is usually written <ch>, as in *church* (again occurring twice). Affricates are complex sounds, involving a stop phase followed by a slow-release phase, so that as the articulators come apart from the stop phase, some turbulence characteristic of the fricatives is created, rather than a neat little explosion as in the case of 'pure' stops. Because they have two parts from a phonetic perspective, the IPA writes these affricates as digraphs. The English affricates involve an alveolar stop but with post-alveolar release, which is the tongue moving back from the point of blockage (you can feel this if you say *jump* or *chump* really slowly). Thus, the IPA combines the symbols for alveolar stops with those for post-alveolar fricatives: [dʒ] as in *jump* and [tʃ] as in *chump*.

There are just two more consonants in English, usually known as the **liquids**. These are the **lateral** [l], as in *leap* or *peel*, and the rather complex [r]. The lateral [l] is so called because the tongue makes a blockage, again with the blade against the alveolar ridge, but the sides of the tongue are held down so that air passes through that way. This consonant gets its name from this lateral airflow. There's no turbulence here, so [l] isn't a fricative.

The Standard English [r] is rather complex, as I already mentioned. Try to hold the [r] in a word like *round* and you will probably notice several things: your lips are pursed and your tongue is bunched forwards towards, but not touching, the alveolar ridge, in fact it's in the post-alveolar area. There's also voicing, as you'll note in the usual way. There isn't any blockage of the airstream here.

In many languages, the sound written <r> is very different to the English one. In quite a few languages, it is an alveolar trill, involving the tongue vibrating against the alveolar ridge. This is what we find in Spanish and Italian, for example (it is also found in many varieties of Scots English). The French <r> is different again, involving the uvula, an articulator not used in Standard English.

Since neither [l] nor [r] involve either turbulence or blockage of the vocal tract, they are neither fricatives nor stops. Since they do involve turbulence and blockage, fricatives and stops can be grouped together as **obstruents** (obstructing the airstream). Sounds like [l] and [r], on the other hand, can be classed as **sonorants**, since they are more 'sonorous' (admittedly a rather subjective notion) than the other consonants of English.

So now we have the complete inventory of the consonants of Standard English, shown in Table 1.3.

Table 1.3 *English Consonants*

	Bilabial	Labio-dental	Alveolar	Post-alveolar	Velar	Glottal
Stop	p, b		t, d		k, g	ʔ
Nasal	m		n		ŋ	
Fricative		f, v	s, z	ʃ, ʒ	(x)	h
Affricate				ʧ, ʤ		
Sonorant			l	r		

Vowels

Vowels differ from consonants in that they don't involve any blockage of the airstream going through the vocal tract, but rather alter its shape so that the cavities in the vocal tract resonate in different ways, producing different patterns of harmonics which give rise to the different 'qualities' we hear in different vowels. The detailed study of these harmonics is fascinating and would take us well into the domain of acoustic phonetics, the study of the physics of the speech sounds.

The shape of the cavities of the vocal tract can be changed in three main ways. You can do it by rounding or spreading your lips, by moving your tongue so as to change the shape of the oral cavity, or by opening and closing the velum to let air out through the nose (or not). In Standard English, all vowels are oral, i.e. they are produced with the velum raised so that air goes out through the mouth only. So the third option isn't active in English (it is in French, which has three or four nasalised vowels, depending on the dialect).

The options for moving the tongue around in the mouth are quite complex: the tongue is a very mobile, muscular organ. But we can simplify a bit and describe many English vowels in terms of two dimensions for the tongue: it can move forwards and backwards and up and down. So we classify vowels as front, central or **back**, according to the tongue's position in the horizontal dimension, and **high**, mid or **low**, according to its position in the vertical dimension. The position of the lips offers a further classification into **rounded** (lips pursed) and **unrounded** (lips spread or neutral).

Now try saying the words 'really small' in as slow and drawn-out a way as you can: 'reeeeeeeaaaaaaaally smaaaaaaaaaall'. As you say the <ea> of 'reeeeeeeaaaaally' you can feel your lips spread and the body of your tongue raised to a position close to – but not touching – the roof of your mouth (actually the **hard palate**). So this vowel is a high (tongue raised), front (tongue forward), unrounded (lips spread) vowel. The IPA symbol for this vowel is [i].

Note: English spelling is highly idiosyncratic. For this reason, we'll see a lot of mismatches between the spellings of English vowels and their IPA symbols. The reason for this is that English is spelled roughly the way it was pronounced in about 1450. The pronunciation of the vowels has changed a lot since then, but the spelling hasn't.

Transition from 'reeeeeeeeeaaaaaaaaally' to 'smaaaaaaaaaaaall'. You can feel you tongue dropping and backing inside your mouth (your lower jaw opens a bit too) while your lips purse. This is because the vowel written <a> in *small* is a low (tongue dropped), back (tongue backed), rounded (lips pursed) vowel, IPA [ɔ].

Warning to American readers: I'm describing the (Southern) British English pronunciations here and below. American English has a somewhat different vowel system, especially as regards the phonetics. It would take too long, almost a whole book in itself, to systematically point out all of the differences (and of course, there are differences among American varieties, especially in the South and in New England). I'll point out the most important ones, and I apologise for not being able to do more. You may also want to try and follow the descriptions of the British pronunciations here, and see how you sound (I make no guarantees, but you might have some fun with it anyway). An immediate example is the <a> in *small*, which in most American varieties has the tongue in about the same position as in British English but the lips are neutral rather than rounded. The same warning applies to most speakers of Scots or Irish varieties of English, which are different again. I'll come back to some of these questions in Chapter 8.

Now say 'smaaaaaaaaall caaarrrrrr'. Here you can feel your tongue move forward from the position for the [ɔ] of *small*, down a bit (with the jaw opening a bit more) and the lips unpursing. So the vowel of *car* is a low, central and unrounded vowel, IPA [ɑ]. (If you're American, Scottish or Irish, you probably also pronounce the <r> in *car*; if you're English, Australian or a New Zealander, you probably don't. We'll come back to this in Chapter 8).

Next, say 'Are you . . . ?' as slowly as you can (some of you may remember the scene in *The Railway Children* where the children first encounter the Russian migrant, and politely speaking very slowly, ask him 'Are you Welsh?'). The vowel in *are* is the same as the one in *car*, [ɑ]. Going from *are* to *you*, you can feel your tongue move up and back (with your lower jaw closing partially) and your lips pursing. That's because the <ou> of *you* is high (tongue raised), back (tongue retracted) and rounded (lips pursed), IPA [u].

These four vowels are the principal **long vowels** of English. In IPA, long vowels are written with a colon after them, [iː, ɑː, ɔː, uː]. English, particularly British English, has an unusually complex vowel system compared to many languages. In addition to the long vowels, there are several **short vowels**, as well as a number of diphthongs (I'll explain what these are below).

Now try saying the following words one after the other: *bead, bed, bad, bud* and *bod*. As you say these words, you should be able to feel your tongue moving down from the high, front position for *bead* (in IPA [biːd]), through the <e> of *bed*, the <a> of *bad*, the <u> of *bud* and the <o> of *bod*. The last four are all short vowels: front mid in *bed* (IPA [ɛ]), front low in *bad* (IPA [æ]), central and a bit below mid in *bud* (IPA [ʌ]) and **low back** in *bod* (IPA [ɒ]). All are unrounded except for the [ɒ] of *bod*. (The last two vowels are different in American English, and if you're from the North of England, you probably have a different vowel in *bud*, the high, back, rounded [ʊ]). These short vowels don't directly contrast in length with the four long vowels we saw earlier, in that they are different both in quality and in length from the long ones (although [ɒ, ɔː] and [æ, ɑː] are fairly close in quality in some varieties of British English). There are two short vowels that *almost* contrast in length with [iː] and [uː], though. These are found in words such as *bid* and *look*. Compare *bid* and *bead*. You should be able to hear a length difference, in that the *bid* vowel is shorter than the one in *bead*. You should also be able to tell that the position of the tongue in the *bid* vowel is slightly lower and more central than the *bead* one. In IPA the *bid* vowel is written [ɪ]. So we have [bɪd] (*bid*) vs [biːd] (*bead*). Comparing your articulation of these two vowels, you may be able to feel a difference in the 'tenseness' of your tongue and lips: the muscles are quite tense in *bead* but somewhat more lax in *bid*. For this reason, these two vowels are sometimes referred to as tense and lax respectively, but I'll stick to the length distinction, with *bead* long and *bid* short. (Things are very different in Scots and Ulster English; I'll briefly come back to this in Chapter 8).

The difference between the vowel of *look* and that of the proper name *Luke* is similar. The *Luke* vowel is the long, high, back and rounded [uː] of *you*, which we've already seen. If you compare the pronunciations of *look* and *Luke*, you should again be able to discern a difference in length, with *Luke* noticeably longer than *look*. Again, comparing your tongue position in the two words, you can feel that the *look* vowel is a little more central and slightly lower than the *Luke* vowel. The *look* vowel is IPA [ʊ]. Also, there is a similar tense (*Luke*) vs lax (*look*) difference to that we saw in *bead* vs *bid* just now. (If you're from the North of England, you may find that you also pronounce *luck* with an [ʊ], just like *look*; in southern varieties, *luck* has the [ʌ] of *bud*, described above, but in many northern varieties [ʌ] doesn't exist at all).

There's one further short-long pair, at least in Standard British English. The short one is the first vowel in words such as _around_, _about_ and _asleep_ or the vowel in the way words like *the* and *a* are pronounced in connected speech (as in *the book* and *a person*). This is a mid-central unrounded vowel. It is known as '**schwa**' and its IPA symbol is [ə]. This vowel is extremely common in unstressed syllables (syllables with no emphatic **accent**) in most varieties of English. Schwa is a short vowel, as you can see from the examples. British English also has a long mid-central unrounded vowel, found in *bird*, *word* and *third*, for example. This is almost exactly a long version of schwa, at least for many speakers. Its IPA symbol is [ɜ:].

We can plot the horizontal and vertical positions of the tongue on an equilateral intended to schematise the space in the oral cavity within which the tongue moves to produce vowels, as in Figure 1.3 (this is sometimes rather misleadingly called the 'vowel triangle'). Figure 1.3 gives the short vowels of English, as we've seen them up to now. They are plotted on the equilateral diagram indicating their tongue positions in the oral cavity along the two dimensions.

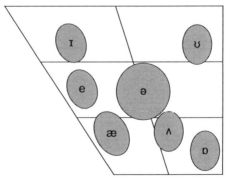

Figure 1.3 Short Vowels of Standard Southern British English.
(Source: www.llas.ac.uk/materialsbank/mb081/images/pic006.gif)

Next we need to look at diphthongs. A diphthong is a complex vowel. All the vowels we've seen up to now involve holding the tongue in a steady position, which we can describe in the way we've seen and plot on the equilateral as in Figure 1.3. Diphthongs, on the other hand, involve *movement* of the tongue from one vowel position to another. So, really, diphthongs are combinations of simple vowels, and we can describe them in terms of their component simple vowels.

Standard Southern British English has up to nine diphthongs. Let's look at them in two groups. The first five are found in *bide*, *bowed* (the past tense of the verb *bow*, as in *bow down*), *bode*, *bade* and *buoyed* (as in *buoyed up by the good news*). Pronounce *bide* first. You should be able to feel your tongue rising from a low front position, roughly that of [ʌ] (or perhaps a bit lower) to a high front position. There is no lip-rounding. So we write this diphthong in the IPA as [aɪ], the two symbols roughly indicating the starting and finishing positions of the tongue.

In *bowed*, the tongue starts at around the same position as the first part of [aɪ] (in more conservative varieties, further back; in more advanced ones, further front) but moves up and back to roughly the position of [ʊ]. Also, the lips round during its articulation. Thus, the IPA writes this one as [aʊ]. The vowel of *bode* starts right in the middle, around the position of schwa, and again the tongue moves up and back to the [ʊ] area, and again the lips round. So this one is written [əʊ]. In *bade*, the tongue starts near the position of the [ɛ] of *bed* and raises to the [ɪ] position, this time without lip-rounding. So we write this one [eɪ]. Finally, the vowel in *buoyed* starts in the [ɔ] position and, once again, moves to the [ɪ] position. Here the lips start off rounded as for [ɔ:] and unround during the diphthong.

The other four diphthongs are [ɪə], [ɛə], [ʊə] and [ɔə]. As you can see, all of them involve moving the tongue from a peripheral (front or back) position to mid, central [ə]. For this reason, they are known as **centring diphthongs**. The [ɪə] diphthong is found in *here*, *beer*, *queer* and *weird*. The tongue moves from the high front [ɪ] position to the [ə] position.

The other three centring diphthongs are all marginal to varying degrees in current Standard British English, especially for younger speakers (and in my English too!). The pronunciation of [eə] is fairly straightforward: the tongue starts in the same position as the [eɪ] diphthong and centres to [ə]. This vowel is found in *there, hair, where* and *scare*, for example. For many younger speakers, this diphthong has been simplified to a long [ɛ:]. For these speakers, *bed* and *bared* or *dead* and *dared* differ only in the length of the vowel. If, like me, you have this pronunciation, then you have one less diphthong and one more long vowel.

The [ʊə] diphthong is found in some pronunciations of *pure, lure, obscure* and *poor*. Again the articulation is clear from the IPA symbols. Most younger speakers of British English don't have this vowel and pronounce these words with the long vowel [ɔ:] instead. In that case, *paw, poor* and *pour* are all pronounced [pɔ:].

Last is [ɔə] as in a rather conservative pronunciation of words such as *soar* and *roar*. Again, the pronunciation is clear from the IPA symbols, and, again, this diphthong has mainly been replaced by [ɔ:] in the speech of most speakers of British English. In that case, *soar, sore* and *saw* are pronounced alike, as [sɔ:]. In my English, both [ʊə] and [ɔə] have been 'levelled' to [ɔ:].

We can plot the diphthongs on the equilateral with boxes, indicating the movement of the tongue in the oral cavity during their articulation, as shown in Figures 1.4 and 1.5.

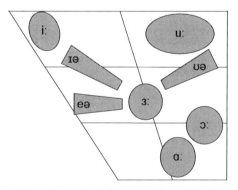

Figure 1.4 Some British English Diphthongs and Long Vowels Plotted on the Equilateral (the marginal centring diphthong [ɔə] is not shown).
(Source: https://upload.wikimedia.org/wikipedia/commons/thumb/b/b0/RP_vowel_chart_(diphthongs).gif/640px-RP_vowel_chart_(diphthongs).gif)

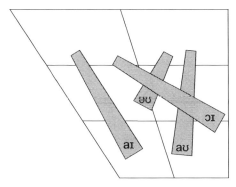

Figure 1.5 British English Closing Diphthongs.

The centring diphthongs are not found in most American, Scots and Irish varieties of English. One thing you might notice about all of the words containing these diphthongs is that they are spelled with an <r>, which is not pronounced. Or, more precisely, it is not pronounced as [r] in British English. In American, Scots and Irish varieties these words are pronounced with an [r]. So, if we take the words *here, there, poor* and *soar*, we have the following different pronunciations:

Table 1.4 *Centring Diphthongs and Their Counterparts*

	here	*there*	*poor*	*soar*
Conservative British English	hɪə	ðɛə	pʊə	sɔə
Younger British English	hɪə	ðɛ:	pɔ:	sɔ:
American English	hir	ðɛr	pʊr	sɔr

Since we saw that English spelling reflects the pronunciation of an earlier stage of the language, the pronunciation of the written <r> in American English reflects an older pronunciation of British English (these <r>'s started to be 'dropped' in the eighteenth century in Southern British English). In the conservative British English varieties, it looks as though [ə] simply 'stands for' the <r>. In the younger varieties, the diphthongs are gradually being simplified and merged with long vowels. There's much more to say about how <r> is pronounced (or not) in various kinds of English, and we'll come back to it in Chapter 8. Just one final note for now, the same applies to the vowel of *bird* and *word* as to the centring diphthongs: in American English, these words are pronounced roughly as [bərd] and [wərd], while in British English we saw the long mid-central vowel [ɜː] here.

This *almost* concludes our survey of the vowels and consonants of English. There are just two sounds left to look at: the **semi-vowels**.

The term 'semi-vowel' seems a bit strange at first sight. Can something really be half a vowel? Well, in a sense, it can. The semi-vowels are like vowels – and unlike typical consonants, especially obstruents – in that their articulation does not place obstacles in the way of the airstream but rather modifies the resonant properties of the vocal tract, particularly the oral cavity, by changing its shape. But, semi-vowels are unlike typical vowels in one very important way. If you look back at all of the vowels we introduced earlier, you'll see that they occur in the middle of their word. More precisely, they occur in the middle of their **syllable** (most of the words I used to illustrate vowels have just one syllable – they're monosyllabic – so it comes to the same). The syllables in question mainly begin with one or more consonants, then have a vowel and then end with a consonant or two. So they have the general shape *Consonant(s)-Vowel-Consonant(s)*, or $C_n V C_n$ for short (where the subscript *n* just means 'any number'). You can see from this that consonants show up at syllable edges and vowels in the middle.

Semi-vowels, however, sound like vowels (no obstruction of the vocal tract), but they act like consonants since they come at syllable edges. Standard English has two: [w] and [j] in IPA notation. The [w] is spelled <w> or <wh> and [j] (called 'yod', not 'jay') is usually spelled <y>. Examples of [w] are *word, why, watch, wave, wink*, etc. Examples of [j] are *you, yesterday, young* and *use* (in this last example [j] doesn't really have a spelling at all, unless we say that <u> corresponds to [ju:]). Both semi-vowels are quite straightforward to pronounce: you should, by now, be able to tell that in pronouncing [j] your tongue is in a high, front position and your lips are unrounded. In pronouncing [w], on the other hand, your lips are rounded and your tongue is in a high, back position. So the semi-vowels correspond, in a way, to [i:] and [u:] respectively.

Now we've looked at all the vowels and consonants (and semi-vowels) of English. You've also seen the IPA symbols for all of them. So you should be able to put all of this together and read IPA symbols. As you've probably realised, the IPA is useful as it gets us away from the vagaries, inconsistencies and plain craziness of English spelling. Moreover, you can learn it in an afternoon. Putting together everything in Table 1.3 and Figures 1.3, 1.4 and 1.5, you've got all of the vowel and consonant symbols for English, except for the semi-vowels [j] and [w]. Thus, you should be able to read an IPA transcription, or: səʊ naʊ ju: ʃʊd bi: eɪbəl tə ri:d ən aɪ pi: eɪ trænskrɪpʃən. Try this one and see how you get on:

tə bi: ɔ: nɒt tə bi: ðæt ɪz ðə kwɛsʧən.

∼

So now you know about noises. Of course, you always knew how to make the English noises. But, as you can see from the above description of the sounds of English, even an act as simple and everyday as pronouncing an English sentence involves a highly intricate, complex and very tightly coordinated dance of the various organs of speech: switching the larynx on and off; raising and lowering the velum; moving the tongue around in the oral cavity; obstructing, blocking and altering the progress of the airstream and pursing and unpursing the lips.

Now go back to the first sentence of this chapter and pronounce it slowly and carefully again. You can now describe what your speech organs are doing. As an exercise, write the sentence in IPA and list how many vowels, fricatives, stops, etc. there are. The impressive achievement of fine control of the speech organs I talked about at the beginning of the chapter should seem all the more impressive now that you actually know what they're doing.

But of course there's more to language than noise. Anything that complex has to be highly organised – you just can't do it with chaos – and organisation implies *structure*. That's why, for the next four chapters, we're going to be looking at the structure of language. We begin with sound structure, or phonology, in the next chapter.

2   How to Organise Noises
Phonology

In this chapter we'll start our investigation of the structure of language by looking at how the sounds of speech – the noises you made reading the previous chapter – are organised and exploited as part of the business of building linguistic units. The chief concept we'll discuss here is the **phoneme**, our first truly abstract linguistic unit. Once we have seen what phonemes are and how they work, we can look at two further abstract entities: **natural classes**, which group phonemes together, and **distinctive features**, which make them up. Finally, we'll take a very brief look at **phonological rules** and how they work.

In the previous chapter, we saw in some detail how complex even the most banal bits of everyday language are. Our little five-second, sixty-eight-sound sentence involves a great deal of carefully co-ordinated writhing and wriggling of the speech organs – impressive enough in itself – *and* manages to mean something. We'll get to how it actually means something later (see Chapter 5). In this chapter, we're going to look at how speech sounds are structured: this is the branch of linguistics known as phonology.

Be sure to get your terminology right: phonetics is the study of the speech sounds themselves; phonology is the study of how languages organise speech sounds into structured systems. To the extent that everyone has the same organs of speech (and the same perceptual apparatus, something we did not really go into in the previous chapter), phonetics is the same everywhere. But different languages may well deploy the same sounds differently, so English phonology and French phonology may be, and in fact to a fair extent are, somewhat different.

The main structural unit in a given language's phonological system is the phoneme. Phonemes are the units of sound that make a difference in a language. We can isolate a language's phonemes by setting up **minimal pairs** of words which contrast only in a single phoneme but which are clearly distinct words in terms of their meanings. So, for example, *pie* and *buy* are a minimal pair in English, contrasting only in the initial [p] in *pie* ([paɪ]) vs initial [b] in *buy* ([baɪ]). So this minimal pair shows us that /p/ and /b/ are phonemes of English.

Notation: phonetic symbols, representing the actual speech sounds, are written in square brackets, as we saw in the previous chapter. Phonemes, representing contrastive units in a language's phonological system, are written between oblique slashes //. So [p] is a sound and /p/ is a phonological unit. The IPA is generally used to represent phonemes, again in part to escape the vagaries of spelling conventions.

The minimal contrast between *tie* and *die* shows /t/ and /d/ are also phonemes of English. Similarly for *shy* and *sigh*, the minimal contrast indicates that /ʃ/ and /s/ are also phonemes. And so on.

It's very important to see that *phonemes are not sounds*. They are abstract linguistic entities that organise sounds. Take the English /p/ phoneme, for example. Pronounce *pie* and *spy* with your hand in front of your mouth. In the release phase of the <p> in *pie* you can feel the explosive puff of air on the back of your hand. This is because the diphthong [aɪ] doesn't start immediately as the lips open, and so there's a split second when all that's happening is air coming out from the vocal tract. This is a very short [h]-sound, known as **aspiration**. In careful phonetic transcription, this pronunciation of /p/ is written [pʰ]. In *spy* on the other hand, there's no aspiration, as you can tell from the fact that there's scarcely a puff of air discernible if you put your hand in front of your mouth. This is unaspirated [p]. You can see the difference between the two in the spectrogram in Figure 2.1.

English has another kind of p-sound, found at the ends of words in normal, colloquial speech. Pronounce *lap* or *tap* as

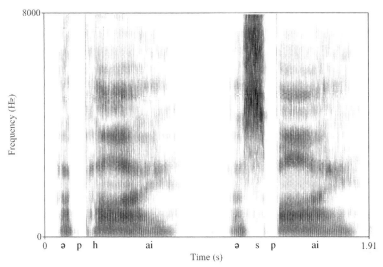

Figure 2.1 Spectograms of Normal British English Pronunciation of *pie* and *spy*
Spectrograms of a *a pie* and *a spy*; the lack of aspiration following the silent phase of
the articulation of [p] in *a spy* can be seen by comparing the two images. The high-
frequency noise of [s] is also clearly visible before the silent phase of [p] in *a spy*.
(Source: Phonetics Laboratory, University of Cambridge)

naturally as you can. You can either release the /p/, and you'll get
aspiration (try the back-of-the-hand test again). Or you can
just leave your lips closed, giving what's called unreleased /p/
(phonetically [p˺]). So there are three 'p-sounds' in English, which
are not contrastive, i.e. they don't form minimal pairs (*lap* means
the same thing whether you release, or aspirate, the /p/ or not).
These different 'p-sounds' (and these are sounds, not phonemes)
are known as the **allophones** of the phoneme /p/. So we say that
English /p/ has three allophones: [pʰ], [p] and [p˺]. Moreover,
each allophone shows up in its own special context: [pʰ] at the
beginning of syllables where there's no /s/ in front of it, [p] when
there is an /s/ in front of it and [p˺] at the ends of words. The
context conditions the possibility of the occurrence of a given
allophone, and so this is known as conditioned allophony. Since
[pʰ] and [p] each have their specific context (at the beginning of a
syllable after /s/ or not), we say that they are in **complementary**

distribution. If two sounds are in complementary distribution, they cannot minimally contrast, and so they cannot be separate phonemes.

Remember that different languages organise their phonemes and allophones differently. For example, French has a /p/ phoneme (as in *poids* 'weight', *paix* 'peace' and *prix* 'price/prize', etc.). But there is no aspirated allophone: at the beginnings of syllables, i.e. in words like the ones just given, French /p/ is just [p]. In some languages, such as Hindi, aspiration of stops is contrastive, and so /p/ and /pʰ/ form minimal pairs, as can be seen from examples, such as *pʰal*, meaning 'knife edge' and *pal*, meaning 'take care of'.

Another example of conditioned allophony, and consequent complementary distribution of allomorphs, in English, concerns the /l/ phoneme (you can tell this is a phoneme as it enters into minimal pairs, such as *lay* and *ray*, etc.). Pronounce *leaf*: here, as we saw in Chapter 1, you should feel your tongue blade against the alveolar ridge and the air escaping over the lowered sides of the tongue. Now pronounce *feel*. Here things are the same in the front part of the oral cavity, but you should be able to feel the back of your tongue bunching up and raising towards the velum, in a position somewhat similar to that in the pronunciation of [uː] or [ʊ] (if you are Irish, American or a Londoner, these differences may not hold, or may not hold in the same way). The two 'l-sounds' are clearly different from a phonetic point of view. The first, in *leaf*, is called palatalised /l/, IPA [lʲ], as it involves raising the tongue towards the hard palate. The second, in *feel*, is known as velarised /l/, IPA [ɫ], since it involves raising the tongue towards the velum.

In Standard British English, [lʲ] and [ɫ] are never contrastive: [lʲ] appears at the beginning of a syllable and [ɫ] at the end. So this is a further example of conditioned allophony giving rise to the complementary distribution of allophones of a single phoneme. The English phoneme /l/ has the two allophones [lʲ] and [ɫ]. Again, other languages do things differently. Russian has distinct /lʲ/ and /ɫ/ phonemes, as in *ugol* 'corner' (velarised /ɫ/) and *ugol'* '(char)coal' (palatalised /ʎ/). Nonetheless, the palatalised /ʎ/ isn't quite the same phonetically as the English [ɫ] allophone of /l/.

We've seen examples of other languages having phonemes that correspond to English allophones. We can also find the opposite situation: English phonemes that are allophones of a single phoneme in other languages. In English, /d/ and /ð/ are phonemes, as the minimal pair *udder* (/ʌdə/) vs *other* (/ʌðə/) shows. But in Spanish, [d] and [ð] are conditioned allophones of /d/, with [ð] occurring in all positions except at the beginning of words, which is reserved for [d]. So, in *dos* ('two'), the first consonant is phonetically [d], while in *Madrid*, both <d>'s are pronounced [ð].

As I said, phonemes are not sounds. As such, we could in fact choose to write /l/ and /p/ as /3/ and /4/, or /@/ and /#/, or /Mary/ and /Dick/. But since they are ways of organising sounds in a linguistic system, we represent them with letters, and, as I already mentioned, the IPA symbols are convenient because they eliminate the complexities of spelling.

The principle of contrast, enshrined in the minimal-pair technique, is central to defining and discovering the phonemes of a language. However, sometimes the system doesn't seem to mind which of a pair of sounds is used. We saw this at the allophonic level with the realisation of /p/ in *lap* and *tap*. Here the /p/ can be unreleased, and this is probably the most natural in spontaneous, colloquial speech. However, you can be careful (and mind your p's, if not your q's!) and pronounce it with release, and, indeed, aspiration. This optionality is called **free variation**.

We also find free variation at the phonemic level. Since phonemes define distinct words, given the principle of contrast, free variation of phonemes is idiosyncratic to certain words. An example of this is the pronunciation of *economics*, whose first vowel for some people can be either /ɛ/ or /iː/. We know that /ɛ/ and /iː/ are phonemes, given the minimal contrast between *bed* and *bead*, so here we have free variation. Another example, at least in my English, is the pronunciation of *either* and *neither*, where <ei> can be either /aɪ/ or /iː/. Again, /aɪ/ and /iː/ are both phonemes, as the contrast between *pie* and *pea* shows.

So that's the phoneme, the principal unit of phonological structure and the main element making up the contrastive sounds of words, which allows us to distinguish words. Phonemes are a pretty important part of linguistic structure. Table 1.3 in Chapter 1 listed the consonant phonemes of English (except for [ʔ], which is not a phoneme but an allophone of /t/). The vowel phonemes, in a conservative variety of Southern British English, are listed below in Table 2.1.

Phonemes can be grouped together in classes, or **natural classes** of sounds. Very often, important generalisations about a language's phonological system can be made in terms of natural classes. In fact, we have been implicitly talking about natural classes all through this chapter and the previous one. Two very large natural classes are vowels and consonants. One generalisation about consonants is that they only appear at the edges of a syllable. We could also say that vowels only appear in the middle part of a syllable, but on the other hand we *could* say that at least high vowels can appear anywhere in a syllable: when /i:/ and /u:/ appear at syllable edges we call them the semi-vowels /j/ and /w/. Also the bizarre English /r/ is, phonetically, not a consonant because it doesn't in any way obstruct the air stream. But phonologically, it is a consonant because it only appears at syllable edges. Since different languages organise their phonemes differently, we might expect to find a language in which a sound phonetically very similar to the English [r] really acts like a vowel; this is true of Mandarin Chinese, for example.

Table 2.1 *Vowel Phonemes of Standard British English (A Conservative Variety)*

/ɪ/ 'pit'	/ɛ/ 'pet'	/æ/ 'pat'	/ʌ/ 'putt'	/ə/'about'	/ʊ/ 'put'	/ɒ/ 'pot'
/i:/ 'key'	/ɑ:/ 'car'	/ɔ:/ 'core'	/u:/ 'coo'	/ɜ:/ 'cur'		
/eɪ/ 'bay'	/aɪ/ 'buy'	/ɔi/ 'boy'	/əʊ/ 'go'	/aʊ/'cow'		
/ɪə/ 'pier'	/ɛə/ 'pear'	/ʊə/'poor'	/ɔə/'soar'			

Another generalisation about these natural classes is that vowels are always voiced. Consonants, of course, can be voiced or voiceless, as we saw in the previous chapter. In describing the phonetics of vowels, I left this point implicit, but you can easily verify it with the finger-on-larynx test. Voiceless vowels are certainly phonetically possible: just pronounce any vowel and switch the larynx off; what you'll hear is something like an [h], the sound of air passing through the open glottis. Moving the tongue and lips to form different vowel shapes can give this [h] a hint of different vowel qualities. But they're hard to hear and, presumably for this reason, very rare in the world's languages. The Amerindian language Cheyenne has quite a few voiceless vowels though (at least phonetically); you can hear them being pronounced at www.youtube.com/watch?v=JaWvsONEEno.

Looking at vowel classes, and leaving the complexities of diphthongs aside, we can discern some further natural classes. One is front vowels; another is back vowels. A further one could be rounded vs unrounded vowels. But look at the front vowels of English: /iː, ɪ, ɛ, æ/. They are all unrounded. Now look at the back vowels: /uː, ʊ, ɔː, ɒ/, all rounded. So, in English (and in many other languages), the following generalisation holds: all and only back vowels are rounded. This is not true in all languages: in French, for example, there are three front rounded vowels, found in the words *lune* ('moon'), *peu* ('a bit/few') and *jeune* ('young'). The IPA symbols for these vowels are /y/, /ø/ and /œ/, respectively. There are also languages with back unrounded vowels, such as Turkish, in words like *ılık* ('lukewarm'); note the dotless <ı> here, which is how this vowel is spelled in Turkish. The IPA symbol is /ɯ/.

Among the consonants, nasals are a natural class. They, too, are always voiced in English and most other languages (do the finger-on-larynx test again to see this). Voiceless nasals exist in some languages. In Welsh, for example, the <nh> in *fy nhad* ('my father') is a voiceless [n], written [n̥] in IPA (when there isn't a separate symbol for a voiceless element, the IPA writes a little ̥ under the letter).

Other natural classes of consonants are stops, fricatives, velars, alveolars etc. You might notice that these classes cross-cut. So /t, d, n, s, z, l/ are all alveolars of one kind or another, while /b, p, t, d, k, g/ are all stops. This cross-cutting suggests that we might be able to break the phonemes down into smaller elements and then combine and recombine these smaller elements to form natural classes.

These smaller elements are known as distinctive features. These are features which are capable of contributing to phonological distinctions. Distinctive features define natural classes, in that natural classes are groups of phonemes which share a specification for one or more distinctive features. For example, the natural class of voiceless consonants of English (and many other languages) can be defined by the single feature [-voice] (since vowels are always voiced in English, this feature on its own singles out all and only the voiceless *consonants*).

If distinctive features are the atoms of phonology, then phonemes are the molecules. Distinctive features have a number of important properties. First, they are phonetically based, in that most distinctive features indicate an articulatory dimension which can vary independently of others. Sometimes this phonetic dimension has to do with the perception rather than the articulation of the sound. So, although, as we have seen, phonemes are not sounds, they can be defined as abstract entities in terms of characteristic phonetic properties of their allophones. Second, distinctive features are thought to be universal, i.e. to be the same for all languages. This is obviously linked to the previous point since we have already observed that the vocal tract is the same everywhere. Third, distinctive features are defined in binary terms, so they are normally preceded by a '+' or a '-' sign, indicating the presence or absence of whatever property it is. Representing distinctive features in binary terms in this way is handy and simple for the linguist, but it may represent a deeper kind of simplicity in the way the brain is organised (I'll come back to this point at the end of the chapter).

So let's look at a few distinctive features. The first one to look at is [±syllabic]. If a phoneme or an allophone is [+syllabic], it is able to form a syllable, either to be the middle part (or **nucleus**) of a syllable, or in fact to form a whole syllable on its own (in which case we could still regard it as a nucleus, just one lacking any edge-material). If a sound is [-syllabic], it cannot do this.

Notation: you'll note that distinctive features are written in square brackets. Moreover, they are usually abbreviated so [±syllabic] is usually written [±syll].

This feature creates our first two natural classes: vowels can be syllable nuclei (i.e. they are the middle part of syllables, and they can be syllables on their own). So /ɑː/ (spelt *are*), /ɔː/ (spelt *or*), for example, are syllables all on their own, but /b/ and /z/ are not. So vowels are [+syll] and consonants are [-syll]. Semi-vowels and /r/ are [-syll] since they are always at the edges of syllables.

Next, there is [±voice]. A sound is [+voice] if it is produced with the vocal cords vibrating and [-voice] otherwise. So all vowels are [+voice]. More succinctly, [+syll] implies [+voice]. Now you can begin to see how distinctive features allow us to express generalisations about sound systems in a neat way.

If a sound is [+nasal], it is pronounced with the velum lowered. Otherwise it is [-nasal]. So, we can say that [+nasal] implies [+voice]. Since in English there are no nasalised vowels, [+nasal] also implies [-syll]. This last implication does not hold true in French, though, since French has nasalised vowels.

Distinctive features apply equally to consonants and vowels. So, for example, [+back] means that the tongue moves to the back of the mouth. So, back vowels like /uː, ʊ, ɔ, ɒ/ are [+back]. But so are velar consonants like /k, g, ŋ/, as well as the semivowel /w/. The distinctive feature [+round] defines phonemes articulated with liprounding; [-round] applies to all others. So, for English, [+round] implies [+back], but not for French, as we saw.

Table 2.2 *Distinctive Features for Simple Vowels of English (Non-Diphthongs)*

Vowels: [+syll, -cons, +son]

	i:	ɪ	u:	ʊ	ɛ	ɜ:	ʌ	ɔ:	æ	ɑ:	ɒ	ə
high	+	+	+	+	-	-	-	-	-	-	-	-
low	-	-	-	-	-	-	-	+	+	+	+	-
back	-	-	+	+	-	+	+	+	-	+	+	-
round	-	-	+	+	-	-	-	+	-	-	+	-
tense	+	-	+	-	+	+	-	-	-	+	+	-

Table 2.3 *Distinctive Features for Non-Obstruent Consonants and Semi-Vowels*

Sonorant consonants and semi-vowels: [-syll, +son]

	m	n	ŋ	l	r	j	w	h
consonantal	+	+	+	+	+	-	-	-
nasal	+	+	+	-	-	-	-	-
lateral	-	-	-	+	-	-	-	-
continuant	-	-	-	-	+	+	+	+
coronal	-	+	-	+	+	+	-	-
labial	+	-	-	-	-	-	+	-
anterior	+	+	-	+	+	-	-	-
spread	-	-	-	-	-	-	-	+
high	-	-	+	-	+	+	+	-
back	-	-	+	-	-	-	+	+

The features [±low] and [±high] indicate the position of the tongue in the vertical dimension in the oral cavity. Again, these features apply to both consonants and vowels. So /iː, ɪ, uː, ʊ/ are [+high], and so are /k, g, ŋ, j, w/.

There are many more distinctive features but not enough space here to take you through all the definitions and examples. Tables 2.2, 2.3 and 2.4 give a full list of the distinctive features

Table 2.4 *Distinctive Features for English Obstruents (No Affricates)*

Obstruents [-syll, +cons, -son]

-voice	p	f	t	θ	s	ʃ	k
+voice	b	v	d	ð	z	ʒ	g
continuant	-	+	-	+	+	+	-
coronal	-	-	+	+	+	+	-
labial	+	+	-	-	-	-	-
anterior	+	+	+	+	+	-	-
high	-	-	-	-	-	-	+
back	-	-	-	-	-	-	+

relevant for English, and the values the English phonemes have for each one. In order to understand these tables fully, you need to know about two more distinctive features: [±sonorant] and [±consonantal]. A [+sonorant] sound does not involve audible turbulence in the vocal tract while a [-sonorant] one does. So the [-sonorant] phonemes of English are the stops and the fricatives (i.e. the obstruents, as introduced in Chapter 1) but not the nasals. Consonantal segments are produced with an audible constriction in the vocal tract. The difference between [+consonantal] and [-sonorant] is that [+consonantal] includes, in addition to the obstruents, the nasals and liquids. Vowels and semi-vowels are [-consonantal].

Here you can see that while [+high] logically enough implies [-low] and [+low] implies [-high], [-high] and [-low] can go together. The mid vowels /ɛ, ɜ:, ʌ, ə/ are all [-high. -low]. You'll also notice the [±tense] feature, which distinguishes tense /i:, u:/, for example, from lax [ɪ, ʊ]. We briefly looked at the phonetic notion of tenseness in the previous chapter.

Most of the distinctive features in Table 2.3 are self-explanatory. The feature [±continuant] distinguishes sounds with closure in the oral cavity from all others so nasals are [-continuant] as they have such closure (although of course the air goes out through the nose, as we saw in Chapter 1). The feature [±coronal] distinguishes alveolars from everything else while [±anterior] defines any consonant articulated at or in front of the alveolar ridge. So bilabials and labio-dentals are [-coronal, +anterior]. The feature [±spread] has to do with the position of the vocal folds and distinguishes /h/ from everything else. I'll explain [±high] and [±back] as they apply to consonants below.

In Table 2.4 we see that [±cont(inuant)] distinguishes just the sounds that can be 'held', in the sense we illustrated in Chapter 1, from those which cannot be held. In other words, it distinguishes stops ([-cont]) from fricatives ([+cont]). Here [±anterior] distinguishes alveolars, such as /t, d, s, z/, from the post-alveolars /ʃ, ʒ/.

Distinctive features can be used to formulate phonological rules and to explicate how these rules apply to natural classes of sounds. Let's look at a simple example of this in detail.

In English, the regular past-**tense** ending on verbs is written <(e)d> (the brackets around the 'e' mean it's not always there in the spelling). So we have pairs like *play* (present), *played* (past); *race* (present), *raced* (past); *want* (present), *wanted* (past). Semantically the ending is always the same; it tells you the verb is referring to something that happened in the past (roughly, the past tense can also refer to unreal situations, as in *If I had a hammer . . .*). The spelling is also the same, apart from the <e> popping up or not here and there. But, now that you know some phonetics, think carefully about the pronunciation of these endings. The ending is pronounced, unsurprisingly, as /d/ in *played*. In IPA, we write *play* as /pleɪ/ and *played* as /pleɪd/. No surprises there. But in *raced* the ending is pronounced /t/: *race* is /reɪs/ and *raced* is /reɪst/. And, very clearly, in *wanted* the ending is pronounced /ɪd/: *want* is /wɒnt/ and *wanted* is /wɒntɪd/. So what's going on? Something phonologically very neat, as we'll see.

Let's first look at some more verbs. Among the verbs that pattern like *play* in having a /d/ past-tense ending are *raze*, *slave*, *bug, bang, ban, bomb, robe, breathe* and *bawl*. Make up the past-tense forms, pronounce them and you'll see.

Verbs that act like *race*, and take a /t/ in the pronunciation of the past-tense ending, include *chafe, bank* and *rape*. And verbs that act like *want*, which are less common, include *word* (as in *she worded the letter carefully*, with *worded* pronounced /wɜːdɪd/).

Now, in distinctive-feature terms, what's the difference between /t/ and /d/? The feature that distinguishes these two is of course [±voice]: /t/ is [-voice] and /d/ is [+voice] (see Table 2.4). Look again at the verbs which pronounce their past-tense endings as /d/. They all end in a [+voice] phoneme: a vowel (*play*), a nasal (*bang*), a sonorant (*bawl*), voiced stop (*bug*) or a voiced fricative (*breathe*). On the other hand, the verbs which take past-tense /t/ all end in a [-voice] consonant: a fricative (*race*) or a stop (*bank*).

So we could say that the past-tense ending is 'really' a /d/, but it turns into a /t/ when immediately preceded by a voiceless consonant. In other words, the final voiced phonemes of regular verbs like to be next to a voiced past-tense ending while the final voiceless ones like to be next to a voiceless past-tense ending. This general phenomenon of like going together with like is known in phonology as **assimilation**. The English past-tense endings we have seen here show voicing assimilation.

This rather strange business of one phoneme turning into another can be captured by phonological rules. So here's Rule One:

Rule One: [+voice] → [-voice]/[-voice]#___##

As in a chemical formula or an algebraic equation, rules like this express a great deal of information in a very succinct and pared-down way; this is why at first sight they might seem rather imposing. However, they are fundamentally quite transparent; the key thing is to go through them very carefully and systematically step by step, or, more precisely, symbol by symbol. So, Rule One says that a phoneme specified as [+voice] turns into (this is the arrow) its [-voice] counterpart, i.e. all that changes in the specification of the phoneme is the value of the feature [voice], from '+' to '-'. That's the first part. The second part, after the oblique slash '/', states the context in which [+voice] is to change to [-voice]. This is indicated by the 'slash-and-dash' notation (/ and ___), which states 'in the context of' (that's the slash), and there's the preceding context indicated by the first symbol after the slash; here that's the single '#'. This single '#' right after the slash indicates the beginning of the ending while the double '##' after it indicates the end of the word. The dash ('__') in between indicates the position of the phoneme whose [voice] feature is to change from '+' to '-', in this case between '#' and '##'. Together this contextual specification makes sure the rule only applies to endings, rather than applying to the middle of a simple word (we'll say much more about endings when we look at morphology in the next chapter). In this way, Rule One states that a voiced phoneme turns into a voiceless one (at the same place of articulation and with all other features constant, as the rule refers only to [voice]) in an ending attached to a word ending in a voiceless consonant. In other words, the past-tense ending of a verb, such as *race, chafe* or *bank*, is pronounced /t/, although it is still a version of the past-tense marker /d/. Thus, /d/ changes into /t/ in exactly this context. Rule One captures this long-winded explanation with just a few concise abstract symbols (think again of chemical formulae or algebraic equations).

Now look at where the past-tense ending is /ɪd/. This is just where the verb ends in a /d/ (*word*) or a /t/ (*want*). So we could say that the past-tense /d/ turns into /ɪd/ when the verb ends in /t/ or /d/, i.e. when the verb ends in an alveolar stop. In distinctive-feature terms, alveolar stops are [-son, -cont, +ant(erior)], as Table 2.4 shows. An important aspect of phonological rules is that we always try to give the minimal feature specification that will clearly define the natural class we are interested in; in Table 2.4, you'll see that [-son, -cont, +ant] are enough to single out /t/ and /d/.

If the past-tense ending is 'really' /d/, as we have suggested, then it too is an alveolar stop: [-son, -cont, -ant, +voice]. It looks as though a little /ɪ/ pops up between two alveolar stops, the final /t/ or /d/ of the verb, and the /d/ of the ending. This phenomenon of phonemes appearing where they are otherwise not seen is known as epenthesis. So here we have an epenthetic /ɪ/.

In terms of phonological rules, we can express this epenthesis operation as Rule Two:

Rule Two: ∅→ /ɪ/ / [-son, -cont, +ant] # ___ [-son, -cont, +ant]##

Rule Two is a bit more complicated than Rule One, but we can again go through it step by step to see how it works. It says that nothing (or zero, written ∅) turns into (the arrow again) /ɪ/ in the context (indicated by the slash /) in between (indicated by the ___ in between the two lots of distinctive features) two alveolar stops (specified by the three distinctive features [-son, -cont, +ant]). As in Rule One, the '#' and the '##' after the slash ensure that the rule only applies to word-endings. (Of course, strictly speaking, /ɪ/ should be written in distinctive features, but I have spared you that detail). Saying zero turns into /ɪ/ is equivalent to saying that /ɪ/ is inserted; the slash and dash tell you exactly where /ɪ/ is inserted (in an ending before an alveolar stop). So Rule Two says that, where the verb ends in an alveolar stop, /ɪ/ appears in the ending. In other words, the past-tense ending /d/ 'turns into' /ɪd/ where the verb ends in /t/ or /d/. Since [voice] isn't specified anywhere in the rule, the rule applies where the alveolar stops in question are either /t/ or /d/. Remember that anything which isn't specified in the rule is left open; the rule states *exactly* what is to be changed.

So now we've got two phonological rules, very succinct and clever ways of expressing phonological generalisations using distinctive features to designate natural classes. But now we can go a step further and *make our two rules interact with one another*. To see this, let's try putting Rule One and Rule Two in order. First, try what seems like the obvious order, Rule One before Rule Two. For example, we start from the verb *want*, i.e. /wɒnt/, and the 'real' form of the past-tense ending, /d/, and mechanically apply the two rules as they are stated above:

	wɒnt #	d	##
Rule One	wɒnt #	t	##
Rule Two	wɒnt #	ɪt	##

This is an example of a phonological **derivation**, taking us from an **underlying form** (the 'real' version of the ending, as we have been calling it up to now) to a phonemic representation of the actual pronunciation. The derivation proceeds by a set of *ordered* phonological rules. The order of the rules is very important and can actually help us to state the rules in the most economical form. To see how this works, look back at how we formulated Rules One and Two and apply them completely mechanically, paying close attention to how the distinctive-feature specifications isolate the classes of sounds that the rules apply to. Then you'll see that Rule One will convert /d/ to /t/ since /wɒnt/ ends in a /t/ and Rule One converts a [+voice] phoneme to a [-voice] one in the context of an ending. Hence, it makes /d/, which is [+voice], [-voice] here, and the [-voice] version of /d/ is /t/. Now Rule Two comes in, and inserts epenthetic /ɪ/ between the two alveolar stops, /t/ at the end of /wɒnt/ and /t/ in the ending as modified by Rule One. So we get /wɒntɪt/ as the past tense of *want*, which is wrong. So this derivation, where Rule One is ordered before Rule Two, doesn't work.

So let's try switching the order of the rules. Let's apply Rule Two before Rule One. Now look:

Underlying Form	wɒnt	#	d	##
Rule Two	wɒnt	#	ɪd	##
Rule One	wɒnt	#	ɪd	##

In this derivation, Rule One cannot be applied (or we can say that it applies vacuously; in other words it doesn't do anything, as indicated here). This is because Rule One, as we have stated it, makes a [+voice] into a [-voice] *immediately following a [+voice]* (at the beginning of an ending, as we saw). But, after Rule Two has been applied, /d/ immediately follows /ɪ/. Note that the 'immediately' specification here is crucial, and this is guaranteed by the way the rule is written. Since we haven't added anything more to the context, each symbol in the context is taken to be immediately adjacent, or right next to, the ones on either side of it. As /ɪ/ is a vowel, it's always voiced, and so Rule One has nothing to do here; it just doesn't apply in the context created by Rule Two. So /d/ stays /d/ in the ending and we get /wɒntɪd/ as the past-tense of *want*, which is what we wanted. Rule Two, on the other hand, has no problem given this order of the rules: it inserts epenthetic /ɪ/ between the alveolar stop /t/ at the end of /wɒnt/ and the past-tense ending /d/. We get the right result if we apply Rule Two first because then Rule Two effectively prevents Rule One from being applied. Phonologists call this bleeding order: Rule Two 'bleeds' Rule One.

All of this footling about with the exact form of the past-tense ending might seem like a lot of work for not much of a result, but two important things emerge. First, formulating phonological rules in distinctive-feature terms gives us a very precise, succinct way of capturing generalisations about natural classes. Here the natural classes in question involve voiced consonants (expressed by [+voice]) and alveolar stops (expressed by [-son, -cont, +ant]). If we can successfully capture generalisations in this way then, as with chemical formulae, our phonological rules are telling us that the behaviour of linguistic sound systems is *law-like*, and so should be studied scientifically. Second, the rules *interact* in the context of the phonological derivation. We saw that Rule Two must be applied first, before Rule One gets a chance, or otherwise things go wrong. Actually there's something even more intriguing here: you can easily see that Rule Two is more complicated than Rule One, in the simple and obvious sense that it involves more distinctive features (and so applies to a smaller natural class of sounds). So Rule Two is more specific than Rule One. Linguists have long thought that there may well be a very general organising principle in language which basically gives the specific precedence over the general. Rule Two getting to apply 'first' in the derivation – before Rule One – in determining the phonological shape of the English past-tense ending is a small example of this very general principle. If this is true, it is important because there is no obvious reason why it should be true; things could easily have been otherwise. Here we glimpse what might be a true law of language.

≈

In this chapter, we have begun looking seriously at the abstract structure of language. Several abstract concepts have been introduced: phonemes, allophones, distinctive features, natural classes and phonological rules. Of these, the really central one is distinctive features, since phonemes, allophones and natural classes can all be defined using distinctive features, and phonological rules use distinctive features to describe phonological processes such as assimilation and epenthesis.

But what *are* distinctive features and phonological rules really? We could say that they are just a handy way of describing and summarising the nature of processes such as assimilation and so on. But there's a more interesting and bolder answer: *these formalisms and abstractions are an attempt to describe what the mind is doing when it structures the sound system of a language.* We could maybe think of them as lines of code in the mental computer program for language; if so, then it's no surprise that distinctive features are binary. This makes things very intriguing. Remember how impressive the intricate moves of the speech organs were in our five-second, sixty-eight-sound sentence in the last chapter? If this view of phonology is right, then, in addition to controlling the movements of the articulators (a nifty enough feat in itself), the brain is also in some way manipulating phonological rules and distinctive features all the time. So the feat of pronouncing a simple sentence becomes still more impressive! What makes phonology so interesting is that it is the part of linguistics where the brain of abstract structures meets the brawn of speech.

But we still haven't said anything about how the noises, however they are made and whatever organises them, get to *mean* something. Now it's time to start doing that; in doing so, we'll meet a really major **design feature of language**.

3   How to Build a Word
Morphology

In this chapter, we're going to start looking at larger units of linguistic structure: words. Morphology is the branch of linguistics that studies the structure of words. We'll basically look at three things. The first is by far the most important: a design feature of language usually known as **duality of patterning**. This is where meaning will at last start to come into the picture, although it'll take three more chapters before we get anything like a full picture of what meaning is.

Once we've covered duality of patterning, we'll be ready to see the basic unit of meaning in language. Contrary to what you might expect, this isn't the word, but the morpheme.

Finally, we'll look at some basic morphological processes. As usual, I'll mainly focus on English, but English is pretty boring in one major morphological respect, so here we'll do a bit of Italian and Latin to brighten things up.

∼

So far, we've seen how sounds are made (phonetics) and how they're organised (phonology). On the basis of this, you should by now have developed a new respect for the mental and physical prowess we all show when saying the simplest sentences.

But language conveys meaning, although the sounds themselves – even when organised into phonological systems – don't mean anything. Take a simple minimal pair once more, such as *cat* and *bat*. The fact that these words mean different things shows us that /k/ (English often spells the voiceless velar stop as <c>) and /b/ are phonemes. But /k/ doesn't mean furry feline, and /b/ doesn't mean flying rodent. This point becomes obvious when we look at other pairs of words distinguished by the same minimal pair, e.g. *king* and *Bing*. Here /k/ doesn't mean male regal person and /b/ doesn't mean suave 1950s crooner (or a well-known search engine). Anyway, how could /k/ mean both furry feline and male regal person, and /b/ mean both flying rodent and suave fifties crooner/well-known search engine? The phonemes simply allow the words to mean different things by combining them together. So one important linguistic pattern is the combination and recombination of phonemes (and phonemes are distinguished from allophones in that they – the phonemes – are the phonological items that do this combining and recombining). How many phonemes does English have? If you put together Table 1.3 of Chapter 1 with Table 2.1 of Chapter 2 you'll see that there are twenty consonant phonemes and twenty-one vowel phonemes in the particular variety of Southern British English discussed there, so let's say roughly forty in round-figure terms (hardly anyone has /ɔə/ anymore). So a rather small number of phonemes can combine and recombine to make thousands of words.

How many words are there in English? You might have heard various estimates, usually in the tens of thousands, and the *Oxford English Dictionary* (often regarded as the authority on such questions, at least in Britain) boasts 'more than 600,000' on its home page (see www.oed.com). Producing several hundred thousand words from forty-odd phonemes is a good trick, but really we could go even further and say that the number of English words is unlimited.

To see this, think of a word like *coffee-maker*. This is a complex word; in fact, it's a **compound**, a type of complex word we'll look at in more detail later. It obviously means something along the lines of a machine for making coffee. We can make this word more complicated, as in *coffee-maker-maker* (the person or machine that makes the machines that make the coffee). So this is an English word too. What about *coffee-maker-maker-maker*? You might think this is getting silly, and in a way it is. But in another way there's a very serious point here: you can still easily tell what this word means (the person, machine or entity that makes the person or machine that makes the machine that makes the coffee). In principle – if we don't worry too much about unwieldy words and outlandish meanings – you can just keep on making this compound bigger and bigger. The same is true of examples like *anti-missile-missile*, *anti-missile-missile-missile* and so on (those of us who can remember the Cold War definitely know that these words mean something very clear).

Making complex words is another kind of pattern. Now we're combining meaningful elements, not meaningless phonemes. In the compound words we just saw, we're making big words out of smaller words, with no clearly discernible upper limit to how long the new words can be.

There are two patterns: you take forty or so phonemes and make basic words out of them, which might easily number in the hundreds of thousands. Then you can take the basic words and combine *them* – and here phonology doesn't matter – to make a seemingly unlimited number of complex words. In the next chapter, we'll see how in syntax you can combine words to make a literally *infinite* number of sentences.

Language uses two distinct combinatorial patterns. Meaningless phonemes combine to make meaningful words, and meaningful words combine to make a vast – unlimited – number of complex words. This is the duality of the patterning of language, and it's an absolutely brilliant way of converting forty-odd phonemes into a huge, ever extendable vocabulary.

Morphology is about the structure of words, and as such has to do with the second level of patterning, the one which combines meaningful elements. Although we've seen that you can make complex words by combining other words, you can also make them out of other – in a way smaller – things. We can see this with the word *maker* (forget about the coffee). This word is clearly complex, containing *make* and the ending (or **suffix**, since it's fixed on to the end of *make*) *-r*. It's important to see that this suffix isn't the phoneme /r/ (for one thing, in British English it's pronounced /ə/). A single phoneme can constitute a meaningful element all on its own, as for example the English **indefinite article** *a*, also pronounced /ə/. Duality of patterning allows a single phoneme to be a meaningful element, but it *isn't* the *phoneme* /ə/ that has meaning. It's just that our suffix here, and the indefinite article *a*, happen to be made up only of that one phoneme.

The -r suffix of *maker* shows up in *baker, shaker, player, cooker, farmer, crooner, striker* and plenty of other English words (as you can see, if the word it's added to doesn't already end in <e>, it's spelled <er>). You can also figure out what it means: a *maker* is someone or something that makes stuff, a *baker* is someone who bakes stuff, a *shaker* shakes, a *player* plays, a *cooker* cooks and so on. So the -*(e)r* suffix has its own sound, /ə/, and its own meaning. In these respects, it's just like a word. Words have sounds and meaning: *cat* is pronounced /kæt/ and means furry feline; *bat* is pronounced /bæt/ and means flying rodent and so on.

The only difference between -*(e)r* and obvious words like *cat* is that -*(e)r* can't stand alone. It has to grab on to something else. But what we can see is that a word like *baker* is complex in a way that a word like *bake* or *cat* isn't. At the second level of patterning, it contains two meaningful elements: the **root** *bake* (which of course can stand alone, and means something involving fooling around with dough, yeast and ovens), and the suffix -*(e)r*, which means someone or something who does whatever the root says. So a *baker* is someone who does the fooling around with dough, etc.

Since -*(e)r* isn't a word on its own, we should call it something else. This is where the concept of the morpheme comes in. A morpheme can be defined as the smallest meaningful unit of language. So morphemes are the atoms of the second level of patterning. Words are the molecules. Simple words like *bake* or *cat* are molecules that happen to contain just a single atom. Complex words like *baker, coffee-maker, anti-missile-missile, supercalifragilisticexpialidocious* and so on are molecules, some of them quite complex. These complex words can have quite a bit of internal structure, as we'll see later.

Stand-alone morphemes which can also be simple words, such as *cat* and *bake*, are known as **free morphemes**. Morphemes which have to be attached to something else, like *-(e)r*, are called **bound morphemes**. Suffixes are one type of bound morpheme. Morphemes, free and bound, combine to form complex words in three main ways.

The first way to make complex words is to combine two (or more) independently existing words. Complex words formed in this way are called compounds. We've already seen a couple of examples. Compounds are very common in English and in many other languages. Here are some more examples of English compounds: *blackbird, blackboard, bookcase, toothbrush, fly-spray* and *witch doctor*. Again, the spelling is unreliable: some compounds are written as single words, some are written with hyphens separating the words making up the compound and some are written as separate words, i.e. with spaces separating the elements. (German is much better organised, with all compounds written as single words, giving rise to words like *Donaudampfschifffahrtsgesellschaftskapitänsmütze*, which means Danube steamboat shipping company Captain's hat.)

There are three things worth noting about English compounds of the type we've just seen. First, order matters. We can make two compounds out of the words *dog* and *house*: *doghouse* and *house-dog*. You can immediately see that these two compounds have quite different meanings. So the order in which the words making up a compound combine affects the meaning.

Second, we can easily distinguish a compound word from a phrase made up of the same simpler words and morphemes just by the stress (or accent) pattern. Compare *bláckbird*, which has stress on *black* and means that particular slightly sinister species of bird (rejoicing in the scientific name of *turdus merula*), with *black bírd*, which has stress on *bird*, and just means any bird which happens to be black. So you can say 'That black bird isn't a blackbird' without contradicting yourself (compare 'That black-bird isn't a blackbird', which is a contradiction). In English nouns are mostly stressed on the first syllable, and *blackbird* is a compound noun. Phrases, on the other hand, are stressed later than the first syllable. Now compare *Oxford Street* and *Oxford Road*. Street names are actually compound words while road names are phrases. Once again, the spelling is hopeless because it doesn't show this distinction.

The third thing about compounds has to do in part with what the compounds mean, and is an important aspect of the second level of patterning. Look again at our examples: a *blackbird* is a type of bird, not a type of black; a *blackboard*, similarly, is a type of board; a *bookcase* is a type of case, a *toothbrush* is a type of brush, and a *doghouse* is a type of house while a *housedog* is a type of dog. One part of the compound is more central to the meaning than the other: this part is known as the **head** of the compound. The head, as its name implies, is the boss. In addition to determining the main part of the meaning of the compound, it also determines the **category** of the compound as a whole: *black* is an adjective (it denotes a quality), *bird* and *board* are nouns (denoting things). *Blackbird* and *blackboard* are nouns, not adjectives. The category of the head determines the category of the whole word: the head is in charge. We'll look at the concepts of head and category in detail in the next chapter, where we'll also see that heads rule in syntax too.

All of the examples of compounds just given clearly contain just two words, *black* and *bird*, *book* and *case*, etc. But *coffee-maker* is different. This is a compound, as it consists of *coffee* and *maker*, both independent words. But *maker* is itself a complex word; as we saw, it's made up of *make* and *-(e)r*. English has lots of compounds like this, where the second part is a complex word containing a suffix: *lorry-driver*, *baby-sitter*, *song-writer*, *back-stabber*, etc. Some compounds of this kind with a bound morpheme other than *-(e)r* are *train-spotting*, *blue-eyed*, *ear-splitting* and many more. Compounds of this type are called **synthetic compounds**, and the simpler *blackbird* type are called root compounds. English is quite rich in synthetic compounds; languages like French and Italian, on the other hand, hardly have any.

Synthetic compounds look like they have an internal structure something like *Word + Word + Suffix*. Actually, it's more complicated than that. In the case of *coffee-maker*, it looks as though we might have a structure like *Word + (Word + Suffix)* since the suffix can independently attach to the second word. In other words, since we independently have *maker* and *coffee* as separate words, but not *coffee-maker*, we might think that this is the structure. In terms of what they mean, though, the structure of synthetic compounds is really *(Word + Word) + Suffix*. The two words form a semantic entity, to which the suffix attaches. To see this, consider the trio *bird-watcher*, *bird-watching* and *bird-watched*. The first one involves the familiar *-(e)r*, and here you can see that *-(e)r* isn't just applying to *watch*, but to *bird* **and** *watch*. A *bird-watcher* isn't someone who watches, it's someone who watches **birds**. Similarly, for *bird-watching*; it's the activity not just of **watching** but of watching birds. Finally, *bird-watched* means not just being watched (note the meaning change this *-ed* suffix brings), but watched by **birds** (think of Hitchcock's famous movie).

Ever heard the joke about the plastic surgeon who sat in front of the fire and melted? If you understand the compound *plastic surgeon* as having the structure *plastic (surge(on))*, with *plastic* as the modifier of *surgeon*, you get the joke. But of course we normally think of a plastic surgeon as a surgeon who does a particular kind of surgery, **plastic** surgery. So *plastic surgeon* has the structure *(plastic surge)on*, and *plastic surgery* is *(plastic surge)ry* (*-on* and *-ry* are more suffixes, a bit less common than *-er*, *-ing* and *-ed*). The point here is that the second level of patterning is highly structured; we'll see this again much more forcefully in the next chapter.

The second way of making complex words is known as **derivation**. Derivation involves adding suffixes, bound morphemes, to words, with the result that the category of the word changes (and, in rather subtle ways, so does the meaning). Take a simple word like *person*. This is a noun. We can add the suffix *-al*, and get *personal*, an adjective (being personal is a quality). Then we can add -*ise*, and get *personalise*, a verb (it's an activity). And now we can turn it back into a noun, but now an abstract noun, by adding -*ation*: *personalisation*. We can carry on, although now we're pushing things: someone who really likes personalisation (perhaps a certain kind of novelist) could be called a *personalisationist* – here we've added the suffix -*ist*. We've still got a noun, but a more concrete one now. Now we can add -*ic*, and make an adjective, *personalisationistic*. Even now, we can turn it back into a noun, an abstract noun, *again*, with -*ism*: *personalisationisticism*. You should be able to see that the second level of patterning allows us to combine and recombine morphemes so that we can always add to our vocabulary – new words are very easy to coin (try it).

Almost each time we added a derivational suffix, as they're called, to *person*, we changed its category. The word *person* is itself a noun, *personal* is an adjective. Now, remember that heads rule: they determine the category of complex elements. If adding -*al* to *person* makes it into an adjective, maybe -*al* itself is a head, and an adjective. In that case we can write the structure of the complex derived word *personal* as [$_{\text{Adjective}}$ [$_{\text{Noun}}$ *person*] *al*].

Notation: we use square brackets to show the internal structure of words. The brackets have little category labels $_{\text{subscripted}}$ on the left bracket, by convention. We'll see this and another equivalent way of representing structures in much more detail in the next chapter.

So *personalise* would have the structure [$_{\text{Verb}}$ [$_{\text{Adjective}}$ [$_{\text{Noun}}$ *person*] *al*] *ise*]. And so on. Complex words have internal structure, and even words formed by derivation may have heads.

The third way of forming complex words is by **inflection**. Inflections are bound morphemes which don't change category. Instead, they usually specify something about the syntax or semantics of the word they attach to. We saw one example of inflection in the last chapter. That was the -*(e)d* inflection, the regular past-tense ending of English. Now we can be more precise, and say that that 'ending' (as we were calling it) is an inflectional morpheme that expresses past tense.

In our discussion of -*(e)d* in the previous chapter, we saw that this morpheme has three pronunciations: /d/, /t/ and /ɪd/. We also saw that we can write phonological rules, Rule One and Rule Two, which, once we work out which one goes first (Rule Two, as we saw), can predict when which variant of the morpheme shows up. These three variants are different realisations of the English past-tense morpheme. We could say that English has a morpheme -*d* for the past tense, which has three variants /d/, /t/ and /ɪd/, showing up as specified by Rules One and Two. The forms /d-t-ɪd/ are **allomorphs** of the past-tense morpheme -*d*, and the alternation is known as **conditioned allomorphy**. Since we can predict which allomorph we get with phonological rules, this is *phonologically* conditioned allomorphy.

Things are actually a bit more complicated. English has some verbs with irregular past-tense forms. The past tense of *sing* isn't *singed*, but *sang*; *bring* has *brought*, *go* has *went* and so on. All in all, English has about two hundred irregular verbs, many of them quite frequent (*be*, with the past tense *was/were*, is a notable example). So we can't really say that the general past-tense morpheme has the form -*d*, as this just doesn't apply to the irregular verbs. Instead, we say that English has the morpheme PAST, which, by default, is realised as the suffix /d/ to which Rules One and Two of the previous chapter apply (i.e. the phonologically conditioned allomorphs are specified by Rules One and Two). But some verbs must be pre-specified as special, and there are several subgroups: the *sing* type, the (rarer) *bring* type, the *put* type (which has no special past-tense ending at all: the past of *I put* is *I put*) and so on. Extreme irregularity of the *go-went*, *be-was/were* type is different as here the past tense seemingly has no formal connection to the non-past form at all. Such cases involve suppletion: here the basic form combines with the PAST morpheme to give a third, quite unpredictable, form.

English nouns – at least some of them – have a plural ending, or inflection. The default, regular plural ending is -*s*, as in *cats*. In fact, this ending has the phonologically conditioned allomorphs /s/, /z/ and /ɪz/. You might be able to spot a family resemblance with the phonologically conditioned allomorphs of the regular past-tense inflection. This resemblance becomes a bit clearer if we say the plural ending is 'really' /z/.

There are also irregular plurals, such as *children, mice, teeth* and *oxen*. Again, these words must be pre-specified as not taking the default form of the plural. And again, this implies that the abstract form of the morpheme is PLURAL.

English doesn't have a lot of inflectional morphology. Regular verbs, for example, only have the inflections *-s* (third-person singular present tense, as in *s/he plays*), *-(e)d* for past tense and *-ing* (known as the continuous and the gerund form), as in *play*, *plays*, *played* and *playing*. By comparison with most languages, this is pretty poor.

To get more of an idea of how inflections work in many languages, let's look at an Italian verb. The Romance languages generally have more inflectional morphology than English, especially in verbs, so Italian is a good example (if you know some French or Spanish, you can think about verbs you might know from those languages; they're quite similar to Italian).

Let's look at a regular Italian verb: *cantare* ('sing'). First of all, where English has just two tenses, the past with *-(e)d* (on regular verbs) and the non-past, or present, with no marking except in the third-person singular (*-s*), Italian has *five* tenses. Here I am only counting 'simple' tenses in both languages; I'm leaving aside complex forms like *ho cantato* ('I have sung') as we're only interested in how the verb itself inflects. The present tense is *canto* ('I sing'), *canti* ('you sing'), *canta* ('he or she sings'), *cantiamo* ('we sing'), *cantate* ('you sing') and *cantano* ('they sing'). There are two forms which translate as 'you sing'; one is singular (*canti*), used when talking to one person, and the other is plural, used when talking to more than one person. We can describe these forms using the **person** and **number** terminology: 'I' is first-person singular (1Sg), 'we' first-person plural (1Pl), 'you' second-person singular (quasi-'thou', 2Sg) and plural (2Pl), 'he/she/it' third-person singular (3Sg) and 'they' third-person plural (3Pl). Normally we still follow the practice of old-fashioned school grammar books, which you may have come across if you've been unlucky, and lay the forms out in a table like this:

Table 3.1 *Present-Tense Forms for Italian* cantare

	Singular	Plural
1	canto 'I sing'	cantiamo 'we sing'
2	canti 'you (sg) sing'	cantate 'you (pl) sing'
3	canta 'he/she sings'	cantano 'they sing'

As you can see, there are six person-number combinations (three persons × two numbers) and six different inflectional endings on the verb here. This is typical of Italian, and strikingly different to English, where, as you can see from the translations, there are is only one ending: -*s* in the 3Sg. There must be at least two morphemes in a form like *canto*: the root, which is probably *cant-* and the 1Sg morpheme -*o*. But things aren't quite this straightforward, as we'll see right away.

Italian has four more tenses: the **imperfect** (expressing continuous action in the past, as in 'I was singing'), the simple past, the future and the conditional (expressing what *would* happen, as in 'I would sing'). These tenses are shown in Table 3.2.

You can see that all these forms have different endings. Italian regular verbs have 5 tenses × 6 person-number endings = 30 inflectionally distinct forms. You can also see that the root of the verb is consistently *cant-* , as we suggested before, so we can say that this is a morpheme meaning 'sing' in Italian. It's hard to divide up the endings of the verbs straightforwardly into separate, readily identifiable morphemes though. Looking at Table 3.2, we might think that -*av*- is a suffix meaning *imperfect*, with the endings -*o*, -*i*, -*a*, -*amo*, -*ate* and-*ano* added on for the person-number markings.

These person-number markings are similar, but not identical, to those of the present tense, as you can tell if you look back to Table 3.1. But now look at the past tense. Here it looks

Table 3.2 *Other Tenses of Italian* cantare

Imperfect ('I was singing', etc.)	Singular	Plural
1	cantavo	cantavamo
2	cantavi	cantavate
3	cantava	cantavano
Past ('I sang', etc.)		
1	cantai	cantammo
2	cantasti	cantaste
3	cantò	cantarono
Future ('I will sing', etc.)		
1	canterò	canteremo
2	canterai	canterete
3	canterà	canteranno
Conditional ('I would sing', etc.)		
1	canterei	canteremmo
2	canteresti	cantereste
3	canterebbe	canterebbero

like we have the endings *-ai, -asti, -ò, -ammo, -aste* and *-arono*. It's not clear where the past morpheme is, or where it stops and the person-number morphemes start. What does seem clear is that the person-number endings are distinct from those of the present and the imperfect. This is another kind of conditioned allomorphy, but this is morphologically conditioned allomorphy, since person-number morphemes change form according to the tense, i.e. according to the morphological rather than the phonological context. By contrast, the /d-t-ɪd/ alternation in the regular English past-tense endings depends purely on the phonological context, so this is phonologically conditioned allomorphy.

As if all this wasn't enough, Italian has two **moods**, known as the indicative and the **subjunctive**. All the tenses given before were in the indicative, as they say something thought to be true. The subjunctive is used to say something considered dubious in various ways. English doesn't really have a subjunctive; the nearest English equivalent to an Italian subjunctive would most likely involve a word like *might*, as in *I might sing*. In Italian, there's both a present and a past subjunctive, and each has a person-number marking. Also, there are other forms which don't have person-number markings (called non-finite forms), such as the **infinitive** *cantare*, and a few others. Finally, there are three classes of regular verbs in Italian, known as **conjugations**; these are distinguished by a characteristic vowel that shows up in the infinitive and many other endings. *Cantare*, is in the *a*-conjugation, as there is an *-a-* in the infinitive in between the root *cant-* and the infinitive morpheme *-re*. The others are the *e*-conjugation (as in *credere* 'believe') and the *i*-conjugation (as in *dormire* 'sleep'). One might wonder what kind of morpheme this *-a*, *-e*, *-i* alternation represents. These are generally referred to as 'theme vowels', whose function is simply to identify conjugation classes; unlike most other morphemes we've looked at, they don't seem to mean anything. And then there are lots of irregular verbs too. English looks beautifully (or, depending on your perspective, moronically) simple in comparison.

This sketch of Italian was just intended to give you a sense of how languages with more inflectional morphology can work, and how tricky it can be to isolate individual morphemes in richer inflectional systems like Italian verbs.

What about nouns? As we saw earlier, English distinguishes singular and plural number in nouns: *cats*, *dogs*, *horses* and *oxen* are all examples of plurals of various kinds. One kind of noun inflection which is fairly common around the world but which Modern English hardly has at all is case marking. The **case** of a noun tells you what the noun is doing in the sentence, usually (but not always) in relation to the verb. Look at the pronouns in these sentences:

(1)   I saw her.

(2)   She saw me.

(3)   *Her saw I.

Notation: here we see, for the first time, 'example sentences' associated with consecutive numbers. The numbers are just for ease of reference. We'll see a lot more of this in the chapters to come. Also, in (3) there's an asterisk * in front of the sentence. That means that the sentence is ungrammatical in Standard English.

It's pretty clear that *I* and *me* are both the same person, i.e., er, 'me'. Using our person-number terminology, we can say that *I* and *me* are both 1Sg pronouns. Similarly, *she* and *her* are 3Sg pronouns. In fact, *she/her* can only be females; males are *he/him* and inanimate things are just plain *it*. So, more precisely, *she/her* are 3Sg feminine pronouns. Now, in (1) and (2) we have *I* and *she* before the verb, and *her* and *me* after it. In (3), the positions of *her* and *I* are swapped as compared to (1) and we get a bad (technically 'ungrammatical') sentence, hence the *. We can also see that in (1), 'I' am doing the seeing, and 'her' is what is seen. In (2) it's the other way round. The preverbal (in-front-of-the-verb) position is the usual place for the 'doer' (or agent) of the action described by the verb in English. This is known as the **subject** position. On the other hand, the postverbal (after-the-verb) position is the usual place for the thing to which something is done in English; this is the **direct-object** position. So now we can see, looking again at (1) and (2), that *I* is the 1Sg subject pronoun, and *me* the 1Sg direct-object pronoun (and the same for the 3sg pronouns *she* and *her*). *I* and *me*, and *she* and *her*, are obviously morphologically different (it's hard to find the individual morphemes here!). These are different **case forms** of the pronouns. *I* and *she* have subject case (traditionally called the **nominative** case) and *me* and *her* have the object case (traditionally known as the **accusative** case).

English only shows case marking on pronouns (and not all of those). But many languages show it on all nouns. Latin is a well-known example of a language of this type. So, for example, *discipulus* is the word for 'pupil', but this is the nominative form, so that's the form of the noun when it's the subject. If you want to talk about doing something to a pupil, you have to put the noun into the accusative case to show that it's the direct object, and this case has a different ending: *discipulum*. Since Latin is like English in marking singular and plural on nouns, we have different endings if we want to talk about 'pupils': *discipuli* is the nominative plural, and *discipulos* the accusative plural. This works for all nouns in Latin, so *puella*, meaning 'girl', has *puella* as nominative singular and *puellam* as accusative singular, *puellae* as nominative plural and *puellas* as accusative plural. The roots *discipul-*, 'pupil', and *puell-*, 'girl', aren't hard to identify, but again it's hard to see where the case morphemes (nominative and accusative) and the number morphemes (singular and plural) start and finish.

With these few Latin words and the verb *amat* ('she or he loves'), we can make up sentences as follows:

(4)   Discipulus amat puellam.
        pupil-NOM loves girl-ACC.
        'The pupil loves the girl'.

(5)   Puella amat discipulum.
        Girl-NOM loves pupil-ACC.
        'The girl loves the pupil'.

Notation: the strange-looking quasi-English in the middle lines here is known as the 'gloss' of the original. It's intended to indicate aspects of the morphology of the original and follows the order of words and morphemes in the original.

Latin actually has six cases! With the two numbers, that makes up to twelve forms for every noun. Once again we generally adopt the layout for presenting the forms of nouns in tables, as shown in Table 3.3.

Table 3.3 *Case and Number Forms of Latin* discipulus

	Singular	Plural
Nominative	discipulus	discipuli
Vocative	discipule	discipuli
Accusative	discipulum	discipulos
Genitive	discipuli	discipulorum
Dative	discipulo	discipulis
Ablative	discipulo	discipulis

All of these forms mean 'pupil(s)'. We've already seen the function of the nominative and the accusative. The vocative is used when directly addressing someone ('Oh pupil!'). The **genitive** is for possessors (as in 'pupil's voice'). The dative is the case of the indirect object (roughly 'to or for pupil', as in *I gave a present to the pupil*; here 'to the pupil' would be *discipulo*). The ablative is used after various prepositions (little words that often indicate spatial relations, like *in, on, by, with* or *from*). Arranging nouns and verbs in tables, such as Tables 3.1, 3.2 and 3.3 gives what are called the inflectional paradigms of a language. As you can see, in some respects this might be a better way of laying out the inflections in a language like Latin or Italian than trying to divide everything up into morphemes, although ultimately we have to try to do the latter if we really think that morphemes are the basic unit of the second level of patterning. Generations of schoolchildren (I was part of one of the last) have spent their formative years being subjected to endless Latin paradigms like the one in Table 3.3.

We can see from all this that Italian and similar languages have much more verbal inflection than English and that Latin and other languages have much more nominal inflection. English is by and large pretty poor in inflections (although we'll see in Chapter 7 that it didn't used to be). But English does have a few little bits of inflection: past tense, 3Sg present and *-ing* on verbs and plural marking on nouns, for example. Are there languages which are even poorer than English? Yes, quite a few. One very well-known example is Mandarin Chinese. In Mandarin, verbs don't have *any* inflections at all. If you want to talk about something that happened in the past, often the context is enough. If you think about it, the past-tense marking in a sentence like *I ate an ice-cream yesterday* is redundant; *yesterday* tells you that the event took place in past, and in fact it is rather more precise than just the general notion of 'pastness' – there is (or was) more to the past than yesterday. In Mandarin, no such redundancy is required. So, to say 'I ate rice yesterday', you say *Zuótiān wǒ chī mǐfàn*, literally

'Yesterday I eat rice'. But, if you need to, you can put in a little particle *le*, which more or less indicates that the action described by the verb is completed, and hence likely to be in the past, as in *Wǒ chīle mǐfàn*, literally 'I eat-completed rice', so roughly 'I ate rice'. This *le* particle is not an ending in the English (or Italian) sense: it never changes its form (i.e. it is not subject to allomorphy of any kind) and there are no irregular forms. Nonetheless, it does lack one thing that 'full' words have in Mandarin, a **tone** of its own. Nearly all words in Mandarin have to be pronounced with one of four characteristic tones, i.e. pitch variations on the vowel, as indicated by the accents in the examples, but there are few little words like *le* that don't have their own tones.

It is similar for plural marking on nouns; in Mandarin you don't need to specify whether a noun is singular or plural. Again, in English plural marking is redundant in many cases, as in *I read three books*; here *three* clearly states that there is more than one book, and, again, much more precisely than the plural ending on the noun. The Mandarin counterpart of this sentence is *Wǒ dúle sān běn shū*. Here *wǒ* is 'I', *dúle* is 'read' (with the completeness marker *le*), *sān* is 'three' and *shū* is 'book'. The little word in between *sān* and *shū* is called a nominal classifier; it has to show up here for reasons that are rather unclear. But, this complication aside, you can see that Mandarin can get by perfectly well without marking nouns as plural.

Mandarin does have a plural marker, though. This is the morpheme *men*, which is optional with nouns that refer to humans, e.g. *xuéshēng* 'student', *xuéshēng men* 'students' (note again that *men* has no accent and therefore no tone of its own). So if you really want to insist on there being several students in question, you can use the plural form. This brings us neatly to another example of the great morphological simplicity of Mandarin. Where in English we have suppletive forms of most personal pronouns for singular and plural (*I* is 1Sg, *we* is 1Pl; *he/she/it* are 3Sg, *they* 3Pl), in Mandarin we have the following:

(6)   *wǒ*   'I'   *wǒ-men*   'we'
       nǐ   'you(sg)'   *nǐ-men*   'you(pl)'
       tā   'he/she/it'   *tā-men*   'they'

Here we see perfectly regular plural marking: 'we' is 'I' plus the plural ending, and the same for the other persons. Not only that, but as you can see from the third-person forms, there are no gender distinctions: *tā* is 'he', 'she' or 'it'. Furthermore, there are no case distinctions either: *wǒ* is 'I' or 'me', *wǒ-men* is 'we' or 'us', etc. So Mandarin is an example of a language extremely poor in inflection, almost to the point of having no obligatory inflections at all. Other languages like Mandarin in this respect are Vietnamese and Thai.

∾

In this chapter you've had a brief introduction to how to build words: morphology.

We've seen:

- duality of patterning (very important)
- morphemes
- compounding (two types in English)
- derivation
- inflection (including Italian verbs and Latin nouns and the lack of inflection in Mandarin)

Whatever you think of the details of Latin cases and Italian tenses and the comparative neatness and simplicity of Mandarin, there's one centrally important thing we've seen here: how duality of patterning can take us from forty phonemes to many thousands of words, in fact potentially an unlimited number of in-principle-inventable words (like the one before last). Next, we look at the part of language where this in-principle-inventability is the guiding principle: syntax.

4 How to Say Absolutely Anything You Want To

Syntax

In the last chapter, we saw how duality of patterning greatly increases the expressive power of language by combining a small number of meaning*less* elements (phonemes) into a very large number of meaning*ful* elements (morphemes). These elements, in turn, can recombine to form a potentially extremely large number of further meaningful elements: complex words of various kinds.

Now we look at syntax: the structure of phrases and sentences. Here we'll see how the rules of syntax allow us to form any of an *infinite* number of sentences. Syntax is at the core of the expressive power of language; it quite literally gives us freedom of expression, the ability to talk about just about everything and anything.

You might object that it's quite impossible to produce an infinite number of sentences in practice, for reasons having to do, basically, with lack of time and energy. Here it is useful to introduce an important distinction, that between linguistic **competence** and linguistic **performance**. A person's competence in their native language is their ability to control all the aspects of that language's structure: the huge, complex, intricate array of things we've seen in the preceding chapters, plus the syntax and semantics we'll look at in this chapter and the next. Performance is putting competence into action: actually speaking and understanding your language. Performance depends on competence but draws on more than just linguistic abilities; when talking and listening other factors, long- and short-term memory, concentration and others, all come into play. Competence refers to the 'pure' linguistic abilities. This implies, for example, that competence is distinct from actually speaking and listening; my linguistic competence as a native speaker of English remains in my mind when I'm asleep, or just keeping quiet. We'll come back to this distinction in Chapter 9, when we look at psycholinguistics, but what's relevant here is that our competence allows us to produce an infinite number of sentences. Nonetheless, performance limitations (lack of time, etc.) prevent us from ever actually doing so in practice.

There are two ways to see that there is a potentially infinite number of sentences in English. First, we asked in the last chapter how many words there are in English and suggested that, although people might be tempted to say there are a few hundred thousand (or however many there are in the *Oxford English Dictionary* or some similar authority), in fact the number is unlimited, as you can always add new ones, and we did. But it *is* reasonable to ask how many English words you have stored in your mental dictionary (or **lexicon**) somewhere in your long-term memory. Knowing the answer would be about as useful as knowing the exact number of hairs you have on your head – only harder to find out, as we have no idea where to look in the brain to find the mental lexicon, or how to look for it, while we could in principle sit there and count our hairs.

Now ask yourself how many English *sentences* you have stored in your head. There's no answer. Imagine the longest sentence you can; you can always add something like '. . . but I don't think so' at the end. And you can add it again. And again. And again . . . *ad infinitum*. From a strictly linguistic, syntactic point of view, nothing stops you from beginning your attempted longest sentence right now and carrying on through the heat death of the universe and beyond (mortality, the laws of physics and, above all, boredom will get in the way, but the sentence itself can just go on and on). There is no longest sentence (in any language), just as there is no largest number; however big a number you can imagine, you can always add one to it and get a larger number. Similarly, however long a sentence you imagine, you can always add 'but I don't think so', or something comparable.

A related point, often made by the linguist Noam Chomsky (who is personally responsible for just about every idea in this chapter): most of the sentences you say and understand every day of your life are completely novel; you've never heard them before and you might very well never hear them again. You may be the first person in all of history to say a given sentence. This awesome observation holds true because of the unlimited power of syntax to make new sentences out of largely (but not always!) familiar words. This is what Chomsky called the creative aspect of language use (the word 'creative' here doesn't have to have to do with literature or poetry, although of course it might: even the most ordinary sentences are creative in Chomsky's sense because they are novel).

So the most important thing to understand as we look at the rather abstract rules and formalisms of syntax is this: syntax gives us our flexibility of mind by giving us maximum freedom of expression in speech and thought. Thanks to syntax, we can talk and think about all the things we do, and generate, store and transmit all our knowledge. In a nutshell: no syntax, no spaceships.

All of this means that there can't possibly be a list of grammatical English sentences in your head or anywhere else. It's impossible, as the list is infinite. In fact, as Steven Pinker has pointed out, even the finite combinatorial possibilities of syntax are so great that a list would be hopelessly long; he estimates that there are 6.4 trillion possible combinations of words making up a simple five-word sentence of English (*The cat ate a mouse* is one of them). So we clearly need another way of specifying what the possible sentences of a language can be.

Sentences come about because of the **syntactic rules** that generate them out of smaller elements like words and morphemes: the centrality of this idea gives this approach to syntax its usual name, 'generative grammar'. So now let's look at how this works. We'll look at the three basic building blocks of syntax: categories, **constituents** and **rules**. All these go together to account for the nature of **constituent structure**, how words group into larger units of various kinds (known as **phrases**) and phrases into sentences.

Categories

Categories come in two main types: lexical categories and functional categories. Lexical categories include some of the familiar ones from school grammars, some of which we briefly saw in the previous chapter: nouns, verbs, adjectives, adverbs and prepositions. Syntacticians love abbreviations and are extremely unimaginative in their use of them, so we refer to these categories for short as N, V, Adj, Adv and P.

Lexical categories form open classes: you can always add new members to them (actually, this isn't so easy in the case of prepositions, which is why these are sometimes classified as functional categories). We saw ways to invent new words out of existing ones in the last chapter, but here we're going to be a bit more creative. Take a look at sentence (1):

(1)   The onx splooed a blatt blarg.

(1) is syntactically just like (2):

(2)   The cat ate a fat mouse.

Obviously, in (1) we have some novel lexical elements – *onx, sploo, blatt* and *blarg* – while in (2) we don't; the other parts of the sentence are functional categories (the words *the* and *a* as well as the past-tense inflection *-ed*) and they're the same in both (1) and (2), as you can see. I'll say more about functional categories later. The traditional definitions of lexical categories, which are really based on semantics (i.e. the kinds of things that words typically mean) are somewhat useful but don't get us very far, especially with new words such as *onx*, etc. For example, the traditional definition of a noun is that it means a 'person, place or thing'. In (1), *onx* is a noun, and it does seem plausible that an onx is a thing (although it's not easy to say what kind of thing). A verb is traditionally defined as an action of some kind, and *splooed* might indeed be telling us what the onx is doing here. Adjectives refer to qualities, or kinds of things, and *blatt* might be telling us what particular kind of blarg is being splooed by the onx.

But it can't be that we're working out that *onx* is a noun, *sploo* a verb and *blatt* an adjective on the basis of their meaning because we don't actually know what they mean. There must be other ways of picking out lexical categories. One is morphology. As we saw in the last chapter, nouns inflect for plural in English. We can guess that the plural of *onx* is *onxes*, just as the plural of *cat* is *cats* (note the phonologically conditioned allomorphy here). Verbs inflect for past tense: *splooed* is the (regular) past tense of *sploo* just as *ate* is the (irregular) past tense of *eat*. Some adjectives in English inflect for their comparative (more than something) and superlative (the most of something) forms, as in *fat*, *fatter* (comparative) and *fattest* (superlative). So we could say (if we knew what we were talking about): *This blarg is blatter than that one.* So, the main lexical categories can be identified by their inflections (in languages with more inflections than English, this is much easier to do).

But the main thing that helps us to spot categories is syntax. This is how we can be reasonably confident about the categories of *onx*, *sploo* and so on in (1) (and in fact we partly guess their possible meanings on this basis, compare *The sploo onxed a blarg blatt* with (1)).

For example, nouns can appear in the **subject** position in English. This position is often first in the sentence, designates the doer (**agent**) of the action described by the verb and usually comes right before the verb. The subject position is blank in (3):

(3)   _____ stole my lunch money.

In the blank here you could put any of the following: *teenagers*, *vampires*, *cats*, *Priscilla* or even, with a bit of poetic licence, *syntax*. But you can't put in a verb, adjective or preposition:

(4)   a. *Walk stole my lunch money.
       b. *Tall stole my lunch money.
       c. *Under stole my lunch money.

(Remember the asterisk, indicating ungrammaticality, from the previous chapter). In fact, whole sequences of words can go in the blank in (3), but they must have a noun as their main word, in fact the noun must be the head of the phrase. The notion of head here is really the same as what we saw in the last chapter in connection with heads of words, only now we apply it to sequences of words, i.e. phrases. So we can say:

(5)   a. The cat stole my lunch money.
        b. A strange person stole my lunch money.
        c. A professor of linguistics stole my lunch money.
        d. Someone's dog stole my lunch money.
        e. The person I met yesterday stole my lunch money.

Sequences of words such as *the cat, a strange person, a professor of linguistics, someone's dog* or *the person I met yesterday* are all Noun Phrases, phrases whose most important word is a noun, NPs for short. In fact, the noun is the head of the NP. Just as in morphology, we can see this from the fact that a *professor of linguistics* is a kind of professor, *a strange person* and *the person I met yesterday* are both kinds of people, and *someone's dog* is a kind of dog. So *professor, dog* and *person* are all nouns, heading their respective NPs.

    Only verbs can appear in the blank in (6):

(6)   Teenagers can ____ quickly.

So, we can complete (6) as (7), for example, by filling verbs into the blank:

(7)   Teenagers can talk/write/learn/understand quickly.

But NPs, adjectives, adverbs and prepositions are banned from that position, and trying to put them there leads to ungrammatical sentences, such as:

(8)   *Teenagers can Dave/kids/injections/tall/in/yesterday quickly.

On the other hand, sequences of words whose head is a verb, i.e. Verb Phrases (VPs), can go into the blank slot in (6):

(9)   Teenagers can dissolve in sulphuric acid/get angry/conclude
        you're boring quickly.

So here we have VPs whose head is *dissolve, get* and *conclude*, respectively.

These tests for categories can confirm our idea that *onx* is a noun and *sploo* a verb in (1). In fact, we can see that *the onx* is an NP and *splooed a blatt blarg* is a VP. *The onx* fits into the gap in (3):

(10)   The onx stole my lunch money.

And *splooed a blatt blarg* fits into the gap in (6) (with a slight change in the verb, dropping the past-tense ending *-ed* as this is not a past-tense context):

(11)   Teenagers can sploo a blatt blarg quickly.

One thing that you might have noticed about (1) and (2) is that both contain two familiar English words: *the* and *a*. These are called the definite and indefinite articles respectively. They are examples of functional categories. Functional categories are closed classes; you can't make up new ones, and they vary much more from language to language (for example, as far as we know all languages have nouns and verbs, but plenty of languages have neither a definite nor an indefinite article: Latin, for example).

Another important class of functional categories is **auxiliaries**, like *can* in (6–9) or *has* in the following slight modifications of (1) and (2):

(12)   The onx has splooed a blatt blarg.

(13)   The cat has eaten a fat mouse.

So we can use morphology (inflections really), positions in the sentence and semantics to identify lexical categories. We can do the same with functional categories, too. For example, a syntactic test for English auxiliaries is that only members of this category can 'invert' (i.e. go before the subject instead of after it) in simple questions. So, alongside the statements in (14) we have the questions in (15):

(14)   a. Onxes can sploo blargs.
         b. Cats can eat mice.

(15)   a. Can onxes sploo blargs?
         b. Can cats eat mice?

These examples show that *can* is an auxiliary. Compare (16), where a verb tries to invert:

(16)   a. *Sploo onxes blargs?
         b. *Eat cats mice?

Together, (14–16) tell us that verbs and auxiliaries are distinct syntactic categories in English. Also, while there are lots of verbs, and new ones can always be invented as we have seen, there are very few auxiliaries, maybe ten or twelve at the most. There are lots of other tests like these which we can use to individuate various other functional categories, but these are enough to get across the basic idea.

So, here we've seen that

- There are two types of categories, lexical and functional.
- The lexical categories are N, V, Adj, Adv and P.
- Functional categories include auxiliaries and articles.
- There are various kinds of tests for distinguishing and isolating the categories.

Now that we've seen roughly what categories there are, let's look at how they combine.

Constituent Structure

Look at these two really simple sentences:

(17)   a. Night fell.
         b. John yawned.

Each of these consists of an N and a V. So we could very straightforwardly indicate the constituent structure of these sentences as in (18):

(18)   a. [$_N$ Night] [$_V$ fell].
         b. [$_N$ John] [$_V$ yawned].

Notation: here we have the same square-bracket-with-subscript notation as we saw in the structure of complex derived words in the previous chapter.

Nouns are heads of NPs, and as wo saw, where we can find a noun, we can usually find an NP. So we have:

(19)   a. [NP A professor of linguistics] [laughed].
        b. [NP The cat who lives next door] [sneezed].
        c. [NP Several onxes] [splooed].

These NPs are complex categories, in the sense that they contain more than one word. They all have a head noun (*professor, cat* and *onxes*) and other words and phrases that either depend on or modify that noun in various ways. These other words include articles (e.g. *the*), and many different kinds of modifiers such as **relative clauses** (*who lives next door* in (19b)) and quantity words like *several* in (19c), among many other possibilities. (We'll say more about certain kinds of 'quantity words' when we look at semantics in the next chapter.)

Verbs head VPs, so the right-hand bracketed word in (19) can be 'expanded' as in (20):

(20)   a. [NP John] [VP spoke about the economy].
        b. [NP Mary] [VP ate her husband].
        c. [NP Clover] [VP ate a fat mouse].

The VPs here include the verb and various other words and phrases that depend on or modify the verb. These are often direct objects, the thing that undergoes the action described by the verb (as we briefly mentioned in the previous chapter): *her husband* in (20b) and *a fat mouse* in (20c). But they can be various other things, such as the Prepositional phrase (PP) *about the economy* in (20a).

Labelled brackets like those in (20) are one way of representing constituent structure. We can represent the full constituent structure of (20b) as in (21):

(21)   [s [NP [N Mary]] [VP [V ate] [NP [D her] [N husband]]]].

The abbreviations NP, N, VP and V are fairly familiar by now, I hope. S simply stands for 'sentence'. D stands for '**determiner**', a functional category which includes articles as well as possessive pronouns like *her* in (21).

The other way to represent constituent structure is with a **tree diagram**:

(22)

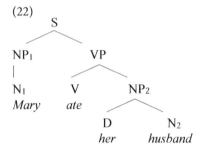

There's nothing magical or mysterious about either labelled brackets or tree diagrams. Both are just different ways of representing *exactly* the same information about constituent structure. We decide which to use for convenience; tree diagrams are what most people prefer as they present the structure in a way that's immediate and easy to see. For example, it's obvious from a glance at (22) that the whole thing is an S, whose basic division is into NP and VP. This information is present in (21), but it takes a bit more looking (and bracket-counting) to spot it.

Time for some tree terminology. The first, and most obvious, thing to note is that the tree is actually pictured upside-down, with its root, as it were, at the top. The parts of the tree with category labels on them are called **nodes**. S is the root node, where the tree starts. The lines linking the nodes are, unsurprisingly, called **branches**. If a node divides, it's called a **branching node**; so VP and NP$_2$ are branching nodes in (22), while NP$_1$ is a non-branching node.

Notation: the subscript numbers on NP$_1$ and NP$_2$ are used simply to distinguish these two NPs and have no deeper significance; we could just as well call them NP$_{Bellatrix}$ and NP$_{Priscilla}$ for example, but the numbers are more convenient to use.

If a node has branches below it, it is a **non-terminal node**. If it doesn't, it is a **terminal node**. In (22), the actual words are the terminal nodes. You can think of the words as the leaves on the branches.

Three conventions apply to tree diagrams like (22). First, branches never cross. Second, all branches emanate from the root, S. Third, branching is only downward. All of these conventions are needed in order to make tree diagrams equivalent to labelled brackets, and, more generally, to make sure they capture the idea of breaking the structure down, as we go 'down the tree' from S to the terminal nodes.

Next we need to see two central notions of constituent structure: **dominance** and **constituency**. As we'll see right away, these are really the same relation looked at in different ways.

In a tree diagram, a given category – call it A – **dominates** another category B just where A is 'higher up the tree' than B and connected to B by a continuous sequence of branches going down the tree from A to B. So, in (22), S dominates all the other nodes, VP dominates V, NP_2, D and N_2, while NP_1 dominates N_1. On the other hand, VP does *not* dominate NP_1. Further, a node A *immediately dominates* another node B just where A dominates B and no node intervenes on the dominance path from A to B. So, in (22), S immediately dominates NP_1 and VP, and VP immediately dominates V and NP_2. But VP does *not* immediately dominate D and N_2, although it does dominate them.

Constituency is dominance 'the other way up'. So B is a **constituent** of A just where there is a continuous sequence of branches going up the tree from B to A. Also, B is an **immediate constituent** of A just where B is a constituent of A and no node intervenes on the upward path from B to A. In these terms, we can say that a linear string of terminal nodes forms a constituent if each of them can be traced upwards by single lines to the same non-terminal node. In (22), then, everything (except S) is a constituent of S, but only NP_1 and VP are immediate constituents of S. A good exercise, to prove that you've grasped these notions, is to work out some more dominance (downward-looking) and constituency (upward-looking) relations in (22) for yourself. Now we've seen what constituent structure looks like. Next we need to know how to get it right.

Rules

We've seen how syntactic representations, either labelled brackets or tree diagrams, are made out of categories and constituents. Morphemes and words belong to different categories, and – aside from being constituents themselves – make up larger phrasal constituents to form sentences. So they combine and recombine in various ways. But what specifies how they combine? And what prevents them from combining wrongly, giving ungrammatical sentences like (23)?

(23)   a. *Sneezed John.
         b. *Husband her ate Mary.
         c. *Fat Clover a ate mouse.

We need rules of combination. The basic rules of combination in syntax are **Phrase-Structure Rules**, or PS-rules for short.

PS-rules are a formal device, meaning that they're supposed to be followed absolutely literally – the way a computer executes a programme – and have nothing to do with meaning. PS-rules **generate** constituent structure, by specifying the precise ways in which categories and constituents can combine, and only those.

Here is a simple basic PS-rule of English:

(24)   S → NP VP

This says 'rewrite S as the sequence NP VP, in that order'. You can imagine a computer doing this in a very mechanical way (think of 'Find and Replace' in a basic word-processing application). In general, PS-rules mean 'replace every occurrence of the symbol on the left of the arrow with the one(s) on the right of the arrow'. The PS-rules specify possible combinations of constituents, and so tell us what kinds of tree or labelled brackets are allowed. The one in (24), for example, tells us that the top bit of the tree in (22) is allowed in English. Here it is again:

(25)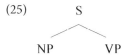

Implicitly, unless we are told something more, it tells us that other 'expansions of S' (ways of rewriting S) are not allowed. Everything which is not required by a PS-rule is forbidden.

There is a link between PS-rules and dominance/constituency. The rule in (24) generates the bit of tree in (25), and thereby tells us that S immediately dominates NP and VP, and that NP and VP are immediate constituents of S. It also tells us that NP and VP must appear in that order, and not in the order VP NP. So (24) tells us how the categories NP and VP can form the constituent S by combining together in the stated order. PS-rules, then, tell us about hierarchical relations (dominance/constituency), linear relations (NP VP and not VP NP) and categorial relations (NP and VP, not AP [adjective Phrase] and PP).

Here are some more English PS-rules:

(26)   i. VP → V NP
       ii. NP → (D) N

The rule in (26i) says that the bit of structure in (27) is ok:

(27)   VP

       V   NP

The rule in (26ii) has a category in brackets on the right of the arrow. This means that category is optional. Strictly speaking, (26ii) is an abbreviation for the two rules in (28):

(28)   i. NP → N
       ii. NP → D N

The rules in (24) and (26) can generate the tree in (22). Here is the tree again (without the words), annotated with the PS-rule that generated each part:

(29)

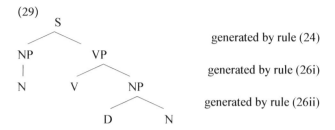

generated by rule (24)

generated by rule (26i)

generated by rule (26ii)

If we tweak rule (26ii) a bit, adding an optional AP between D and N, and add a simple rule for APs, as in (30), we can generate the structure of (1) and (2):

(30)   (26ii, revised)   NP → (D) (AP) N
                            AP → (Mod) A

'Mod' here means a category of elements that can modify adjectives, like *very*, as in *very hot*.

Now here's the structure of (1) and (2):

(31)

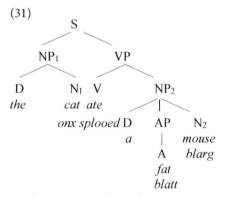

Under NP$_2$, we have AP as an immediate constituent thanks to our tweaking of rule (26ii). AP expands as just A following one option under rule (30). The other option, giving the substructure in (32), would be:

(32)

        AP
      /   \
   Mod   A

Taking this option of rule (30), we would generate: *The cat ate a very fat mouse* or *The onx splooed a very blatt blarg.*

The PS-rules don't determine where the words go, just the ways categories and constituents combine. But the words, as leaves on the trees, have to match the categories they appear with. So, in (31), *the* and *a* are Ds, *cat, onx, mouse* and *blarg* are Ns, *splooed* and *ate* are Vs and so on. How the words get to 'slot into' their positions in the trees is called lexical insertion (inserting lexical items – or words/morphemes – into constituent structures). There are various ways to do this, whose precise technical details would take us too far afield here, but suffice it to say that the main point is that the category of the word or morpheme (which is intrinsic to that word and partly connected to its meaning) must match the category of the terminal node it sits under.

One last and really important point about syntax. PS-rules can be applied and re-applied to their own output. To see what this means, let's look at a more complex English sentence:

(33)   The detective thinks that [Mary ate her husband].

If you look at the bracketed part of this sentence, *[Mary ate her husband]*, you can see that it is a sentence, too. In fact, it is (20b), which has the structure in (22), and we've seen the PS-rules that can generate (22).

So we already know what the structure of bracketed part of (33) is. What about the rest? It's clear that *the detective* is an NP, of the form [$_{NP}$ D N], generated by one of the rules in (26ii). We can easily tell that *thinks* is a V, but what is *that*?

Here we need to introduce another functional category: C, for Complementiser. Complementisers correspond roughly to what you may know from school grammars as 'subordinating conjunctions'. Complementisers combine with sentences (S) to form a larger constituent, the Complementiser Phrase, or CP. We can state this in a new PS-rule:

(34)   CP → C S

Also, we need to modify the VP-rule in (26i) as follows:

(35)   VP → V (NP) (CP)

Now, choosing the expansion of VP as V CP in (35), and applying rule (34), we can give the structure in (36):

(36)

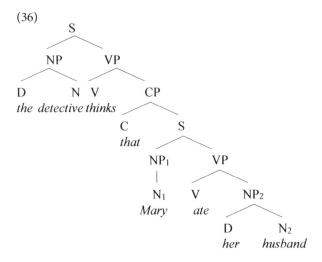

Looking at each bit of the tree in turn we can see that we've already seen the PS-rules that generate each of them.

But there's something *hugely* important about (36), which again emerges if we look closely at how each bit of the tree is generated by a PS-rule. The first rule we apply here is (24): S → NP VP. Looking at VP, we choose one of the options in (35), V → V CP. CP is expanded, following (34), as C S. And now, we apply rule (24) to S again, and get [S NP VP] (equivalently, the subtree in (25)). Then we apply a different option to VP (V NP). But, of course, at this point we could take the V CP option again here, apply (34) again, apply (24) again, expand VP as V CP again ... and so on. Until the heat death of the universe (PS-rules aren't interested in cosmology).

So our PS-rules can give us **infinitely big trees** of the form in (37):

(37)

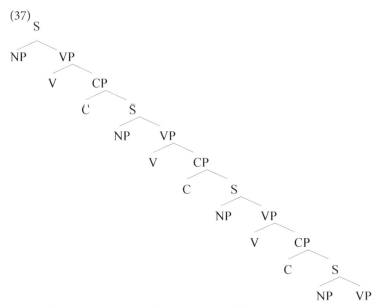

Trees like this correspond to sentences like:

(38)   Mary said that John thinks that Priscilla believes that Clover
        suspects . . .

Sentences like this, although long-winded and inelegant, are definitely grammatical sentences of English.

What all this means is that even a small, simple set of PS-rules like the ones that we have seen here – rules (24), (34) and one version of (35) – can generate *an infinite number of sentences*! These simple rules – or at least a few rather like them – can give us the unlimited expressive power of syntax that we talked about at the beginning of this chapter. It's the finite PS-rules that can give rise to the infinite number of sentences in languages.

The property of PS-rules that makes it possible to generate infinite structures from a finite set of rules is known as **recursion**. Recursion means roughly 'running back again', and in a way this is what happens when we generate potentially infinite structures like (37). We apply rule (24), one version of rule (35), rule (34), and then 'run back' to rule (24), and then do it all again, and again and

again. The rules, taken together, apply to their own output. Formally, this is a very simple matter: as long as you have the same
symbol on the right of the arrow as on the left (not necessarily in
the same rule, but somewhere in the rule system), and the rules
don't have to apply in a specific order (so you can 'run back').

So we see that it's the finite PS-rules that can give rise to the
infinite number of sentences in languages. Human language is
thus a system of discrete infinity. In this respect, sentences are
exactly like the whole numbers in mathematics. Sentences are
discrete in that there are five-word sentences and six-word sentences but no five-and-a-half-word sentences. Sentences are infinite in that, just like whole numbers, we can always add one more
bit to a sentence of any length at all and get another slightly longer
one, just as you can always add one to a whole number, however
large, to get a bigger one.

The recursive nature of PS-rules of the kind we have seen here
captures – in a relatively straightforward way – one of the very
central properties of human language and maybe a defining aspect
of us as humans.

∾

What we've seen in this chapter is the very heart of language: it's
the way syntax works, as specified by PS-rules generating constituent structures, which gives language its unlimited expressive
power. Arguably, this is what makes it possible for us to say – and
think – anything. Thanks to the PS-rules, we can build spaceships.

But there's still a pretty big part of the story missing. On their
own, constituent structures don't mean anything; representations
like (22), (31), (36) and (37) don't convey meaning. They're
purely formal objects, generated by the formal system of
PS-rules. We still need to see how semantics fits into the picture,
and that's what we'll do next.

5   How to Build a World
Semantics

This chapter is the last one which focuses on core aspects of language structure, although the chapters that come later – particularly the next one on pragmatics – are very important in giving you the big picture of language and linguistics.

Now we're finally going to look at meaning. Obviously, this is a major component of language; many people, both linguists and non-linguists, would say that it must be the most important. After all, what's the point of language without meaning? What's the use of meaningless noise, or meaningless forms? Well, we've seen in the previous chapters that there are plenty of interesting, even amazing, things to say about language without semantics, but of course there can be absolutely no doubt that semantics is fundamental to language. As I said in the Introduction, this is where the tyre hits the road.

So here I'll try to give a brief introduction to the main ideas in semantics. We'll look at three big questions:

- **What is meaning?**
- **Logic**
- **Compositional semantics**

The first topic is an obvious one. On the other hand, the point of looking at logic may not seem obvious but will emerge. And the third topic connects semantics to what we've seen up to now, particularly in the previous chapter.

Meaning and Truth

Semantics is hard and so it's quite likely you'll find this the hardest chapter in the book. This is where you scale the summit of linguistics, and I hope you'll find the effort worth it; the view from the top is pretty impressive.

One of the reasons semantics is so hard is that its subject matter is hard to define. As we've seen, phonetics is about the sounds of language, phonology is about how those sounds pattern in linguistic systems, morphology is about the structure of words and syntax is about the structure of sentences. In all these areas, the subject matter is pretty apparent, and in fact we didn't spend any time worrying about it in the previous chapters.

Semantics is about meaning. But what is meaning? What is it about the phoneme sequence /kæt/ that means furry feline? Why does /dɒg/ mean canine mammal? One thing we can certainly say is that these meanings – or whatever they are – are **conventional** and **arbitrary**. The English word *dog* (or /dɒg/) means nice canine, but if you're French it's *chien*, if you're German it's *Hund*, if you're Welsh it's *ci* and so on. These are just the conventions of the different speech communities. The relation between the phonological shape of a word and what it means is arbitrary; this idea is known as *the arbitrary nature of the linguistic sign* (and was put forward just over a hundred years ago by the Swiss linguist Ferdinand de Saussure). This idea is connected to duality of patterning (introduced in Chapter 3), in that the second level of patterning (the one involving meaningful elements) is arbitrarily connected to the first (combining phonemes).

But that doesn't help with really understanding meaning. The main reason this is so difficult is that meaning relates linguistic stuff (words, morphemes, sentences) to non-linguistic stuff. That's what talking about stuff involves. But how? One completely impractical answer is to say that, since meaning is the relation between language and non-language, semantics involves studying everything except linguistics. If that's right, we might as well end this chapter here and log on to Wikipedia. But all the knowledge in the world (or Wikipedia), for example everything zoologists and biologists know about cats and dogs, doesn't really tell you what the words *cat* and *dog* mean. Still less does it tell you how the sentences *The cat bit the dog* and *The dog bit the cat* mean what they do and why and how they mean different things. The basic problem is that any attempt to say what meaning is involves language and so we're defining language in terms of language. Is there any way to break the circle?

The best, although nonetheless highly problematic, idea about meaning is to say that meaning can, in many cases, be reduced to **reference**. This is clearest in the case of proper names: *J.K. Rowling*, for example, refers to the well-known author. So we could say that that's the meaning of this expression. The intuitive idea here, which is quite appealing at least at first, is that words label things. This approach seems to break the circle – we're relating words to things.

So, *Clover* refers to a certain specific cat, *Sim* to another one, *Wonky-Head* to another one and so on. The NP *the cat*, refers to some known cat; *a cat* to any individual cat, known or unknown, and, maybe, *cat* to all possible cats. The problem for this approach concerns non-existent entities, which we can quite happily – and meaningfully – talk about. What does *unicorn* refer to? If there are no unicorns, it doesn't refer to anything. But the word is *not* meaningless, and neither does it mean the same as *nothing*, which seemingly refers to, well, nothing.

Maybe we could say that at least words like *unicorn* refer to concepts in our minds (and perhaps words like *cat* do too). Fine, except we don't really know what concepts are. Are there concepts for which there are no words, perhaps waiting (where?) to be referred to when we come up with the right word? Are there words which designate impossible concepts (certainly there are phrases, like *a round square*)? We just don't really know. Linguists, philosophers and psychologists have speculated about these fascinating questions but with little real result. One thing at least seems clear: it's ok talking about cats as a concept as we know that they exist independently of our concept of them (or at least we *think* they do. . .). But abstract concepts, such as *justice*, *sincerity* or *three* (numbers are *highly* abstract concepts!) are very hard for most of us to think about without thinking of the word. Are the words and the concepts really separate from one another? Is our set of concepts just our vocabulary? If so, then we're locked back in the linguistic circle.

A way out of this is to say that the intuitive notion of meaning really has two parts to it: reference, the thing(s) a word labels in the world, and **sense**, an intrinsic property of the word that gives it its power of referring to something. Then we can say that the reference of *cat* is furry felines, and the sense of the word is what makes it mean furry felines, clearly somewhat related to but not identical to the concept of cat. And this way you don't have to be a zoologist to understand what the word *cat* means.

There are two advantages of this approach. First, we can say that a word like *unicorn* has no reference (in our world), because there aren't any unicorns. But it still has sense: if there were some unicorns, it would refer to them and not to other stuff (or nothing). And in worlds of our imagination populated by unicorns, it refers to them.

A second advantage is that it allows us to understand how two words or expressions can refer to exactly the same thing and yet, in an obvious intuitive way, mean something different. So, for example, *J.K. Rowling* and *the author of the Harry Potter books* both refer to the same person, but they mean different things because they have different senses (and you can imagine a world in which someone else had written the Harry Potter books and then these two expressions wouldn't refer to the same person).

So let's conclude that words, and at least some phrases, have reference (that's what they label in the world) and sense (what makes the label stick). What about sentences? At first this question looks even harder. But two things can be said here, and they point together towards a *very* interesting approach to semantics.

The first thing about sentences is that – for the most part – their meaning derives from the meaning of their parts. Let's look again at a sentence from the previous chapter:

(1)   The cat ate a fat mouse.

This sentence obviously means something involving cats, mice and eating, whatever the senses and references of these words. Also, the syntax of the sentence is relevant; keeping the same words but putting them in a different order changes the meaning of the sentence, as (2) shows:

(2)   A fat mouse ate the cat.

This sentence still involves cats, mice and eating, but it clearly relates to a different situation from that described by (1). So, sentence meaning depends on the words that make up the sentences and how they are put together: sentence meaning is compositional.

The second thing will give us a basis for the rest of our discussion of semantics. If you understand what a sentence means, you understand what the world would have to be like for that sentence to be true. So, if I say *It's raining*, you can look out of the window, or up at the sky, or whatever and say *Yes, it is* or *No, it's not*. If you've understood the sentence, you know what the world would have to be like for the sentence to be true (and, by implication, if the world isn't that way, you know the sentence is false). So, *to know the meaning of a sentence is to know the conditions that would make that sentence true*. In this way, we can identify the meaning of a sentence with its **truth conditions**. This approach to semantics is known as **truth-conditional semantics**, and we'll explore it a little bit in the remainder of this chapter.

We can link this idea about sentence meaning to sense and reference by saying that the reference of a sentence is True or False, while the sense of a sentence is what makes it true or false. This in turn depends on the meanings (references and senses) of the words that make the sentence up, and on how they are combined. This approach works best, and was developed for, declarative sentences. Other types of sentence, such as interrogatives as in *Did the cat eat a mouse?* don't seem to fit so well. To cut a long story short, we can integrate this kind of interrogative into the truth-conditional approach by taking it to mean something like 'Either the cat ate a mouse or the cat didn't eat a mouse, which is true?' You might note that an appeal is being made here to a more knowledgeable interlocutor, who is presumed to be able to provide the answer – I'll come back to the question of speaker-hearer interaction, and, briefly, the nature of interrogatives, in the next chapter.

So let's look in a bit more detail at how all of this works. But before looking at compositional, truth-conditional semantics any further we need to take a quick detour into formal logic, for reasons that will become apparent.

Logic

Logic is the study of deductions, inferences and related matters. The laws of logic are sometimes called 'the laws of thought'. Our intuitions about logic allow us to say that the reasoning in (3) is cogent while that in (4) is not:

(3)   All cats are mortal.
        Clover is a cat.
        Therefore Clover is mortal.

(4)   All cats are mortal.
        Fido is a dog.
        Therefore Paris is the capital of France.

This much is pretty clear. But what has this kind of thing got to do with semantics? The connection lies in the notion of truth. Logically sound inferences like that in (3) are truth-preserving: if the premises (the first two lines) are true, then the conclusion (in the last line) just *has* to be true; if you deny it you're being ridiculous. So the rules of logical inference are really also about preserving truth. Now, if the meaning of a sentence has to do with what makes it true, then it's clear that logic and semantics are closely connected. In fact, as linguists, we can use two and half millennia of logic (since the time of Aristotle) to give ourselves a leg-up with our notion of truth, and therefore of meaning.

Logical truth is *not* factual truth, as the inference in (5) shows:

(5)   If the moon is made of green cheese, then everyone is happy.
        The moon is made of green cheese.
        Therefore everyone is happy.

This is a valid inference, even though both the second premise (in the second line) and the conclusion are factually false. The logic is nonetheless sound: if the second premise were true, the conclusion would hold.

In fact, the validity of logical inferences depends on the interaction and meanings of certain logical words, such as *if, then* and *not*. We don't really need to worry about the other parts in examples like (3) and (5) since logic isn't about facts. For example, any inference of the following form is valid, where *p* and *q* stand for any sentence (or in logic, any **proposition**):

(6)   If p, then q

        p

        Therefore q

Notation: in logic, lowercase letters of the alphabet starting with *p* are used to stand for propositions.

In (6), we are displaying what is known as the **logical form** of the inference. Logical form is a key concept in logic because of the generalisation that if an inference of a certain logical form is valid or true, then all inferences or sentences of that form are valid and true. So formal logic is mainly about encoding valid inferences by putting them into logical form.

Again, what has this got to do with semantics? The connection is that truth, as we have suggested, is a core notion in semantics. We can identify the meaning of a sentence with its truth conditions, as we saw. Our theory of meaning is therefore going to involve truth (especially if sentences refer to the True or the False). Logic is all about truth, too. Logical notations which display truth relations among sentences can be thought of as expressing certain aspects of meaning. So we can, in a way, hijack logic and logical form in the service of truth-conditional semantics. So now let's do a bit of logic.

There are two main kinds of formal logic: **propositional logic** and **predicate logic**. We have to look at propositional logic first, as we need that in order to understand predicate logic.

Propositional logic, as the name implies, deals with relations among propositions (roughly sentences – we'll come back to the differences between sentences and propositions in the next chapter). Propositional logic is mainly concerned with the **connectives**, the 'logical words' like *if* and *and*, which connect propositions. The connectives are known as **truth-functional** because they always affect the truth of the propositions they connect in the same systematic way.

There are five truth-functional connectives in standard propositional logic: **negation, conjunction,** disjunction, **implication** and **equivalence**. Let's look at each of these, and introduce the symbol for each one, in turn, using one of the standard logical notations.

First, negation. Actually this isn't strictly speaking a connective, as it doesn't connect two propositions, but just affects one. The symbol for negation is $\neg$. So $\neg p$ (read 'not-p') has the opposite truth value to p. Whenever p is true, $\neg p$ is false, and vice versa. We can summarise this in a simple **truth table** as in (7):

(7) | p | $\neg p$ |
     |-------|----------|
     | true | false |
     | false | true |

This actually tells us the truth-conditional meaning of $\neg$, and comes close to the meaning of *not* in English: if *it's raining* is true (look out the window!), *it's not raining* is false and vice versa.

Conjunction is symbolised &. The conjunction of two propositions, p & q, is true just where (in Logic-Speak, if and only if) both p is true and q is true; otherwise p & q is false. The truth table for conjunction is:

(8) | p | q | p & q |
     |-----|-----|-----------|
     | t | t | t |
     | f | t | f |
     | t | f | f |
     | f | f | f |

Notation: here 'true' and 'false' are abbreviated as 't' and 'f' respectively. This is standard practice, and I'll follow it from now on.

The meaning of & is close to English *and*; if I say *Clocks are big and machines are heavy*, this is true just in case (if and only if) *Clocks are big* is true and *Machines are heavy* is true. If either or both of these sentences is false, then the sentence which conjoins them with *and* is false.

Next, disjunction, symbolised *v*. The disjunction of two propositions, *p v q*, is true if and only if either *p* or *q* is true on its own. The truth table for disjunction is:

(9) | *p* | *q* | *p v q* |
|-----|-----|---------|
| t | t | t |
| f | t | t |
| t | f | t |
| f | f | f |

Actually, there are two kinds of disjunction, inclusive and exclusive. The table in (9) is the truth table for **inclusive disjunction**, which approximates to 'and/or'. You can see that the first line of (9), where both *p* and *q* are independently true, makes *p v q* true; this is just the same as conjunction, as you can see by checking the first line of (8).

Exclusive disjunction, on the other hand, corresponds roughly to 'either/or'. It is sometimes written ⊕. The exclusive disjunction of *p* and *q*, *p ⊕ q*, is true if and only if either *p* or *q* is true, but *not both together*. The truth table is (10), which you can compare with (9) to see that the first line is different:

(10) | *p* | *q* | *p ⊕ q* |
|------|-----|---------|
| t | t | f |
| f | t | t |
| t | f | t |
| f | f | f |

Better living through semantics (Part One): next Halloween, when you go trick or treating, after you've been given your treat by your neighbour, feel free to trash their house in the usual tricky way. When confronted by the indignant homeowner that you got your treat, point out that you read *trick or treat* as *inclusive* disjunction. So you get your treat (*q* is true) and you trash your neighbour's house (*p* is true), and, by inclusive disjunction, *p v q* is true.

Next comes implication. This one is a bit trickier than the last three, as it's not quite as intuitive (for reasons we'll touch on in the next chapter). Implication is written →. So $p \rightarrow q$ ('if p then q') is true where either p is false or q is true. The truth table is:

(11) p q $p \rightarrow q$
        t   t   t
        f   t   t
        t   f   f
        f   f   t

Take the sentence *If it's raining, then I'll take an umbrella*. Obviously, this is true when it's raining and I take my umbrella (first line of (11)). It's *also* true if I take my umbrella and it *isn't* raining – not so obviously in this case (second line of (11)). On the other hand, it's *false* just when it's raining and I don't take my umbrella (third line). It's also, rather vacuously, true if I don't take my umbrella and it's not raining.

> *Better living through semantics (Part Two)*: get your parents to agree that if you mow the lawn, then they'll give you £20 (remember to put it just like that). Then lock up the lawnmower, let the grass grow and claim your £20. At the same time, you can teach your parents about implication (NB: if your parents are logicians, don't try this).

The second line of (11) is conceptually important. It really says that nothing follows from a false proposition. False propositions are of no use to logicians as inference is about the preservation of truth.

The final connective is equivalence (also known as the biconditional). This means 'exactly when', 'only when', 'just when' or, more formally, 'if and only if' (abbreviated as 'iff'). It's written as ↔. Here's the truth table:

(12) p q $p \leftrightarrow q$
        t   t   t
        f   t   f
        t   f   f
        f   f   t

Comparing this truth table with the one in (11), you can see that the only difference is the second line. (This, by the way, is what makes the non-lawn-mowing trick just described work with implication, but not with equivalence).

In a way, when we give these truth-functional definitions of the logical connectives, we are defining part of the meaning of words like *not, or, and* and *if* by giving their logical form. So here we see the connections among logic, truth and meaning and how logic can be a tool for semantics.

Now let's go back to our earlier deductions. We can restate (6) as follows:

(13) $p \rightarrow q$

         p

         $\therefore q$

You should be able to see that, on the basis of the truth table in (11), (13) holds, whatever truth value of *p* and *q* you start from. You can also work out some neat deductions. For example, whenever $p \rightarrow q$ is true, its contrapositive $\neg q \rightarrow \neg p$ is also true. This follows from the truth table in (7) and the one for implication in (11).

So propositional logic formalises some of our intuitions about valid inferences. As such, it expresses aspects of logical form. Hence, if we think that truth is central to understanding meaning, it expresses some aspects of meaning.

But propositional logic is pretty limited. It doesn't capture anything like enough of our intuitions regarding logical deductions or the truth conditions of sentences. To see this, look again at the inference in (3):

(3)   All cats are mortal.
         Clover is a cat.
         Therefore Clover is mortal.

We can write this in propositional logic as $(p \,\&\, q) \rightarrow r$ (i.e. 'if both all cats are mortal (*p*) and Clover is a cat (*q*), then Clover is mortal (*r*)'; as in school algebra, you do the calculation inside the brackets first). You can work out, using the truth tables for conjunction and implication, that if *p* and *q* are both true, then *r* must be too. But exactly the same holds for the non-inference in (4):

(4)   All cats are mortal.   (*p*)
        Fido is a dog.   (*q*)
        Therefore Paris is the capital of France.   (*r*)

Again, (4) has the form (*p* & *q*) → *r* in propositional logic and so the truth of *r* will follow from the truth of both *p* and *q*. But of course there's a big intuitive difference between (3) and (4). The truth of the conclusion in (3) seems to follow inevitably from the truth of the two premisses (as Aristotle noted twenty-five centuries ago), but this isn't so in (4).

This is where predicate logic comes in. Predicate logic looks inside propositions and breaks them down into **predicates** (roughly corresponding to verbs and adjectives, or VPs and APs, in syntax) and **arguments** (roughly corresponding to nouns or NPs). A simple sentence like (14) would be written as (15a) in propositional logic and as (15b) in predicate logic:

(14)   Clover is wise.

(15)   a. *p*
        b. W(*c*)

Notation: in (15b), W symbolises the predicate 'is wise' (a kind of VP) and *c* stands for 'Clover'. The conventions are that predicates are written in capitals, arguments in lowercase and predicates are written in front of their arguments with the arguments immediately following them in round brackets.

In order to see how predicate logic can tell us the difference between (3) and (4), we need to pay attention to one crucial word that shows up in the first line of both: the word *all*. This is an example of a **quantifier**, a word that expresses a quantity of something. So *all cats* expresses a quantity of cats (the whole lot), for example. The other really important quantifier in predicate logic is *some*: *some cats* also expresses a quantity of cats, but a different (and seemingly smaller) quantity than *all cats*.

Quantification, including words like *all* and *some* in NPs, is central to predicate logic and very important for semantics, as we shall see. The main reason for this is that quantified expressions, like *all cats* in (3) and (4), are expressions which don't involve individuals (unlike *Clover, J.K. Rowling, Priscilla, Bellatrix, Mary*, etc.), but rather a **quantity** or group of individuals of some kind – hence the name. Quantified expressions have special logical properties. To see this, compare the next two sentences:

(16)   a. Clover is wise and Clover is not wise.
       b. Some cats are wise and some cats are not wise.

(16a) is a logical contradiction; it's always false. In propositional logic, we write it as p & $\neg p$. If you apply the truth tables for conjunction and negation, you'll see that this just has to always come out false (pragmatic considerations which we'll look at in the next chapter might allow you to say (16a) in a certain situation without contradicting yourself, but let's leave that aside for now). So propositional logic does a good job of telling us about (16a). But it treats (16b) *exactly the same way*, and yet (16b) doesn't have to be false at all (pragmatics or not). It doesn't express a contradiction; instead it expresses a proposition that may or may not be true, depending on how the world is.

A further point, which will help us see the difference between (3) and (4), concerns sentences like (17):

(17)   All cats are wise.

We could try writing (17) as (18) in predicate logic, on the model of (15b):

(18) $W(a)$

Here W is still 'are wise' and a stands for 'all cats'. But, as we said, 'all cats' isn't (aren't?) an individual we can pick out and so representing it in predicate-logic notation as a is misleading. If you think about it, what (17) really says is something like 'any cat you can find will be wise', or 'if something is a cat, then it's wise' or even (entering Logic-Speak now) 'for everything in the universe, if it is a cat then it is wise'. Predicate logic, but not propositional logic, allows us to express this. Let's see how.

This is where the quantifiers come in. In predicate logic, we write (19) as (20):

(19)   Some cats are wise.

(20) $\exists x \, [C(x) \, \& \, W(x)]$

As with the phonological rules and PS-rules seen in earlier chapters, (20) is like a chemical formula or an algebraic equation expressing a great deal of information in a very concise way. To see what it says, we need to go through the symbols slowly, systematically and step by step. So let's do that.

The first symbol, the backwards capital E, $\exists$, is the **existential quantifier**. It means 'There is at least one', or, more simply, 'some'. The x following it is a **variable** like in school algebra, except in school algebra it means 'any number', while here it means 'any individual'. Then (note the brackets; square and round brackets are used just to distinguish them), we have the predicate C for 'is a cat'. After that, we have another x, which means 'any individual' again. *But*: whatever value x gets here, it must get everywhere in the formula (or, more precisely, everywhere inside the square brackets following the quantifier). So if we 'fill in' x with one value (say, Clover, a good example of an individual) in one place in the formula, all the other x's have to be filled in the same way, so if one x is Clover, all the other x's inside the square brackets must be Clover. Next we have good old conjunction; here it conjoins $C(x)$ and $W(x)$, and it works just the same way as in propositional logic, that is it follows the truth table in (8), where we treat $C(x)$ and $W(x)$ as if they were propositions like p and q. Then we have W, still meaning 'is/are wise' and then another x requiring the same value as the others.

So we translate (20) into Logic-Speak as 'There is at least one something or other, such that that something or other is both a cat and is wise'. That's the Logic-Speak version, which sticks very close to the formula and as such is somewhat stilted, to put it mildly. In slightly more everyday English, we could restate this as 'Something is both a cat and wise' or 'There is at least one wise cat'. And here we're getting pretty close to (19).

Why go to all this trouble to translate 'some' or 'some cats' this way? The reason is that using quantifiers in predicate logic like this allows us to see the difference between (16a) and (16b). (16a) comes out as:

(21) $W(c)$ & $\neg W(c)$

Conjunction and negation are just the same as in propositional logic. Since '$W(c)$', the combination of a predicate and an argument, is a proposition, (21) is exactly equivalent to p & $\neg p$ and hence a contradiction. That seems right: Clover can't be both wise and non-wise at the same time – he has to be one or the other (of course, he might be wise at one time but not at another, as he gets older, perhaps, but I'm leaving aside the complications of tense here).

Given the way we've just translated (19) using the existential quantifier, (16b) comes out in predicate logic as:

(22) $\exists x$ [$C(x)$ & $W(x)$] & $\exists y$ [$C(y)$ & $\neg W(y)$]

The first part of (22) is the same as (20), and we just took that apart. We saw that it means 'There is at least one wise cat', roughly. The second part, after the conjunction symbol &, is almost the same as the first part, except for two crucial details. First, the variable is y, not x, which means 'something or other' still, being a variable, but a potentially *different* something or other from the x one in the first conjunct. The other difference is the negation in front of $W(y)$. What the second part of (22) says, in Logic-Speak, is 'There is another something or other which is both a cat and not wise', or 'There is at least one cat which is not wise'. Putting this together with what we said about (20), we get the whole proposition, in Logic-Speak: 'There is at least one something or other which is a cat and is wise, and there is at least one other something or other which is a cat and is not wise'. Closer to everyday English, 'There is at least one wise cat and there is at least one non-wise cat'. This is clearly not a contradiction and is a decent gloss of (16b). So we see that using the existential quantifier and its associated variables in formulae like (20) and (22) and treating NPs like *some cats* in this way can bring out very clearly the different logical and semantic properties of sentences like (16a) and (16b).

What about a statement like 'All cats are wise', as in (17)? In predicate logic, we use the other quantifier, the **universal quantifier**. This is written with an upsidedown A, $\forall$, and means roughly 'all' or 'every'. So we write (17) as:

(23) $\forall x \, [C(x) \rightarrow W(x)]$

Let's go through (23) in the same way as we did with (20). The universal quantifier $\forall$ means roughly 'every', so $\forall x$ means 'for every something or other'. $C(x)$ means 'that something or other is a cat' and $W(x)$ means 'that same something or other is wise' (remember that occurrences of the same variable inside the square brackets must have the same value). The arrow $\rightarrow$ is the symbol for implication, 'if-then', just as in propositional logic. Since $C(x)$ and $W(x)$ are equivalent to propositions, $C(x) \rightarrow W(x)$ means 'if x is a cat then x is wise'. So the whole thing means, in Logic-Speak, 'For every something or other, if it is a cat, then it is wise'. Or: 'if anything is a cat, then it is wise', or 'every cat you find will be wise'. So you can see that this pretty much captures what (17) means.

Now, at last, we are in a position to see how predicate logic can tell us the difference between (3) and (4). Let's go back to (3), along with its predicate-logic translation:

(24)   All cats are mortal. $\forall x \, [C(x) \rightarrow M(x)]$
         Clover is a cat. $C(c)$
         Therefore Clover is mortal. $M(c)$

In predicate logic, *the validity of the inference comes from simply substituting values for the variables*. We put c (for the individual argument 'Clover') as the value of the variable x in the second line because $C(x)$ and $M(x)$ are in the brackets immediately following the universal quantifier. Then in the third line we *have to* put it in as the value of the second *x*. Implication does the rest (you can check this with the truth table in (11)), and so the inference *must*, inexorably, hold.

Now let's look at (4) in predicate-logic terms:

(25)   All cats are mortal. $\forall x\ [C(x) \rightarrow M(x)]$
       Fido is a dog. $D(f)$
       Therefore Paris is the capital of France. $Cof(p)$

(Here D is 'is a dog', *f* is 'Fido', Cof 'is the capital of France' and *p* 'Paris', not to be confused with the *p* of propositional logic). Predicate logic clearly shows us that there are no logical connections between the statements in (25) and so no inference to make. So the difference between (3) and (4) emerges very nicely, thanks to the use of quantifiers, predicates and variables. These are the basic elements that predicate logic adds to propositional logic, and here we can see their usefulness.

Compositional Semantics

One might reasonably think that propositional and predicate logic are all very well, but what they can really tell us about the semantics of real languages (rather than some kind of Logic-Speak) is pretty limited. It's easy to see what they can tell us about the meanings of words like *not, and, if, some* and *all*, but there's rather more to language than that (although you'd be surprised how much you can do with propositional and predicate logic; we've only scratched the surface here).

In particular, there's syntax, complete with recursive PS-rules, as we saw in the previous chapter. Can we connect the logical, truth-based semantics we've seen here to what we've seen in syntax?

The answer is yes, although here I can only show this in a very limited and simplified way. To see how this works, let's take a very simple sentence:

(26)   Clover sleeps.

As we saw in the last chapter, this sentence has a structure like (27), generated by the relevant PS-rules (in particular the rule S → NP VP, see (24) of Chapter 4):

(27)

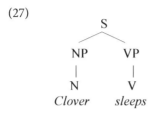

This sentence has the logical form, in predicate logic, in (28), following the conventions for writing predicates and their arguments that we introduced in the last section:

(28)   Sleep(c)

Two questions arise if we really want to do a truth-based semantics for (28). First, how do we assign a truth value to (28)? Second, how do we relate the syntax in (27) to the logical expression in (28)?

The answers to both questions involve **type theory**, the theory of logical types. This is really a precise, and in some ways simpler, version of the school-grammar idea of defining syntactic categories in terms of vague semantic notions that we briefly mentioned in Chapter 4 ('a noun is the name of a person, place or thing'). Type theory recognises two basic types: **entities** and **truth values**. These are written <e> and <t>.

(*Notation*: in semantics, angle brackets indicate types, not spellings as in phonetics/phonology).

As we'll see, more complex types can be built up from these two basic ones. Sentences are of type <t>, as they correspond (usually) to propositions and so have truth values; they are true or false (as we've seen, they refer to the True or the False).

We can answer our first question – how do we assign a truth value to an expression like (28) – by introducing a standard way of expressing **denotations**. Denotations are a cover term for the different logical meanings of the different types; in this case, since we're looking at the denotation of a proposition and propositions are of type <t>, i.e. they refer to truth values, the denotation is a truth value. We write this as in (29):

(29)   [[Sleep(c)]] is true if and only if 'Clover sleeps' is true.

Notation: semanticists use double square brackets [[ ]] to indicate the denotation of an expression inside them. So (29) can be read as 'the denotation of *Sleep(c)* is True if and only if 'Clover sleeps' is true'.

This looks pretty uninformative, but that's because we're using approximations to English both for the expression we're interpreting ('Sleep(c)') and the way we're expressing the truth conditions. Put it this way:

(30)   [[Sleep(c)]] is true iff 'Mae Clover yn cysgu' is true.

In (30), I've used Welsh to express the truth conditions of 'Sleep (*c*)' and it at least looks a bit more informative than (29). The truth conditions can in principle be stated in various ways. Welsh is not usually used (I used it here for illustration); English often is (for convenience). It's also quite common to use an enriched version of predicate logic. Another interesting possibility is to take enriched predicate logic to represent the Language of Thought, the language of our mental belief systems. (Since if something is true then you believe it; our belief systems are part of our cognitive abilities that are related to but distinct from language, and an awful lot of our talk is about expressing our beliefs and trying to alter those of others). We don't know much – or anything really – about the Language of Thought, so I'll leave this fascinating possibility aside.

So we can see a way to state the truth conditions of a logical expression like (28). But how do we get from the syntactic structure in (27) to (28)? Here again we can use type theory to get us started. What we can try to do is to convert syntactic categories like S, NP and VP (and so on) into semantic types like $<e>$ and $<t>$. It's easy at first: S expresses a proposition, so it's type $<t>$. NPs (and Ns) express an entity – Clover is clearly one of these – so NP is of type $<e>$. But what about VP?

This is where the key idea in compositional semantics comes in. What does the syntactic object $[_{VP}$ *sleeps* $]$ in (27) correspond to in the logical expression in (28)? Obviously, the predicate *Sleep*, you might think. Well, not exactly; a predicate must have an argument, and *Sleep*, written just like that, doesn't have one. If we say that $[_{VP}$ *sleeps* $]$ corresponds to *Sleep(c)* then we're saying, incorrectly, that $[_{VP}$ *sleeps* $]$ somehow means 'Clover sleeps', which it obviously doesn't. Instead, we need to put in a variable for c in (28): *Sleep(x)*.

Now we're getting somewhere. A simple VP like $[_{VP}$ *sleeps* $]$ corresponds to the predicate-logic expression *Sleep(x)*. But what does *Sleep(x)* mean? On its own, strictly speaking, nothing. Any expression containing a free variable, i.e. an x with no quantifier around, is uninterpretable. In the absence of a quantifier, semanticists 'borrow' a device from mathematics and use the λ-operator (λ is the Greek letter lambda) in order to express the intuition behind what the predicate on its own means. Although this looks very impressive, it's really just a way to save the day for the variable, which, technically, can then be bound by λ. So we get the formula $λx[Sleep(x)]$, which just means 'those x's which sleep' (in Logic-Speak 'the x such that x sleep'). This formula gives the denotation of the VP in our example, so we can say:

(31) $[[[_{VP}$ *sleeps* $]]] = λx[Sleep(x)]$

So our VP here means 'those things which sleep'.

Now we can see a way to put things together. The VP *sleeps* means 'those x which sleep'. You can think of an expression like this as a way to divide everything in the universe into two classes: things which sleep and things which don't. In the first class, we have Clover, me, colourless green ideas, lions and indeed all mammals. In the second class, we have New York (according to Frank Sinatra), rocks, numbers and stars. So the meaning of [$_{VP}$ *sleep*] takes an entity and tells you whether or not it sleeps. In other words, it maps entities to truth values: for any entity (me, Clover, New York, etc.) it says whether or not that entity sleeps. So VPs (or, really VP denotations, [[VP]]) map entities <e> to truth values <t>. So we say that they take an <e> and give you a <t>; they are of type <e, t>.

So we can combine our syntactic representation and these ideas about type theory, decorating the tree with logical fairy lights which give the denotation of each node:

(32)

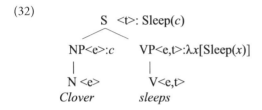

Remember that we said that *Clover* and NPs like that (proper names, for example), are of type <e>, an entity. Syntactically combining NP and VP to make S means semantically combining an expression of type <e> (NP) with one of type <e, t> (VP) to get one of type <t> (S). So, an entity (type <e>), such as Clover, denoted by an NP, combines with a predicate of type <e, t>, denoted by a VP, to give an S, of type <t>. There's an operation akin to cancellation of the two <e>'s going on here. Given the denotations of the syntactic elements specified in this way, this amounts to saying that 'Clover sleeps' is true if and only if the denotation of 'Clover', a noun and an NP, the entity Clover, is 'in' the denotation of the VP, 'those things that sleep'. Put another way, our sentence is true if Clover is among the sleeping entities and false otherwise. This is a pretty good rendering of what the sentence *Clover sleeps* means. So this gets the meaning of the sentence nicely. The syntactic combination of NP and VP corresponds to the semantic operation of putting the NP-denotation c (representing Clover) 'in' the VP-denotation λx *[Sleep(x)]*. This corresponds to substituting *c* for the variable in *λx[Sleep(x)]* and knocking out the λ (which was only there to bind the variable anyway), so we get *Sleep(c)* of type <t>. And that has the truth conditions I just stated.

There's a beautiful and elegant mathematical basis for all this, but this isn't the place to go into those details. Just one last thing: calling NPs and Ns type <e> is something of an oversimplification. It works for proper names like *Clover* and *J. K. Rowling* but not for all NPs. To see this, try a sentence with a quantifier in it:

(33)   All mammals sleep.

We can give (33) the constituent structure in (34), taking *all* to be a D:

(34)

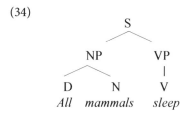

This is fairly straightforward (see PS-rule (28ii) of Chapter 4). The predicate logic expression for (34) is:

(35) $\forall x$ [Mammal(x) → Sleep(x)]

How do we connect (34) and (35)? This has been a major conundrum for semantic theory for many years. I won't give the whole story here but just point two things out. First, as (35) indicates, we actually have to treat simple common nouns like *mammal* as predicates, having the logical form *Mammal(x)*, etc., and so being, like VPs, of type <e, t>. A common noun tells you whether something is one or not: *mammal* divides the world into mammals and non-mammals, just as *sleep* divides the world into sleepers and non-sleepers.

So *all* has to convert *mammals* into an <e>. But actually it's worse: we have to do something with the implication → too. To cut a long story short, quantifiers like *all* relate predicates to one another: what *all* says is that anything which belongs to the <e,t> *mammal* also belongs to the <e,t> *sleep*. This involves assigning a rather complex type to *all*, so I'll spare you the details of how this is done.

This approach has some nice results. If simple common nouns are really of type <e,t>, then, just as the meaning of *sleep* is $\lambda x[Sleep(x)]$, the meaning of *mammal* is $\lambda x[Mammal(x)]$, and the meaning of *life* is given below:

> *Better living through semantics (Part III)*: so, having suffered through all this, you now deserve to know the following:
>
> (36) λx [life(x)] & ιy [universe (y)] & $\forall z$ [F(z)]
>
> The 'ι' (the Greek letter iota) is a way of expressing the meaning of the definite article *the*: it means roughly 'the one and only'. So, maybe you've guessed, (36) is the meaning of life, the universe and everything. How cool is that?

~

By now, we've seen how everything fits together, at least in outline. We've gone from the writhing and wriggling of the organs of speech in phonetics, to how the phonological brain imposes patterns on the phonetic brawn, to the duality of patterning which permits a small number of phonemes to make a very large number of morphemes and words, to how the rules of syntax can make an *infinite* number of sentences out of those morphemes and words, to how a truth-based, logical semantics can *interpret* the syntactic structures and give them meanings, construed in a very precise way as truth conditions. This is how we can say – and understand – *anything*. Not bad, eh?

But this book is about making noises and influencing people. You might have noticed that people (and societies, cultures – that sort of thing) have been rather absent in our discussions of

PS-rules, logical forms, type theory and so on. *People* use language to mean things, influence other people and do stuff (like building spaceships). And they do it very cleverly indeed! Time for a shift of gears, to look at how people manipulate syntax, and, in particular, logic, when they want to influence each other.

6   How to Influence People
Pragmatics

This chapter completes our picture of how language works, and at the same time paves the way for later chapters, all of which relate language to its various contexts: historical, social and psychological. What we're interested in here is how language is used in various subtle and clever ways to mean more that what is said.

In humour, we very often leave things unsaid, and this is the basis for many a good joke (but I'm not going spoil any of them by trying to analyse them). The important thing here is that much is often left unsaid in ordinary conversation, joking or not. It is quite usual to mean more – much more – than we say; we all do it all the time.

We have to clarify two meanings of *mean* here. On the one hand there's **sentence meaning**, which is what we were talking about when we tried to show how syntactic structures can be interpreted by a logical semantics; here we can say that nouns, verbs, NPs and VPs mean something. But what's going to be relevant in this chapter is speaker meaning: roughly, what people intend to communicate by what they say (and what they don't say, as we'll see). The two notions of meaning are obviously connected although the connections are intricate and subtle.

Pragmatics is a big and growing field. Here I'm going to limit myself to introducing two classic ideas: **speech acts** and **implicatures**.

Speech Acts

Speech-act theory was first put forward by the Oxford philosopher J.L. Austin. Austin wasn't a linguist, but he was interested in trying to understand philosophical ideas by analysing language (this was the 'ordinary language' school of philosophy, which flourished in Oxford in the years after World War Two). Austin's branch of philosophy was ethics: the study of morals, goodness and how to lead a good life. So, for example, he wanted to understand what was involved in keeping and breaking promises. He quickly realised that giving the truth conditions for a sentence like *I promise I'll give you your money back* doesn't tell you much about the ethics of keeping a promise: what a promise really is, i.e. what the word *promise* really means.

Austin made a distinction between **performative** and constative sentences. Constatives are the kinds of sentences we've been looking at in the previous chapter: sentences that say something that might be true or false, like *It's raining, Clover ate a mouse* and *All mammals sleep*, etc. As we've seen, truth-conditional semantics seems to work quite well here. Performatives, on the other hand, don't so much *say* something as *do* something. Examples are *I promise to pay you back tomorrow, I name this ship the USS Enterprise* and *I solemnly swear that I am telling the truth*, etc. Giving the truth conditions for these sentences seems pointless. Instead, to understand what they *really* mean, you have to understand what they *do*, and how they do it.

To do this, Austin further distinguished what he called the **locutionary act** of saying a sentence (that is, actually uttering it) from the illocutionary act, this is what the sentence is used to do. The illocutionary act carries **illocutionary force**, and that's what the utterance of the sentence does. The illocutionary force of a performative is what it's meant to *do*. So, the illocutionary force of a promise is that, by uttering the sentence under the right conditions (these are important, as we'll see right away), you actually *make a promise* to someone to do something. Performatives perform **speech acts**, and speech acts have illocutionary force. The illocutionary force of *I hereby pronounce you husband and wife* is to marry a couple, for example.

Alongside their illocutionary force, speech acts have **felicity conditions**, which specify what makes a speech act work, and **perlocutionary effects**, which are the result of the speech act. So the felicity conditions for promising are, for example, that I have to be capable of fulfilling the promise. There's no point in saying to someone – however much you might like to – *I promise you all the money in the world, immortal life and a planet of your own.* The reason is that we can't fulfil the promise, and so the basic felicity condition isn't met. For the marriage ceremony, there's no point in most of us saying to some random couple we might know *I hereby pronounce you husband and wife.* In order to carry out the speech act, you have to have the civil or religious power to marry people; obviously you also need the people, and they need to want to get married. All of these are felicity conditions.

The perlocutionary effect of a promise is that you are under the obligation it expresses; you've got to do what you promised to do or you're a bad person, guilty of the misdemeanour of breaking a promise and, in principle, open to whatever punishment that might exist in your society or legal system. The perlocutionary effect of the marrying speech act is that the couple so married are stuck with each other until death or divorce do them part.

Here's another example, just to get these ideas clear:

(1)   I name this vessel the Starship Enterprise.

The speech act carried out here is the act of naming the starship. That's the illocutionary force: by saying (1), given the right felicity conditions, you actually give the vessel its name.

The felicity conditions in this case might be a bit demanding. First, you need a nice, newly-built starship (not so easy to find). Second, you need to have the power to utter (1), perhaps invested in you by the Galactic Federation (or perhaps not). Third, you need to accompany the naming act with a conventionally appropriate gesture such as breaking a bottle of champagne on the warp-drive boosters. And so on. The perlocutionary effect of (1), if all the felicity conditions are fulfilled, is that the Enterprise is then a starship in good standing, able and ready to boldly go where no man has gone before.

So, if you walk into your living room one quiet evening and say (1) in front of your family and friends, you haven't named a starship. At best, you've made a fool of yourself; at worst, they'll call the people in white coats. But the truth conditions of (1) are exactly the same whether the speech act is successfully carried out or not.

There are lots of speech acts. In fact, the more you think about them, the more there are: persuading, asking and ordering are among the really obvious ones. So, let's take asking questions. The felicity conditions for asking a question are, at least, that you don't know the answer (hence *Do bears shit in the woods?* isn't a real question, since in our culture everyone is assumed to know the answer), that the person you're asking has a reasonable chance of knowing the answer (so *What is the meaning of life?* is not a reasonable question to put to a non-guru or a non-semanticist). The illocutionary force is that the question is successfully put: we could call this interrogativity. The perlocutionary effect, if all goes well, is that you'll get the answer.

One important point here is that questions – or, more precisely, interrogatives – have a special syntax in many languages. In English, as we briefly saw in Chapter 4, they involve 'inverting' the auxiliary in front of the subject NP. But the illocutionary force of a question and interrogative syntax are distinct things, although they often go together. We can use a syntactic interrogative to give an order, as in *Why don't you shut up?* Conversely, we can ask a question without interrogative syntax, as in *I heard you're getting married*, which, in the right context, could naturally be taken as asking someone whether they're getting married.

What's important about speech acts is that they show how language can be *used*, in the right *contexts*, with the right *people*, to do more than its structural elements on their own seem to mean. Speech acts are a great example of how speaker meaning adds a further dimension to language, and greatly adds to its already formidable expressive power. What's also important is that *people have to cooperate* to make speech acts work. Most of the felicity conditions involve some kind of *mutual knowledge*; if I ask you a question or make you a promise in such a way that the speech acts actually have a chance of working, I have to recognise your role in the felicity conditions, illocutionary force and perlocutionary effects, and you have to recognise mine. It's impossible to perform speech acts in a vacuum. These ideas about implicit co-operation and mutual knowledge are even more central to the notion of Implicature, which is the next topic.

Implicatures

The notion of implicature was put forward by another Oxford philosopher connected to the ordinary language school: H. Paul Grice. Implicatures (a term Grice invented) are forms of reasoning we all use all the time in normal linguistic interactions, but they are *not* logical deductions, inferences or entailments, in the sense that they are not captured – and should not be captured – by the rules of a logical system like propositional or predicate logic.

As a philosopher, Grice was interested in human rationality, and, in particular, how people co-operate reasonably in everyday life, particularly in exchanging information. His main idea was the **Co-operative Principle**, which divides into various conversational maxims. There are four of these, as follows:

Maxim of Quality: be truthful

Maxim of Quantity: be brief

Maxim of Relation: be relevant

Maxim of Manner: be clear.

A natural initial reaction to this is that either it is a pretty poor theory of how people communicate, or some sort of philosophical pie in the sky. It's absolutely obvious that people aren't truthful, they witter on, they go off the point and they don't express themselves clearly. But, *and this was Grice's point*, and this is the clever part: people flout the maxims all the time, but since everyone has an awareness that the maxims should be obeyed, if

I recognise that you're flouting a maxim, I put this down to a communicative intention on your part that I should recognise this, and so I do recognise this and this allows you to achieve a certain communicative effect.

A simple example comes from metaphors. If I say to you, *'You're the cat's whiskers'*, this is obviously not true. In straight truth-conditional terms, the sentence is false and that's that. But why would I sit around uttering false sentences? You assume, first, that I'm not insane (ok . . .). Second, you assume that I'm not a liar (of course people do tell lies, but communication cannot proceed at all unless a basic assumption of veracity is made; this is one of the reasons why lying is bad). So, if I'm sane and truthful, why am I talking nonsense? Why am I saying something which is patently untrue? This is where you recognise my intention to communicate something *other* than what I actually said, thanks to the Co-operative Principle. I'm obviously violating the Maxim of Quality by saying something false, and I'm violating the Maxim of Manner by saying something obscure about cat-parts. So you recognise my intention to do that (note that if you assume I'm lying or mad, you implicitly abandon the Co-operative Principle; it is a principle of rational interaction and rationality involves good faith), and you recognise my intention that you will recognise my intention. So you conclude that I must be trying to say something more, i.e. that I think you're pretty special and nice (since these are general properties of cats' whiskers, by a vague cultural convention).

The really interesting thing about all of this is that it relies on each of our abilities to recognise the other's intentions as they violate a maxim. I have to recognise the contents of your mind – in a way, I'm reading your mind with the help of the Co-operative Principle, and you're reading mine. This ability to think about – and recognise – someone else's intentions, thoughts and beliefs, and to recognise that they might be different from your own, is known as **Theory of Mind**. Each of us actually has an intuitive theory of what other people's minds are like: the sorts of thoughts, beliefs, desires and intentions others have. We readily – almost unthinkingly – attribute minds of this kind to other humans, and sometimes to pets and computers ('this bloody thing doesn't want to save my file!', which is of course nonsense as computers no more have desires than tables or parsnips do). Babies, up to about age one, and some people with autism may have impaired Theory of Mind: they can't recognise that the contents of other minds might be different from their own.

However, the kind of reasoning about others' intentions that's involved here goes like this: 'My interlocutor said something they know to be false, and they expect me to recognise that, and that I will recognise that they intended me to recognise that and they expect me to conclude on this basis that they really meant . . .'. All of this involves some syntactically complex reasoning, arguably involving structures (of thought, not necessarily of actual sentences) like those we saw in Chapter 4 using recursive application of PS-rules. There could be a link between Theory of Mind and the fact that our minds can employ recursive syntactic rules.

Let's look at some more examples of implicatures in action. Grice distinguished three types of implicature: **conventional implicatures**, **generalised conversational implicatures**, and (particular) conversational implicatures. The last kind is what we've just seen: an implicature is computed 'on the fly', using the Co-operative Principle. We really do do this all of the time.

We can illustrate conventional implicature with *but*. Compare the following sentences:

(2)   Fred is kind, and he is handsome.

(3)   Dinsdale is vicious, but he is fair.

In propositional logic, we can obviously write (2) as p & q, p being 'Fred is kind' and q being 'Fred/he is handsome' (let's ignore the business of figuring out who the pronoun refers to). So clearly (2) is true iff both conjuncts are true. No problem there.

What about (3)? How would we render it in propositional logic? This too has to be p & q. (3) is also true iff both 'Dinsdale is vicious' and 'Dinsdale is fair' are true. But there's an obvious difference between *but* and *and* (which becomes quite clear if you swap them around in (2) and (3)). The difference is that *but* comes with a conventional implicature that there is a contrast of some kind between the two conjuncts. We can roughly capture this by glossing (3) as 'Dinsdale is vicious and, despite this, he is fair'. In (2), no such extra gloss is needed.

Generalised conversational implicatures arise in what are also known as indirect speech acts. These are speech acts whose illocutionary force is, in a way, disguised, and some reasoning via the Co-operative Principle is needed to figure it out. But the cases are so common that these are not done 'on the fly', but are quite general (at least in a given culture). A classic example is:

(4)   Can you pass the salt?

This sentence has the syntax of a question (the auxiliary *can* precedes the subject NP *you*). The auxiliary *can* means, roughly, 'to be able'. But (4) is not normally taken as a question about an individual's salt-passing capacities: compare *Can you swim the Channel?*, which normally would be taken as a question about someone's abilities. In fact, if I answer (4) by saying 'Yes thanks; I'm an able-bodied adult and as such quite capable of lifting and moving a salt cellar in your general direction', and do nothing, you'd understandably be ticked off (and your dinner would remain inadequately seasoned). On the contrary, if I respond by saying nothing at all, or saying 'Of course' or 'Here!', and actually passing you the salt, I'm doing what you wanted.

How does this work? Under normal conditions, there's not much point in asking someone if they are capable of carrying out physically undemanding actions that are obviously feasible for them (contrast the reaction to (4) if I'm recovering from a broken arm and you're a physiotherapist). So in asking the question, I'm asking a question whose answer is obvious; in speech-act terms, the question doesn't meet the felicity conditions for interrogative illocutionary force. I recognise this, and so realise that your intention was *not* a request for information but rather a (polite) request for me to do something. Since I obviously *can* pass the salt, you're asking me if I *will* pass the salt. I recognise your intention for me to recognise this in virtue of your deliberate flouting of the Maxim of Quantity (no point asking a question whose answer is obvious), and, duly, pass the salt. This is a generalised conversational implicature since the sentence in (4) is commonly used in exactly this way: the implicature isn't computed 'on the fly'. Example (4) is an indirect speech act, whose illocutionary force as a request is computed as just described. The basic felicity condition is that it is trivially possible for me to pass the salt (hence the violation of the Maxim of Quantity), the illocutionary force is that of a request and the perlocutionary effect is that you get the salt.

A very important kind of implicature are **scalar implicatures**. These have to do with scales of various kinds, in particular, logical scales. A famous example has to do with numbers. In normal circumstances, in simple positive declarative sentences, using a number to modify a noun logically entails that the same sentence is true for all positive numbers lower than that number. For example, look at (5):

(5)   75,000 people came to the match.

If (5) is true, then it's also true that 74,999 people came to the match, 74,998 people came to the match and so on. Now, look at the following little dialogue:

(6)   A: How many people came to the match today?
        B: Three.

B's answer is true if 75,000 people came to the match, as we've just seen. But it's obviously not co-operative! The Maxims of Quality and Quantity (sometimes it's hard to tell which, but that needn't concern us unduly here) require us to be as precise as possible. B's answer is naturally interpreted by A as 'exactly three' (by A's recognition that if there had been 75,000 people there, B would have said so, and hence that B must have intended to say that there were exactly three people and no more there). In simple positive declarative sentences, numbers mean 'at least n' logically, but 'exactly n' pragmatically. So I can truthfully, but not at all co-operatively, tell you I have one child, when in fact I have two. Again, if I say 'I have one child', the implicature is 'exactly one', given the Co-operative Principle.

Here's another example of a scalar implicature. Going back to the quantifiers of predicate logic, it should be clear that universal quantification entails existential quantification. So, if all cats are wise, it follows that some cats are wise. Formally:

(7) $\forall x \, [F(x)] \rightarrow \exists x \, [F(x)]$

(Here 'F' just stands for any predicate). So I can truthfully say 'Some mammals sleep' even if I know that all mammals sleep, given (7). But the Co-operative Principle forces me to recognise that if I had *meant* 'all mammals sleep' I would have *said* 'all mammals sleep'; saying 'some mammals sleep' causes the impli-cature (clearly not a logical entailment) that 'not all mammals sleep'.

In general, what the number examples and the quantifier example show us is that the Co-operative Principle leads us to always make the strongest statement we can, where 'strongest' means 'most likely to be false'. A universal statement is more likely to be false than an existential one; for the universal to be false, just one nonsleeping mammal, for example, is needed, while for the existential to be false, no mammal can sleep. It's easier for an existential to be true than it is for a universal, and therefore harder for it to be false. Therefore, existentials are 'weaker' than universals, and so the Co-operative Principle leads us to state universals when we think they hold, rather than existentials, despite both being true in the same situation.

For the same reason, we naturally interpret one-way implica-tions as biconditionals, i.e. the *if* of propositional logic is often interpreted as *iff*. We saw this in the lawn-mowing example in the last chapter (see 'Better living through semantics (Part II)'). Your parents naturally interpret *If I mow the lawn, then you give me £20* as *If and only if I mow the lawn, you give me £20.* This is because the iff-statement is stronger: it's true in one less case than the if-statement (just the one where I don't mow the lawn and you give me £20).

Similarly for the numerals. If there were roughly 75,000 people at the match (say, the 75,000-seat stadium was full) then I should say that, rather than the equally true 'three people'. Of course, 75,000 can be an uncooperative number too: if I say '75,000 people live in London' or 'there are 75,000 humans on the planet', I'm being just as uncooperative as when I say there were three people at the match, since in fact there are many more in both cases. Again, to say 75,000 is true, but an uncooperatively weak statement.

A final example of implicature. If a loyal husband pops out to the pub, saying to his wife 'I'm not leaving you, dear', the wife will probably get worried. Again, if hubby's intention is indeed just to have an innocent pint, what he's *said* is true: it's not the case that he's leaving his wife. But, by alluding to p ('I'm leaving you'), he has implicated that p is at least within the bounds of possibility. The poor wife, intuitively calculating her husband's intentions using the Co-operative Principle (applying her Theory of Mind), naturally gets worried. Under certain conditions, $\neg p$ can implicate the possibility that p. Shakespeare's famous line 'Methinks the lady doth protest too much' describes a case like this.

～

What we've seen here is, I hope, enough to give you an idea of what pragmatics can tell us about how language is used in order, very often, to convey much more than just 'what is said'. Of course, this is just the sketchiest overview, but it captures the flavour of things.

It may be useful to end this chapter, and the chapters on the internal workings of language, by making a three-way distinction between utterance, sentence and proposition. The utterance is what is said in a given context, complete with implicatures, illocutionary force, etc. This is the real, everyday use of language that we all practice all the time. The sentence is the formal object, generated by PS-rules and systematically connected to a phono-logical and a semantic representation (we saw how to get from syntax to semantics, but not how to get from syntax to phon-ology). The proposition is a logical form, capable of bearing truth values. So, for *Clover ate a mouse* we have:

Utterance: klǝʊvǝr eɪt ǝ maʊs

Sentence:

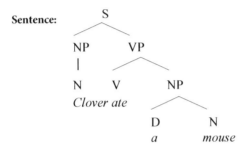

Proposition: ∃x [Mouse(x) & Eat(c,x)]

One implicature of this utterance is that Clover ate exactly one mouse; the logical form of the proposition doesn't say this, it merely 'translates' the indefinite article *a* of the sentence into the existential quantifier. The existential quantifier, remember, means 'at least one', not 'exactly one'. But if Clover had eaten more than one mouse, the utterance would most likely have been *Clover ate some/two/fifty mice*, in line with what we've seen here regarding scalar implicatures. There are other implicatures here: the past tense *ate* refers to a time before the present (i.e. the time of the utterance), but probably not to a prehistoric, Stone Age cat-eating-mouse event; it's more likely to refer to a past time of interest and relevance to the interlocutors. I've left aside the whole complicated question of the syntax, semantics and pragmatics of tenses here.

There's lots more, of course, but by now it should be apparent that our ordinary use of language in ordinary situations involves, in addition to all of the complexities of phonetics, phonology, morphology, syntax and semantics, the constant interplay of implicatures and speech acts, both based on our intuitive use of Theory of Mind in all of our interactions with each other (and sometimes with our pets and computers, too).

7 How to Find Lost Languages
Historical Linguistics

'My name is Ozymandias, king of kings;
Look on my works, ye Mighty, and despair!'

(P. B. SHELLEY)

All things must pass. This is as true of you and me as it is of everything we know. It's also true of languages: Avestan, Etruscan, Tocharian, Gothic, Cornish, Klamath, Yurok, Akkadian, Sumerian, Dyirbal. Gone. These are languages that we have some record of, but there are languages of which we know almost nothing except a name (itself often invented by linguists): Venetic, Messapian, Celtiberian, Thracian, Illyrian and many others. And then there are the countless languages forever lost to history. If humans have been around and speaking for, say, 50,000 years (estimates vary widely), then there are literally tens of thousands of languages which were once spoken by someone, somewhere and which are irretrievably lost. For example, we know *absolutely nothing* about the language spoken by the builders of Stonehenge (but it's a safe bet they had one; it's hard to imagine how people could organise an artistic and creative engineering feat like that without language). In fact, we have no record of any language from earlier than just over 5,000 years ago. Only three languages show continuous written records going back over three millennia: Chinese, Egyptian/Coptic and Greek. And don't forget: *all* things must pass. It may seem inconceivable to us now, but one day English will be extinct too. Look again at Shelley's words in the quotation above.

But, undaunted, linguists have found a way to reconstruct the past. Time eats languages, as it does everything else. But we can study the attested languages of the past few millennia and, on that basis, observe that certain changes are systematic, and so can be 'run backwards'. That way we can try to reconstruct what has been lost, at least in a limited way.

It's important to distinguish the study of historic, or pre-historic, languages from the study of the evolution of language. Humans have been speaking for at least 50,000 years, probably quite a bit longer. Also, we know that the humans of 50,000 years ago (or more, back to at least about 100,000 years ago) were like modern humans, and so, we assume, their linguistic abilities were like those of modern humans. Since, as just mentioned, our actual records of language only go back 5,000 years or so, there are at least 45,000 years of lost languages, more than 99 percent of which we'll never recover. But since there's no reason to think that humans have been evolving biologically in that time, we assume that these lost languages would in essential respects be like modern ones (i.e. in having complex phonetics and phonology, duality of patterning, recursive syntax, compositional semantics and intricate pragmatics; in other words, all the basic structural features we've looked at in the preceding chapters). Languages have been changing over all of this time but not evolving in anything like the standard biological Darwinian sense. What happened earlier, more than somewhere around 100,000 years or more ago, and what kind of language – if any – the various species of hominin which preceded modern humans (including the Neanderthals) may have had, we simply don't know. So I'm not going to say anything about the evolution of language here.

In this chapter we're going to look at historical linguistics, specifically:

- Correspondences among languages
- Systematic **sound changes**
- Reconstructing lost languages

These are the main elements of historical linguistics, the study of how languages change over time. Another aspect of historical linguistics involves the decipherment of ancient texts written in unknown scripts of one kind or another, a famous example being Linear B, a mysterious script discovered in Knossos and other places in Crete and on the Greek mainland in the late nineteenth century which was eventually deciphered and recognised as a very ancient form Greek known as Mycenaean, in the 1950s. I'll leave this fascinating topic aside here, though.

∽

Correspondence

In Chapter 5, we saw that linguistic signs (words and morphemes) are arbitrary. In terms of duality of patterning the link between the two levels is arbitrary. There's no particular reason why /kæt/ means furry feline (or $\lambda x[\text{cat}(x)]$) and /dɒg/ means nice canine, λx [dog(x)]. These are the conventions of English: French, German, Welsh, Avestan and Yurok have (or had) different ones. So, if we spot a resemblance between words in different languages we have something to explain.

The plot thickens if we rule out two other factors. One reason you might find words that look alike in different languages has to do with the limitations of the first level of patterning (phonetics and phonology). There are, after all, only so many different noises the human organs of speech can make (we only saw some of these in Chapter 1, as we stuck mostly to English). Moreover, these sounds can only combine to form syllables in limited ways: you're not too likely to find a word consisting of a syllable like [slθx] in any language (although dialects of Berber, mainly spoken in Morocco and Algeria, do have syllables like this; suffice it to say that this kind of thing is rare, though). So, every now and then, two languages associate the same phonetic shape to the same meaning – they happen to link the two patterns in the same way in the odd instance. One example is the indigenous Australian language Mbabaram, whose word for 'dog' is *dog*.

Coincidences happen, but they're boring. From a scientific perspective, nothing is worse than coincidence: we want *patterns*! The laws of nature – and, therefore, of language – reveal themselves through patterns, and so coincidences are really of no interest if we're looking for scientific laws. Thus, we leave these odd cases aside.

Another obvious way in which two languages might end up having words that look alike is if one borrowed the word from the other (or both from a third). This is particularly likely to happen if the word denotes an artefact or idea that was new at some point in history to one of the groups of speakers. The word is borrowed with the thing. No big surprise then, that the words for 'iPad' or 'computer' are very alike in many languages; mostly they've been borrowed from English quite recently and the word is some local contortion of /aɪpæd/ or /kəmpjuːtə/. More interesting examples are words such as *parliament, table, money* and *toilet* in English, all of them borrowed from French in Medieval times. In fact, it's a good rule of thumb for English that, if a word denotes an aspect of civilised living, it came from French. In addition to the examples just given, think of more recent borrowings (which are more obviously French-looking), such as *café, restaurant, ballet* and *garage*.

But the really interesting thing, and this is where historical linguistics gets started, is that sometimes we find whole chunks of vocabulary in two (or more) languages which look and sound alike, where the likeness can't be attributed to chance (too unlikely, as well as boring) or borrowing (because the words are too basic). Take the following pairs of English and German words:

Maus	mouse
Haus	house
Laus	louse
Ding	thing
Distel	thistle
drei	three

You don't need to be an expert in German, or even to really know any, to be able to see that the German words in the left-hand column are very similar to their English counterparts in the right-hand column. The first three pairs are pronounced practically the same, in fact (I'll gloss over the detailed phonetic differences here and ignore the Fact that Germans put capital Letters at the Beginnings of Nouns). And they mean the same. The second three are actually more interesting for historical linguistics. Wherever there's a <th> in English there's a <d>, or <D>, in German. Phonetically, where English has /θ/, German has /d/ in these cases. That's an example of a systematic sound correspondence.

Three points need to be made now. First, it's highly unlikely that English speakers borrowed words like *mouse, louse, house* and so on, from German speakers, along with the things. We had our own mice and lice in our houses. For another thing, there are just too many correspondences of this kind for this to be plausible. Third, the correspondences are systematic: in our little list, German /d/ corresponds to English /θ/ every time.

There's a family resemblance here. Just as you look a bit – but not quite – like your parents or siblings, so German and English look a bit – but not quite – like each other. Could they by any chance be related? Of course the answer is yes. There was once a parent language of English and German, from which both are descended. Hence the similarities. The systematic correspondences show us where one (or both) of the daughter languages (as they are conventionally called) has changed. At some point in the development of English and German from their common ancestor, then, either /d/ turned into /θ/ or /θ/ turned into /d/ (actually we know it was the latter in this case).

Unfortunately, the parent language of English and German was spoken by a bunch of illiterates and so has been lost to history. It's conventionally known as Proto West Germanic (I'll explain the 'Proto' later) and was most likely spoken in what is now Northern Germany and Southern Denmark around the time of the Roman Empire. This brings me neatly to a familiar question: what have the Romans ever done for us? Well, aside from roads, aqueducts, education, wine and laws, the Roman Empire actually bequeathed a very nice kind of real experiment to historical linguistics. Among their many marvellous exports to the four corners of the Roman Empire, the Romans brought the Latin language. After the break-up of the Western Empire in the fifth century AD, people mostly carried on speaking some sort of Latin in Gaul, Iberia and Italy (in Britain people more or less gave it up and went back to, or carried on, speaking an ancient form of Welsh; the Germanic language English was then all but unknown in these islands). Over the centuries, through processes we'll get a bit more idea about as we go on, the Latin morphed into different languages and dialects in different places, eventually giving what we now know as French, Spanish, Portuguese, Italian and their various dialects (as well as Romanian further east; most of the Eastern Empire had always been Greek-speaking, so things were different there).

So history has a given us a group of languages that we *know* have a common parent. French and the others (generally called the Romance languages) all descend from the spoken Latin of the Western Roman Empire. So here we expect to find systematic correspondences, and, sure enough, we do. Here are a few examples:

Table 7.1 *Systematic Correspondences among Modern Romance Languages*

	French	Spanish	Italian
'cup'	coupe	copa	coppa
'drop'	goutte	gota	gotta
'mouth'	bouche	boca	bocca

Here we can easily observe a couple of correspondences. Wherever Spanish has a single non-initial consonant, <p>, <t> or <c>, Italian has a double one: <pp>, <tt> and <cc>. This corresponds to a phonetic/phonological distinction between single and double voiceless stops (<c> is the voiceless velar stop /k/ in both languages). French <tt> in *goutte* is just a /t/, and then French has an extra difference in that it has <ch>, pronounced /ʃ/, in the word for 'mouth'. Also, where Spanish and Italian have a final <a>, French has <e>, which is either not pronounced at all or pronounced /ə/ depending on factors we don't need to go into here. Also, the other vowels are <o> (/o/) in Spanish and Italian, but <ou> (pronounced /u/) in French. The Latin words at the origin of these Romance forms are *cuppa*, *gutta* and *bucca*. So Spanish and Italian have changed Latin <u> (/u/) to /o/ while French apparently hasn't undergone this change. At the same time, Italian retains the 'double' consonants of Latin with Spanish making them single and French changing /k/ into /ʃ/. Also, Spanish and Italian kept the final <a> while French changed it to /ə/ and then (almost) lost it. The correspondences are quite intricate but clearly observable.

So here we see how we can establish a historical relationship among groups of languages. In the case of English and German, the parent language has been lost. In the case of the Romance languages, the parent language is known, thanks to the Romans. We can set up little genealogies, family trees of languages, as follows:

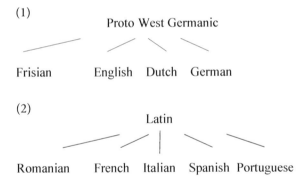

(1)   Proto West Germanic

Frisian   English   Dutch   German

(2)   Latin

Romanian   French   Italian   Spanish Portuguese

I've added some extra siblings in (1) and (2), to give a fuller picture.

This is all very nice, but so far no real surprises, perhaps. We've just seen that there are two language families in Western Europe, one originating in the Roman Empire, one not. A natural question now is: can we connect Latin and Proto West Germanic? To do this, we'll have to go back further into history.

One thing that even the Romans knew was that Latin and Ancient Greek were very similar. They were rather proud of this, as they were great admirers of Classical Greek culture. Latin and Ancient Greek were spoken close to one another in the Mediterranean world and by people of very similar cultural backgrounds. So, again, no big surprise that the languages are related.

But, imagine people's surprise when, centuries later, Europeans discovered the ancient language of the Hindu civilisation of Northern India, Sanskrit, and realised that it is *extremely* similar to both Latin and Greek. Here are some examples:

Table 7.2 *Latin-Greek-Sanskrit Correspondences*

	Latin	Greek	Sanskrit
'father'	pater	patér	pitár
'meat/raw'	cruor	creas	krávis̩
'who'	quis	tis	kas

(Here the <s̩> in Sanskrit *kravis̩* is a retroflex voiceless fricative (IPA [s̩]), similar to English [s] but pronounced with the tongue curled back so that the underside of the tip makes contact with the alveolar ridge; this phonetic detail isn't central for the following discussion though). The systematic correspondences across large stretches of basic vocabulary are absolutely evident. So linguists concluded that these three ancient languages must be related. For a while, partly since its oldest texts reflect a much earlier period than anything then known in Greek or Latin, people thought Sanskrit was the parent language. But it was quickly realised that this couldn't be right and that the parent language had been lost.

That parent language is now usually called **Proto Indo-European**. Very little is known for certain about its speakers, or even when and where they lived. There are two conjectures as to where and when the 'Indo-Europeans' lived: one is that they originated in the southern part of what is now Ukraine around 5,000 years ago, the other is that they first lived in Anatolia (Central Turkey) around 8,000 years ago. Interestingly, we know much more about the language than the people, but we'll get to that.

Where does Proto West Germanic come in? It's now established that one of the daughters of Proto Indo-European, a sister of Latin, Greek and Sanskrit (or really more of an auntie, as we'll see later) was Proto-Germanic, which in turn split into Proto North, Proto West and Proto East Germanic (Proto North Germanic gave rise to the modern Scandinavian languages while Proto East Germanic spawned various kinds of Gothic, which have all died out).

In fact, Proto-Indo-European is the ancestor of almost all the languages spoken in Europe today, with the sole exceptions of Basque, Finnish, Hungarian and Estonian (actually we should exclude European Russia and the Trans-Caucasus, where there are lots of non-Indo-European languages). The family tree is shown in Figure 7.1.

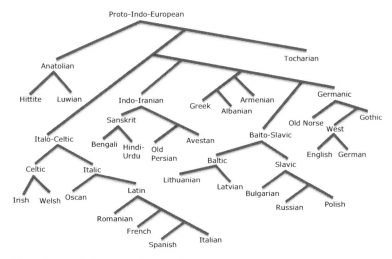

Figure 7.1 Indo-European Family Tree.
(Source: www-rohan.sdsu.edu/~gawron/fundamentals/course_core/lectures/historical/pie2.gif)

How can we establish all of this? The key lies in the systematic correspondences. Let's look at those in more detail.

Systematic Sound Changes

To see how we can set up a language family as big and complex as Indo-European, we need to look closely at the systematic correspondences which hold across languages. A famous example comes from how Germanic is connected to other Indo-European languages. Look at the first consonants in the words in Table 7.3:

Table 7.3 *English-Latin Consonant Correspondences*

English	Latin
father	pater
fish	piscis
foot	pēs

It's easy to see here that wherever English has an initial /f/, Latin has /p/. German is like English in having an initial /f/ in these words: *Vater, Fisch, Fuss* (German <v/V> is pronounced [f]). Greek, Sanskrit and several other Indo-European languages outside the Germanic family have /p/ here too (the Modern Romance languages have inherited this from Latin; compare French *père, poisson* and *pied*). So Germanic /f/ corresponds to /p/ elsewhere in Indo-European.

Here's another set:

English	Latin
three	trēs
mother	māter

English /θ/ corresponds to Latin /t/. Finally, a third set:

English	Latin
heart	cors
horn	cornu
have	capere ('take')
hundred	centum

Here English /h/ corresponds to Latin /k/ (the pronunciation of <c>). German is again like English here: the corresponding words are *Herz, Horn, haben* and *hundert*.

So we get the correspondence set in (3):

(3)   a. English/Germanic /f/; Latin /p/
        b. English/Germanic /θ/; Latin /t/
        c. English/Germanic /h/; Latin /k/

(Concerning (3b), remember that we've already pointed out that the English /θ/ corresponds to the original Germanic consonant, with Modern German /d/ being the result of a more recent change).

In Chapters 1 and 2 we saw that [p, t, k] are all voiceless stops, distinguished by their places of articulation: bilabial, alveolar and velar, respectively. On the other hand, [f, θ, h] are all fricatives. If we leave [h] aside for a moment, we can observe that [f] is a voiceless labiodental fricative and [θ] is a voiceless interdental fricative. So the pairs [p, f] and [t, θ] share voicelessness and (almost) place of articulation (bilabial/labiodental and alveolar/interdental respectively). On the other hand, they clearly differ in manner of articulation: stop vs fricative. So a generalisation emerges: Indo-European voiceless stops correspond to Germanic voiceless fricatives at (almost) the same place of articulation. This generalisation leads us to expect a voiceless velar fricative [x] in Germanic where elsewhere in Indo-European there is a [k], and indeed there is some reason to think that this was the original sound here, which later changed to [h].

So here we see a precise and neat set of correspondences, which justify positing Germanic as a subgroup of Indo-European. The change is particularly neat given the chart of distinctive features given in Chapter 2, Table 2.4. There you'll see that [p] and [f] differ only in their values for the feature [±continuant], [p] being [-continuant] and [f] being [+continuant] and the same is true for [t] and [θ] ([x] isn't given, as the chart was restricted to English). So we could say that the correspondence is: Indo-European [-son, -cont] corresponds to Germanic [-son, +cont] (we need to specify [-son] in order to single out the natural class of obstruents).

Here's another set of correspondences between Germanic and Indo-European, still with English representing Germanic and Latin Indo-European:

English	Latin
two	duō
cat	gattus

Here we're concerned just with the initial consonants. We see the correspondences [t, d] and [k, g]. Clearly, Indo-European voiced stops correspond to Germanic voiceless ones at the same place of articulation. In distinctive-feature terms, Indo-European [-son, -cont, +voice] corresponds to Germanic [-son, -cont, -voice]. The examples just given establish this for the alveolar and velar places of articulation; it is harder to establish this for the labials, as Indo-European /b/ is hard to find in the daughter languages. One possible correspondence though is between the /p/ of English *deep* and the /b/ of Lithuanian *dubùs* 'deep'.

The two sets of correspondences above are thought to be the result of changes that took place very early in the history of Germanic. They are common to all of Germanic, and so most likely took place before the family broke up into its West, East and North branches. The changes led to considerable reorganisation of the Germanic consonant system, as you can see. Together, and along with a third set which I will leave aside here as it involves some extra phonetic complications, these changes are known as **Grimm's Law**, after the German linguist Jakob Grimm (who wasn't actually the first to notice them, that was a Dane called Rasmus Rask). Grimm and his brother Wilhelm collected the famous fairy tales; there's actually a connection between the fairy tales and historical linguistics that has its roots in the broad and deep intellectual currents of German Romanticism, but this isn't the place to go into that.

The changes are also known as the **First Germanic Sound Shift**. Why 'First'? Take a look at the next set of English-German correspondences:

English	German
pepper	Pfeffer
two	zwei
cow	Kuh

Here English /p/ corresponds to German /pf/ or /f/. Since the letter <z/Z> is pronounced /ts/ in German, we can see that English /t/ corresponds to German /ts/. So here we have a (fairly) systematic correspondence between voiceless stops in English and combinations of stops and fricatives at the same (or nearly the same) place of articulation in German. The correspondence doesn't work for the velars; English *cow* (with an initial /k/ of course) corresponds to German *Kuh*, also with a /k/. However, in some German dialects, notably Swiss German, words like this have an initial /kx/ or /x/. So the correspondence works there. The set of correspondences (which actually distinguishes Standard, or 'High', German from the rest of West Germanic, including Dutch, Frisian and the 'Low' German dialects of Northern Germany) is known as the *Second* Germanic Sound Shift. Since it only affects a subgroup of West Germanic, the change must have happened later than the first one.

Let's put Grimm's Law in a wider Indo-European context. Table 7.4 gives the words for the numerals 2, 3, 5, 8 and 10 in various Indo-European languages, ancient and modern.

Table 7.4 *Indo-European Numerals*

English	German	Latin	Greek	Sanskrit	Welsh	Hindi
two	zwei	duō	duo	dva	dau	do
three	drei	trēs	tres	tri	tri	teen
five	fünf	quinque	penta	pañca	pump	paanc
eight	acht	octō	okto	asstá	wyth	aath
ten	zehn	decem	deka	dáça	deg	das

Looking at the initial consonants, in 2 and 10 we see the correspondence [t, ts, d, d, d, d, d], exactly corresponding to the two Germanic consonant shifts. In 3, we see [θ, d, t, t, t, t, t], again following the First Germanic Consonant Shift, with the extra [θ]-to-[d] change in German. The words for 5 we have initial [p] in Welsh, Greek, Sanskrit and Hindi and [f] in Germanic. Again, we see the effect of the First Germanic Consonant Shift. Latin is a bit more complicated: the sound spelled <qu> in Latin was a labialised voiceless velar stop, a [k] with lip-rounding, IPA [kʷ]. In the word for 8, there's a [t] almost everywhere, sometimes before a final vowel, sometimes not. Welsh has <th>, pronounced [θ], here; this is the result of a change which took place in Early Old Welsh and which was in certain respects similar to the First Germanic Sound Shift. Hindi also has <th>, but this is pronounced [tʰ] (with an aspirated retroflex voiceless stop, IPA [ʈ], involving the tongue curling back so that the underside of the tip closes against the alveolar ridge; on aspiration, see the discussion of aspirated stop phonemes in Hindi in Chapter 2). Looking at the consonant before the [t], there's none there at all in English, Welsh and Hindi, but in the other languages we find [x, k, k, k]. The difference between German and the other languages again corresponds to First Germanic Consonant Shift. English spelling actually helps us here: the silent <gh> of Modern English reflects an earlier [x], which was pronounced until around 1500. (Welsh and Hindi have different histories here again). You can also see that the <h> in German *zehn* (which is no longer pronounced in Modern German) might correspond to the velars in Latin, Greek and (with voicing) Welsh. Sanskrit and Hindi show a different development, pronouncing the earlier velar in different palatalised positions.

So this gives you a picture of how we can trace historical correspondences, and infer changes, across languages, and thereby set up complex webs of historical connections. So we can show how English, Welsh and Hindi are related – no mean feat! But there's more; what we've seen so far makes it seem that we have to put up with a certain amount of 'noise' in the correspondences. It doesn't really look like an exact science. But there are good reasons to think historical linguistics can be an exact science. Looking at Table 7.4, we saw some systematic correspondences but had to gloss over a few complications. But really, we can maintain that *sound laws are exceptionless*: the phonetic and phonological changes languages undergo are *fully* systematic. Let's see how this idea works in connection, again, with the First Germanic Consonant Shift. Here's a simple two-word list, again, but now we're comparing Old English and Latin:

Old English	Latin
fader	pater 'father'
broþor	frater 'brother'

(Old English <þ>, the ancient Germanic letter 'thorn', was pronounced [θ]. As you can see, English has collapsed the medial

[d] and [θ] here as /ð/ in these words since Old English times.) The initial consonants of 'father' follow the First Germanic Consonant Shift, as we've already seen: [f] in Germanic, [p] in Latin (and elsewhere). The initial consonants of 'brother' follow the complicated third series of changes which I left aside; in fact, the Latin [f] here is a peculiarity of that language (but the result of regular changes). But look at the medial consonants; in 'brother', we have Latin [t] and Old English [θ], in conformity with the First Germanic Consonant Shift. But in 'father' we have a [d] in Old English where we'd also expect a [θ] given what we know so far.

For a time, people thought this was an exception, and that was that. Grimm's Law just appeared to have exceptions to it. But scientific laws aren't supposed to have exceptions (Newton's laws don't allow things to fall upwards now and then, or entropy to be reversed, etc.). So, if we want (historical) linguistics to be a proper science, we shouldn't just put up with random exceptions. In the 1870s, a linguist named Karl Verner spotted what was going on. To see this, we have to look at the Sanskrit words for 'father' and 'brother', *pitár* ('father') and *bhráter* ('brother'). The accents here indicate which syllable is stressed, i.e. which receives the most 'phonetic emphasis' (we mentioned stress briefly in Chapter 3: remember *bláckbírd* and *black bírd*).

So in Sanskrit, we can see that 'father' and 'brother' had different stress patterns: 'father' had stress on the second syllable, and 'brother' had stress on the first syllable. Sanskrit reflects the original Indo-European pattern (Greek is very similar, and Latin is known to have generalised initial stress, which is why it's not helpful here). Verner pointed out that Grimm's Law doesn't hold where the consonant *begins a syllable following an unstressed syllable* according to the original stress pattern. Instead, in this context, a different correspondence holds, which involves Indo-European [t] corresponding to Germanic [d]. This became known as Verner's Law. Together, Grimm's Law and Verner's Law correctly predict the consonant correspondences between Germanic and Indo-European.

Not only that: Germanic has, like Latin, changed all stresses to initial stress; in both German and English *fáther* and *bróther* have initial stress. So there were two changes between Proto Indo-European and Germanic: stress shift and consonant shift. And: *we know what order they happened in!* The consonant shift *must* have been first, because, if the stress shift had been first, all the consonants would have changed the same way since 'father' and 'brother' would have had the same stress pattern. Since the consonants *didn't* all change the same way, i.e. since both Grimm's Law and Verner's Law are valid, the stress difference must have been operative when the consonants changed. So the consonants shifted, then the stress.

This is *very* cool: we know these details about sound changes in a language of which we have absolutely *no* records. As far as we know, Proto-Germanic was spoken by a bunch of semi-nomadic tribespersons who lived somewhere in Northern or Eastern Europe sometime in the first millennium BC. We have no artefacts, no descriptions of these people, nothing. But we can infer a lot about their language and how it must have been changing, and we can fit this into the general picture of the historical development of the various branches of Indo-European in a very accurate way.

To repeat, the real key to this impressive conclusion is the idea that sound changes are exceptionless. This idea, first put forward in the 1870s, was arguably the starting point of modern scientific linguistics.

One important consequence of the exceptionless nature of sound laws is that we can 'run them backwards'. In other words, we can reconstruct parts of lost languages. Let's look in detail at how this is done.

Comparative Reconstruction

Comparative reconstruction is the technique used in historical linguistics for recovering what we can of the languages of the past for which we have no records, or incomplete records. The basic idea, as far as actually reconstructing the forms of words and morphemes is concerned, is what we've already seen: if sound changes are completely regular, we can run them backwards and infer what the lost earlier languages must have looked like. These reconstructed languages are known as **protolanguages**. This is why we talk about Proto West Germanic and Proto Indo-European. We could call Latin Proto Romance, but we don't, because we don't have to reconstruct it; this is what the Romans did for us linguists.

To take a simple practical example, let's look at the word for 2 in Table 7.4 again. Let's now be really systematic and try to compare phoneme by phoneme, going from left to right. So, first we have:

(1)   t-ts-d-d-d-d-d

We know that German /ts/ is due to the Second Germanic Consonant Shift, and English /t/ to the first shift. So we're fairly safe in reconstructing Proto Indo European */d/ here.

Notation: in historical linguistics, an asterisk * in front of a form means it's reconstructed, i.e. not attested in some ancient text.

What about the second phoneme? Well, here we have <w> in English and German. The English <w> isn't pronounced nowadays, but again the spelling is telling us how the language used to be pronounced, so there used to be a [w] there. The German <w> is pronounced [v] in Modern German, but used to be [w] in older German. In Latin and Greek, we have either a [w] or a [u]; as we saw in Chapter 2, these are *phonetically* the same, but *phonologically* different depending on their function in the syllable. Welsh and Hindi don't have anything corresponding to these possible [w]s (in Welsh, the <au> spelling is a diphthong similar to English /aɪ/). So in these languages, as in the recent history of English, this sound has been lost. Sanskrit has /v/, like Modern German; here we can assume that an original [w] changed to [v] (this is quite a common change in the world's languages). So we can conclude that the second phoneme in the Indo-European word for 2 was either /w/ or /u/, a high back rounded (semi-)vowel.

Finally, the third phoneme. Here things are a bit trickier, as they often are where the reconstruction of vowels is concerned. English <o>, pronounced /uː/ of course, again represents an older pronunciation as a mid, round back vowel. Latin and Greek <o> correspond roughly to the same vowel. We know that Greek <o> corresponds to Sanskrit <a> (pronounced [ɑː]). Hindi, being descended from Sanskrit, seems to have changed the vowel 'back' to an [o]. That leaves German and Welsh, both of which have diphthongs similar to English /aɪ/ here. These are fairly certainly the result of relatively recent changes in these languages. So it's very likely that this vowel was some kind of [o]: a mid, back, rounded vowel, in Proto Indo-European.

Putting all this together, we get the reconstructed form *duo* or *dwo* for Proto Indo-European 2. Although very simplified, here we get an idea of how this can be done over and over again, and gradually we get a picture, at least a partial one, of what the proto-language must have looked like. We are quite literally rediscovering the past.

So how far back can we go? Why stop at Indo-European? Ever since comparative reconstruction was first developed in the nineteenth century, people have wondered about going further back. There is some reason to think that the Uralic languages (a family including Finnish and Hungarian and very likely to have been originally spoken in what is now Russia) may be related to Indo-European. But this is very hard, almost impossible, to prove using the standard techniques of comparative reconstruction. The reason is that, as we go back further and further in time, the correspondences we can observe become fewer (as borrowings and other factors interfere with the original correspondences), and the chances that any observed correspondence is actually a coincidence become greater. This is partly due to the fact, which we mentioned above, that there are only so many noises the human speech organs can make. So it may be that comparative reconstruction – a really reliable technique within its limitations – can only go so far.

Up to now I've been concentrating on phonetics and phonology, but of course other things can in principle be reconstructed. Inflectional morphology, in particular, can be. For example, all of the older Indo-European languages that we know about (Old Irish, Gothic, Old Church Slavonic – the oldest Slavonic language – Ancient Greek and Sanskrit) have lots of nominal case marking, along the lines we saw for Latin in Chapter 3. In fact, where Latin has six cases, Sanskrit has eight (in addition to the six Latin cases, there was an instrumental case – expressing doing something *with* something – and a locative case, expressing *where* something was done or someone was going). English, too, used to have cases. Old English, spoken by the Anglo-Saxons who invaded Britain in the fifth century AD and eventually wrote the epic poem *Beowulf* and – mainly thanks to King Alfred – lots of other stuff in the ninth and tenth centuries, had four cases, shown in Table 7.5 for the noun *engel*, 'angel'.

Table 7.5 *An Old English Case Paradigm*

	Singular	Plural
Nominative	engel	englās
Accusative	engel	englās
Genitive	engles	engla
Dative	engle	englum

Observing how Latin lost all its cases in the development to Romance, and the history of English from Old to Modern, we might be tempted to think that languages tend to lose their cases.

We can also reconstruct verbal morphology. In Indo-European, this is extremely complicated, and so I can't go into the details here. Suffice it to say that Proto Indo-European is usually thought to have a very complex system of verbal inflection, considerably more complex than what we saw for Italian in Chapter 3.

Finally, what about syntax? Here things are trickier. While words and morphemes are inherited from generation to generation through history, in that phonetic/phonological and morphological units can be identified over the centuries, sentences aren't inherited in the same way because of the generative nature of the rules for building sentences (which we saw in Chapter 4). So it may be that we just can't reconstruct syntax.

On the other hand, we can observe recurrent syntactic patterns in the older Indo-European languages, which might suggest at least that they are inherited from the proto-language. A simple example, the only one I can give here, has to do with word order. We saw in Chapter 4 that the rule for expanding the VP in English is *VP -> V (NP)* ... (there are other things to the right of the arrow, but right now I'm only interested in the NP). Among other things, this rule states that the verb precedes its direct object, if there is one, in English. So we have *Clover ate a mouse* and not **Clover a mouse ate*. We can sum up this state of affairs by saying that English is a VO language, a language in which the verb precedes its object. Many of the world's languages are like English in this respect, e.g. the Modern Romance languages. However, by no means all of them are; there are many OV languages, that is, languages in which the direct object precedes its verb (so in these languages the PS-rule expanding VP would have to be, among other things, *VP -> (NP) V*). We'll say more about word-order types of this kind in Chapter 10.

Now, the older Indo-European languages (Latin, Sanskrit, Hittite, the very ancient Greek of the Homeric epics *The Iliad* and *The Odyssey*, among others) tend towards OV order. These languages all have quite flexible word orders, so VO is also found, but OV seems to be the most common and the most 'neutral' word order (where no particular emphasis is being put on the verb or the object). Hittite, the oldest attested Indo-European language of all, shows this order quite clearly. So it's tempting to try to 'reconstruct' Proto Indo-European as an OV language. Similar reasoning applies to various other syntactic features of the older Indo-European languages, but to go into all that would take us too far afield, and in any case it's all pretty controversial.

∾

So, languages come and go, and have always come and gone, like everything else. But the lost languages of the past are not quite, not all, like the snows of yesteryear. Thanks to the brilliant hypothesis that sound laws are exceptionless, and various other regularities which we touched on in morphology and syntax, at least some aspects of lost languages can be plausibly reconstructed. We really do have a remarkably good idea about many aspects of Proto Indo-European, for example, despite still knowing almost nothing about the people who spoke it, or even – for certain – where and when they lived. This is no mean feat.

Finally, a sadly topical note. Languages, like everything else, have indeed always come and gone. However, in the twenty-first century we are faced with a crisis of language endangerment that may be worse than anything that's ever happened in the past (although, again, we don't know for sure). Pessimistic estimates are that up to *half* of the languages currently spoken will become extinct by the end of this century. Optimists think it might be 'only' 20 percent. The forces causing this seemingly unprecedented rate of language extinction are the same ones as those which are causing species and indigenous societies to disappear: various forms of 'globalisation'. As a certain form of vaguely 'Western' culture and ideology takes over the world, so the languages that go with that culture wipe out the others: English, Spanish, Russian, Portuguese and Mandarin are the real linguistic bulldozers crushing hundreds and thousands of small indigenous languages into the dust. Of course, this has always happened: Latin did the same to any number of indigenous languages of Western Europe 2,000 years ago. But we're more efficient than even the Romans were. Linguists debate what to do about this and many could be – and probably will be – accused of fiddling while Rome burns. But it's important to be aware of this, and decide what, if anything, should be done.

8 How to Influence the Right People
Sociolinguistics

In this chapter, we'll look at sociolinguistics. This is where linguistics meets sociology. So the topics here have to do with language in society. The classic areas of study in sociolinguistics have to do with how language varies from region to region and from social group to social group. Another very important topic, especially in recent years, is language and gender: how men and women speak differently.

Here I'm going to look at just three areas:

- Accents of English
- The social stratification of speech
- Negation in non-standard English

The first topic is pretty self-explanatory. Whole books can be and have been written on phonetic and phonological variation in English, and I'll just provide a very sketchy overview, picking up on a couple of points I mentioned in Chapters 1 and 2. Under the second topic, I'll introduce the foundational work in sociolinguistics by William Labov, concentrating on his study of social variation in the English of New York City, and Peter Trudgill's later study of Norwich English. Finally, I'll briefly discuss non-standard forms of negation in English and explain why these are *not*, as is sometimes claimed, in any sense 'illogical'.

∼

Everyone is aware of how accents vary from place to place. Most people who have lived in England for a few years can spot a 'Northern' accent, for example. And of course 'Northern' covers

a multitude of sins: Liverpool and Manchester, two great northern
cities separated by 35 miles and one of the bitterest football
rivalries on the planet, have dramatically distinct forms of local
English, and no inhabitant of either city would thank you for
taking them to be from the other one. Then there are Leeds,
Newcastle and Sheffield, which are just the main urban varieties.
Yorkshire alone boasts seemingly innumerable local varieties, and
the speech of Northumberland north of Newcastle is remarkable
in a number of ways.

And that's just the North. We're all more or less familiar with
the West Country 'burr', the Welsh 'lilt', the Black Country . . . er,
whatever, and of course good old Cockney. Then there's Scotland,
then there's Ireland (and it's a tin ear that can't distinguish
Glaswegian from the Edinburgh accent, or an Ulsterman from a
Dubliner).

It's not just Britain, of course. Americans can easily spot a New
Englander (go on YouTube and find a speech by the late Presi-
dent John F. Kennedy if you want to hear an authentic Boston
accent), a New Yorker (more on these later) and of course the
Southern drawl. In the American West, there's less variation
(more space, fewer people and English hasn't been there all that
long), but a fascinating Southern Californian variety has emerged
in Valspeak (check out 'Valley Girl' by Frank and Moon Unit
Zappa). Then there's Canada, and then there's the Southern
Hemisphere, mate.

But this is all just anecdote: we want *patterns*. Coming back to
the basic North-South distinction in England, there are two main
differences in the vowel system which are common to all the
'Northern' as opposed to all the 'Southern' varieties. First, Northern accents don't have the /ʌ/ vowel. In these varieties, *put* and
putt, *book* and *buck* and *look* and *luck* are all pronounced with the
same vowel /ʊ/.

The second difference has to do with the vowel, mostly
spelled <a>, in words like *grass*, *dance*, *laugh* and *pass*. In the
South, this is /ɑː/, the same vowel as in *father* and *car*. In the
North, the vowel is short /æ/, although usually pronounced

somewhat lower than /æ/and more like an IPA [a]. So the vowels in *grass* and *gas* are the same in these varieties.

Systematic studies of regional variation make it possible to plot these trends on a map. An **isogloss** is a line we draw on a map to separate the two variants. Figure 8.1 shows the isogloss for the /ʊ/ vs /ʌ/ vowel of *luck*, etc.

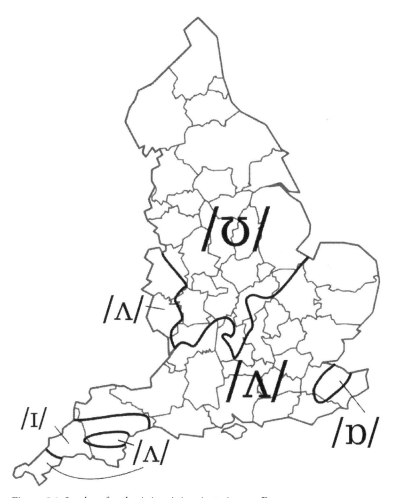

Figure 8.1 Isogloss for the /ʊ/ vs /ʌ/ variants in *sun*, Etc.
(Source: https://upload.wikimedia.org/wikipedia/commons/thumb/8/8d/Foot-strut_split.svg/220px-Foot-strut_split.svg.png)

The isogloss for /ɑ:/ vs /a/ in *grass* runs close to the one for the *sun* vowel, hence the widespread impression that these variants characterise 'Northern' vs 'Southern' English accents.

More generally, we can divide all of the accents of English the world over into three main groups. One group of accents is basically Scots, extending across to Ulster in the northern part of the island of Ireland. These accents have very different long vowels and diphthongs to the rest of the English-speaking world, and in fact make the 'long' vs 'short' distinction in a very different way from a phonetic perspective.

In the second group, we have most of the accents of England, Wales (in large areas of which English is a fairly new arrival), the Southern Hemisphere, New England, New York and many varieties of the American South. What these varieties all have in common is that they fail to pronounce the <r> in words like *car*. In these varieties, <r> is pronounced only at the beginning of a syllable, as in *red* or *Fred*. This is of course familiar in Standard British English, but for example Bostonians are often lampooned in the US for saying 'pahk the cah in Hahvahd Yahd', where the spelling tries to indicate the r-less pronunciation here; similarly, the Big Apple is sometimes referred to as 'New Yawk'.

The third set of accents pronounces these <r>s. So *car* is pronounced /kar/, roughly. This is the case in 'Standard' American English (if there is such a thing), basically all American varieties except for New England, New York and parts of the South and all of Ireland south of Ulster, as well as in Canadian English. It's also true of the varieties of the West Country and Norfolk in England, as well as parts of Lancashire (Blackburn and Burnley, for example) and a small part of the East Riding of Yorkshire.

Of course, accents aren't only regional: we're all aware of what 'talking posh' means, and are often inadvertently snobbish ourselves about 'local' varieties. In Britain, Received Pronunciation (RP) refers to a particular variety of English which lacks regional connotations, this is roughly the 'conservative' variety of Southern

British English I described in Chapter 1. The funny thing about RP is that hardly anyone speaks it anymore. It very roughly corresponds to what people call 'The Queen's English', 'BBC English' or 'Oxford English'. In fact, Her Majesty speaks a particularly conservative form of RP (characterised by her pronunciation of words like *off* with /ɔ:/ rather than /ɒ/), normal enough for an aristocrat born in 1926, but hardly representative of contemporary English. And you can listen to the BBC for a long while without hearing real RP these days. As for Oxford, I couldn't possibly comment, but you don't hear much RP in Cambridge. If you want to hear a good example of RP, listen to Julie Andrews in *The Sound of Music*.

Most middle-class people in Britain nowadays speak a mildly regionalised approximation to an innovative form of RP, but the original is all but dead. Working-class people tend to use more regionally diverse forms of English. There's an approximate correlation between social class and the degree of regional differentiation.

This is where the serious sociolinguistics comes in. Thanks to the work of Labov and his followers, we now know that the situation is more complicated and interesting. To see this, I'll first try to summarise the main elements of Labov's study of New York City speech, before returning to the UK to look at Trudgill's study of Norwich English.

Labov recognised that certain variant pronunciations have **social value**: they are recognised as markers of the speech of a particular social class. From a purely linguistic perspective, the ascription of social value to a given pronunciation is completely arbitrary. The <r> business described above illustrates this well. In Britain, the r-less (or **non-rhotic**) pronunciation is the **prestige form**, with the r-ful ones (the **rhotic** ones) being considered hokey, regional, working class, **low prestige**. In the US, it's the other way round: in New York City in particular, the nonrhotic variety is low prestige, and the rhotic one high prestige (Boston is a bit more complicated, as the example of JFK suggests).

Labov studied the incidence of rhoticity as a sociolinguistic variable, marking a correlation between accent and social class in New York. The conception of the study was brilliantly simple. Labov chose three Manhattan department stores, Saks Fifth Avenue, Macy's and S. Klein. These stores are known for being very upmarket, middle class and somewhat downmarket, respectively. On entering each store, Labov checked what was on sale on the fourth floor, and then he asked a shop assistant where he could find whatever it was, in this way eliciting the words 'fourth floor'. So then he could check whether the assistant said /fɔrθ flɔr/ or /fɔ:θ flɔ:/ (or, in New York, /fɔɔθ flɔɔ/). He also pretended not to hear the assistants' first answers, getting them to repeat the words more carefully. This allowed him to distinguish spontaneous and more careful speech.

The results were impressive. The incidence of **rhoticity** (i.e. rhotic or nonrhotic pronunciation) closely reflected the social cachet of the department stores. The assistants at Saks had the highest incidence of the rhotic pronunciation (/fɔrθ flɔr/), those at S. Klein the least. Another interesting result was that the Macy's assistants showed the biggest difference between spontaneous and careful speech, indicating an awareness of the social value of the rhotic pronunciation.

The department-store results showed awareness of **overt prestige**, the desire to sound 'classy' and align oneself with the speech of the dominant group in society. Labov also discovered the phenomenon he called hypercorrection, which is the overuse of a prestige form. This, he observed, was commonest at Macy's, the 'middle' store. In fact, Labov went a step further and pointed out that it was middle-class women who showed the highest incidence of hypercorrection and therefore the greatest sensitivity to overt prestige.

Still another innovation was the concept of **covert prestige**. This arises when people want to distinguish themselves from the 'dominant group', and so use seemingly low-prestige forms in order to show a distinct social or regional identity. The high incidence of nonrhotic forms at S. Klein (the downmarket department store) shows covert prestige. Middle- and working-class males are most likely to use covert-prestige forms, Labov observed. So Labov was the first person to demonstrate a clear correlation between social class, gender and accent, indicating the social stratification of speech.

One very important result which emerges from the kind of sociolinguistic work that Labov's New York City study initiated is that sound changes can be observed going on, in real time. Indeed, by comparing the incidence of rhoticity across different age groups in New York (in 1962), Labov was able to show that rhoticity was not a social marker for the older generation at the time but was for the younger generations. This is an example of a linguistic variable taking on social value; Labov demonstrated how speakers may be conscious of such social value.

A similar study was carried out in Britain by Peter Trudgill in the early 1970s. He looked at sociolinguistic variation and social stratification in the speech of the city of Norwich, in East Anglia. One of the variables he looked at is actually found in non-standard varieties of English all over England (and elsewhere in the English-speaking world). This is the pronunciation of the ending -*ing* in words like *walking, talking* and so on, as what's usually written -*in'* (IPA /ɪn/ as opposed to /ɪŋ/. Here the apostrophe indicates the 'missing' <g>, but in fact the two sounds are different: an alveolar nasal in the non-standard varieties but a velar nasal in the more standard varieties). He also looked at the presence or absence of the 3Sg present -*s* ending (as in *She go to the shop* or *She goes to the shop*). The -*in* forms and those without the -*s* ending are low-prestige forms, of course.

Trudgill's main findings were similar to what Labov found in his New York study: class was more of a determiner of non-standard usage than gender, though women in all social classes were more likely to use the overt prestige forms, i.e. the standard ones, especially in careful speech. Men, on the other hand, showed evidence of covert prestige, in that they over-reported their non-standard usage, while women over-reported their standard usage. One of Trudgill's general conclusions was that women are more susceptible to overt prestige than men, while men are more susceptible to covert prestige. Like Labov, Trudgill found that the differences between men's and women's usage of the standard forms were greatest in the lower middle class and the upper working class, and in careful speech. So the same forces of social stratification seem to be at work with different formal variables in both New York and Norwich. Since the 1970s, the same results have been replicated in many places and in many languages.

In the previous chapter, we took the notion of change for granted, and effectively treated things like the Germanic Consonant Shifts as though they were instantaneous changes. Of course, this was justified, since they took place thousands of years ago and we know nothing in detail about the circumstances under which they happened (all we really know is that they must have happened). But sociolinguists have shown us how changes actually take place in real time and the role of sociological factors in inhibiting or facilitating them. Today's variation is tomorrow's change, looked at in retrospect.

Sociolinguistic variation doesn't only affect phonetics and phonology. Morphological variation exists, and certain forms are regarded, again arbitrarily, as high or low prestige. For example, in Standard English, the -s ending on verbs only shows up in the 3sg of the present tense; however, there are many varieties where this form has a different distribution. In many non-standard Midlands varieties, the -s ending appears on all persons in the present tense, and so we find forms like *I thinks*, *they sings*, etc. Some varieties in the West Country and East Anglia don't have this ending at all, so we have *he think*, *she sing*, etc, as we saw above in connection with Trudgill's Norwich study. Finally, in parts of the North of England, as well as Scotland and Ulster, there's the Northern Subject Rule, which requires a singular verb form with a non-pronoun subject NP, singular or plural and the standard form of agreement (i.e. no -s in the plural) with an adjacent pronoun subject. This rule extends to the forms of the verb *to be*, so it's not just about the -s ending but about the system of subject-verb agreement in general, as examples like (1) show:

(1)   Them eggs is cracked, so they are.

All of these variants are highly regional and low prestige, but every single one of them is a coherent linguistic system, every bit as much as Standard English. It's sometimes said that working-class language or non-standard forms are somehow intrinsically inferior to the standard language, on the basis of some notion of 'logic' or 'clarity' or 'precision'. From a linguistic point of view, *there's absolutely no reason to think this whatsoever*. Non-standard forms of English are just that: not the standard. It's best not to use them when taking tea at Buckingham Palace, or in a job interview or (more debatably) on the BBC, but there's nothing *intrinsically* 'wrong' with them. To believe that non-standard varieties are inherently inferior to the standard is to dress up social snobbery with pseudo-linguistics.

A good example of this comes from how negation works in non-standard English (in many parts of the English-speaking world, including both the US and the UK and elsewhere). In non-standard English, sentences like (2) express various kinds of negation:

(2)   a. I ain't done nothing.
        b. I can't stand it no more.
        c. I ain't never been there.
        d. She don't like no-one.

Before saying any more about the examples in (2), let's take a quick detour into how languages express negation. The key point is that, while in propositional logic, as we saw in Chapter 5, two negatives make a positive (i.e. $\neg\neg p \leftrightarrow p$), in natural languages two negatives very often just make an emphatic negative. Or even a non-emphatic one. French is a very good example of this. In French, if you want to negate a sentence, you have to put in *two* negative words, one before a finite verb and one after it:

(3)   Je ne bois pas.   ('I don't drink')

Of course, we can't possibly say that each of *ne* and *pas* are equivalent to logical ¬; if we did, then (3) would be a positive sentence (and Standard French would seemingly have no way of expressing simple negation).

French has other negative words, as in (4):

(4)   a. Je n'ai rien fait. ('I haven't done anything')
        b. Je ne le supporte plus. ('I can't stand it anymore')
        c. Je n'ai jamais été là. ('I have never been there')
        d. Elle n'aime personne. ('She doesn't like anyone')

On their own, *rien* means 'nothing', *plus* means 'no more', *jamais* means 'never' and *personne* means 'no-one'. So all the sentences in (4) have two markers of negation too, but, as their English translations show, each expresses only a single negation.

There's nothing 'illogical' here (how could the language of Descartes, Voltaire and Rousseau be illogical?). Many languages express negation in the way French does, and we call this **negative concord**. All it amounts to is that, when you want to express a negative, you negate several bits of the sentence at once. Propositional logic (a 'language' invented by logicians and philosophers) and *some* languages, like Standard English, don't do this: instead each negative expression 'counts', and so two negatives do indeed make a positive, *in these languages*.

Now, purists often claim that the varieties of English illustrated in (2), which we can now say differ from Standard English in showing negative concord, are 'illogical' or – worse – that the people who say such things are 'illogical' or incapable of thinking clearly. This is simply not true. In fact, you might have noticed that the sentences in (2) exactly parallel the French sentences in (4). Is French therefore 'illogical'? Were Descartes, Voltaire and Rousseau incapable of thinking clearly? Of course, the notion is utterly absurd, and shows a very imperfect understanding of language and languages – in this case, the widespread phenomenon of negative concord – as well as a naïve, and quite unjustified, willingness to assimilate natural languages to propositional logic.

But it can be worse: social prejudice masquerading as pseudo-linguistics can actually disguise *racial* prejudice. William Labov, once again, has made very significant contributions to revealing these prejudices. In particular, he pioneered the study of what is usually known as *African American Vernacular English* (AAVE), sometimes called 'Ebonics'. This variety of English, spoken by much of the African American population of the US, also has negative concord. In a classic article from 1972, Labov made a number of striking observations concerning negative concord, and other aspects of the syntax of negation, in AAVE. Labov observed sentences like those in (5):

(5)   a. Well, wasn't much I couldn't do.
        b. Down here nobody don't know about no club.

In (5a) negative concord goes 'across clauses': here *wasn't* is in the main clause and *couldn't* is in a separate (relative) clause, but they are interpreted as one (so the sentence means 'There wasn't much I *could* do'). In (5b) the subject participates in negative concord (the examples in (2) don't have this). These two kinds of negative concord can combine to give spectacular examples of the following type:

(6)   a. It ain't no cat can't get in no coop.
        b. When it rained, nobody don't know it didn't.

Each of these examples actually contains a single logical negation ('No cat can get into a coop'; '. . . nobody knew it did'), the further expressions of formal negation just being the negative-concord system of this variety. Many a purist would probably have a hard time figuring out what these sentences mean, but kids in the urban centers of the US would probably not have any problems.

The examples above are not emphatic. AAVE has ways of emphasising negation, as in:

(7)   a. She ain't in no seventh grade.
        b. But not my physical structure can't walk through that wall.
        c. Ain't nobody on the block go to school.
        d. Don't so many people do it.

Again, spectacular stuff, and hardly the product of unclear, illogical or imprecise thought processes. All of this clearly shows that AAVE is a distinct grammatical system from Standard English (and from the many non-standard white varieties), and that it may have undergone, or be undergoing, certain changes in how negative concord works which do not affect other varieties. And of course this distinct variety has social value since it is associated with a particular ethnic group. So here Labov showed a case of social stratification, correlated with ethnicity, involving a syntactic feature.

~

As I said at the beginning of this chapter, there's much more to sociolinguistics than what we have seen here. But nonetheless we've looked at a couple of the major areas: accents and dialects, evidence for the social stratification of speech and language change in real time and evidence that non-standard forms are entirely coherent linguistic systems, every bit as 'logical' as standard varieties.

As with all of the other chapters, this has been an attempt to give a taste of what is involved. It should be clear, at least, that sociolinguistics can do much to counter unjustified social and racial prejudice when this is manifested through pseudo-linguistics.

9   How to Lose a Language and How to Learn a Language

Psycholinguistics

Bibeeya!

(J. ROBERTS, age one)

Psycholinguistics is where linguistics and psychology meet. As such, it is a huge field, covering areas as rich and diverse as language learning and acquisition, language disorders (what happens to someone's language when they get certain kinds of brain damage), and how we 'process' language in real time as we hear it. In recent years, as new techniques for monitoring and imaging brain activity have been introduced, the questions surrounding how language is embodied in the brain have become more and more important. Neurolinguistics is the field which studies these questions in detail, but, aside from a brief discussion of **aphasia**, I will leave that aside here (partly because it requires some technical knowledge of neurology, and partly because there is little clear consensus on the central questions).

I'm going to limit the discussion here to just two areas of psycholinguistics: the study of aphasia, one kind of language disorder, and the study of how small children acquire their first language. This topic has a natural fascination, and, as we'll see, raises questions that are central for linguistics and have relevance for certain venerable philosophical debates.

∽

Let's look first at aphasia. As I already mentioned, language disorders (or language pathology) is the study of what happens to a person's language if they suffer brain damage of some kind (this usually arises either from a nasty accident or from a stroke).

151

Nowadays this area is more and more part of neurolinguistics as we are becoming increasingly able to pinpoint the relation between damage to certain areas of the brain and various effects on language, but I'll just give an overview of the main kinds of aphasia, which were identified long before the current brain-imaging techniques were developed.

Aphasia is a general term for a range of syndromes involving language impairment as a consequence of brain damage. It has been known since the nineteenth century that there are two main kinds of aphasia: **Broca's aphasia** and **Wernicke's aphasia**. These are named after the individuals who first identified them, Paul Broca (1824–1880) and Carl Wernicke (1848–1905). Broca's aphasia (also known as **expressive aphasia** or agrammatic aphasia) typically involves rather halting speech, with many functional categories such as auxiliaries, determiners and complementisers (see Chapter 4) missing, along with inflections and other aspects of morphology and disturbances to intonation and stress. The following is an example of the speech of a Broca's aphasic trying to describe going to the hospital for a dental appointment (from H. Goodglass and N. Geschwind [1976]. 'Language disorders'. In E. Carterette and M. P. Friedman. *Handbook of Perception: Language and Speech. Vol VII.* New York: Academic Press):

> Yes . . . ah . . . Monday . . . er . . . Dad and Peter H . . . [his own name], and Dad . . . er . . . hospital . . . and ah . . . Wednesday . . . Wednesday, nine o'clock . . . and oh . . . Thursday . . . ten o'clock, ah doctors . . . two . . . an' doctors . . . and er . . . teeth . . . yah.

It doesn't take any great expertise in syntax to see that the individual who produced this utterance is having severe problems. Very interestingly, deaf patients who communicated with sign language before becoming aphasic show very similar symptoms. This kind of aphasia can be very severe: in fact, one of Broca's original patients was nicknamed 'Tan', after the only syllable he could say. However, some rote-learning can be retained, such as the ability to count from one to ten. At the same time, Broca's aphasics who can do this are incapable of producing the same numbers in ordinary conversation. This suggests that it is some aspect of the generative capacity for syntax (the PS-rules for example) that is disturbed in this type of aphasia. This idea is supported by the fact that individual words are recognised and understood, but understanding is impaired where syntax is needed in order to get the correct meaning. For example, Broca's aphasics tend to confuse passives and actives, i.e. they understand *The mouse was eaten by the cat* (passive) as *The mouse ate the cat* (active). Again, we see that this kind of aphasic seems to be unable to recognise the role of auxiliaries such as *be* and prepositions such as *by*, as well as the inflections on the verbs.

Wernicke's aphasics (also known as receptive aphasia), on the other hand, are usually quite fluent and seem to be well in control of grammatical nitty-gritty like auxiliaries and inflections. But their speech, although fluent, doesn't really make sense. In particular, lexical words, especially nouns, seem to be missing and are very often paraphrased in highly roundabout and rather confusing ways, as we can see from the following example, where a Wernicke's aphasic is asked to describe a picture ('What's happening there?'):

> I can't tell you what that is, but I know what it is, but I don't know where it is. But I don't know what's under. I know it's you couldn't say it's . . . I couldn't say what it is. I couldn't say what that is. This shu-that should be right in here
> (from www.departments.bucknell.edu/linguistics/lectures/
> aphasia.html).

The differences in the linguistic production of the two kinds of aphasics are quite apparent. Wernicke's aphasics also have trouble understanding others, and indeed understanding their own speech. After recovery, some report that they couldn't stop themselves from speaking, even though they couldn't understand themselves. So we can also see major differences in comprehension between the two types of aphasia.

So the two types of aphasia are rather different (in medical terms, they have different etiologies). What is really interesting from a psycholinguistic (and neurolinguistic) perspective is that they involve damage to different parts of the brain. Broca identified his aphasics as having damage to a particular part of the left hemisphere of the brain (known as the inferior frontal gyrus, a rather small part of the brain, low-ish on the left side of the brain a little above and in front of the left ear). This is now known as **Broca's area**, and is obviously of central importance for language. It is tempting to conclude from observation of Broca's aphasics that that part of the brain makes possible the mastery and use of PS-rules. Nonetheless, one should be careful about connecting abstract theoretical constructs like PS-rules with actual pieces of brain anatomy. The brain is so complex that this kind of simple connection is almost certain to be proved wrong.

Wernicke's aphasics, similarly, show damage to a nearby but distinct area known as **Wernicke's area**. This is in the posterior part of the superior temporal gyrus in the left hemisphere (in most people, i.e. about 95 percent of right-handed people); this is an area a little behind and above the left ear, two or three inches back from the position of Broca's area. The two areas are connected by part of a tract of white matter, known as the uncinated fasciculus, which also links various other parts (of both hemispheres) and whose exact general function is unclear, although because it links Broca's and Wernicke's areas it seems to be important for language. The two areas are shown in Figure 9.1.

So here we see how the study of a particular kind of language disorder has led to some insight into how language is represented in the brain, in that at least two main 'language areas' have been identified. Broca's area, in particular, seems to be particularly important for structural aspects of language, perhaps especially syntax (although, as I mentioned above, we should be careful about making simplistic connections between parts of the brain and aspects of our linguistic abilities). Until the recent development of brain-imaging techniques, this was the only way to find out how language is embodied in the brain. Nowadays, however,

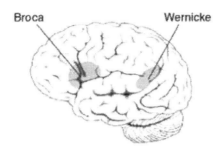

Figure 9.1 Left Hemisphere of the Brain, showing Broca's and Wernicke's Areas. (Source: https://upload.wikimedia.org/wikipedia/commons/thumb/0/03/Brocas AreaSmall.png/250px-BrocasAreaSmall.png)

there are other techniques, and we are no longer forced to rely on damaged brains to find out how language is embodied. However, to go into this further would take us into neurolinguistics proper, which I do not intend to do here, for the reasons I gave earlier.

Let's turn now to our other psycholinguistic topic: how children acquire their first language. Normally, linguists talk about children *acquiring*, rather than *learning*, a first language since learning generally implies being taught and, as we'll see, small children are not really taught their first language. Rather than laboriously learning it, children seem to rather effortlessly acquire their first language.

Before getting into the detail of what the little children do, a couple of central issues should be clarified. As we'll see, these clarifications also apply retrospectively to much of what we've been looking at in the preceding chapters.

One thing that I haven't done so far is define the word 'language'. I've been relying on an intuitive understanding of what this is, and of course we've been building up a picture of how language works – and therefore getting a clearer idea of what it 'really is' – as we've been going along. But, in order to clarify some of the issues in psycholinguistics, we need to be clearer about our definitions now.

The problem is that language is very difficult to define, and how you define it depends partly on what you're interested in studying. For us, though, a distinction made by Chomsky between Internal Language (**I-language**) and External Language (**E-language**) is useful. I-language is language seen as something internal to the individual: language as ultimately a property of the mind or brain. E-language, on the other hand, sees language as external to the individual minds and brains, a property of societies, cultures, etc.

I-language is the relevant concept of language for psycholinguistics. Everything we said in Chapters 1 to 5 about phonetics, phonology, morphology, syntax and semantics was really about I-language too. Also, pragmatics relies on our ability to make inferences about others' intentions through Theory of Mind allied to I-language, so it's really about how our minds exploit contextual information, and as such it concerns I-language rather than E-language. Historical linguistics and sociolinguistics seem to have to do with E-language. But in the case of sociolinguistics, our ability to recognise and respond to different social and regional varieties has at least an I-language component. And when we reconstruct sound changes and other lost things in historical linguistics, we are, at least in part, trying to find out what the I-languages of long-ago people were like.

So, arguably, I-language is more important than E-language. In fact, it's really logically prior: you can't have any E-language unless someone's got an I-language in their head, but you could at least imagine I-language without E-language.

Another important distinction, also due to Chomsky, is that between linguistic **competence** and linguistic **performance**. We mentioned this in connection with infinite sentences in Chapter 4, but it's worth recapitulating here. A person's competence in their native language is their ability to control all the aspects of that language's structure: the huge, complex, intricate array of things we saw in Chapters 1 to 5. Performance is putting competence into action: actually speaking and understanding your language. Performance depends on competence but draws on more than just linguistic abilities; when talking and listening other factors, long- and short-term memory, concentration, Theory of Mind and others, all come into play. Competence refers to the 'pure' linguistic abilities. This implies, for example, that competence is distinct from actually speaking and listening; my linguistic competence as a native speaker of English remains in my mind when I'm asleep, or just keeping quiet.

Competence is closely identified with I-language; we can say that a native speaker of English, for example, has native competence in their I-English (which might be diffcrent from other people's I-English; terms like 'English', in normal usage, actually refer to complex cultural, sociological and historical E-things). Performance is *not* E-language, though; performance involves a whole range of psychological and cognitive factors in addition to I-language/competence while E-language is by definition a non-psychological notion,

Now, when we look at how a child acquires their native language, what we are interested in is the development of the I-language competence in the child's mind. Of course, one thing that we look at is what the child says, but this is only part of the story; this is the child's performance, which may only indirectly reflect competence, given all the other factors involved.

With these clarifications behind us, we can now start looking at how child language acquisition actually proceeds.

∼

Thanks to over fifty years of quite intensive study, we now have a pretty good picture of the various stages of first-language acquisition. So here goes: it's a pretty amazing story, as any parent can attest.

It seems that very young babies, newborns just a day or two old, can distinguish their mother tongue (quite literally: the language that their mother speaks) from other languages. What the babies seem to be sensitive to are the basic rhythm and intonation patterns of the language (aspects of phonetics and phonology we unfortunately couldn't go into in Chapters 1 and 2). You might wonder how we know this, since babies that small obviously can't speak and in fact don't communicate much (except hunger and pain). Babies that age will happily suck on anything that seems like a nipple, and the sucking rate varies according to the stimuli the baby is getting. If the baby takes an interest in something in its environment, the sucking rate increases and then if there is no interesting new stimulus the sucking rate gradually tails off. So psycholinguists hook a dummy to a machine and record the sucking rates. When exposed to a recording in the mother tongue, the sucking rate increases and stays pretty high throughout the recording, but when exposed to a recording of some other language, it tails off much more quickly. So the babies seem more 'interested' in their mother tongue, and clearly seem able to distinguish it from other languages.

The first real linguistic behaviour (as opposed to various noises, mainly crying, gurgling and burping) emerges usually at about six to eight months.

> *Health warning*: all the statements I'll be making about when things happen in language acquisition are average estimates. Of course, there's no such thing in real life as 'the average child'; every one is different. So don't worry if your child or sibling seems to be 'late'. The chances are that this is just a quirk of statistics.

At this point, 'babbling' starts. Children start to make seemingly controlled vocalisations, i.e. they're controlling their organs of speech. Initially, babbling consists of a range of sounds, with no particular reference to the sounds of the mother tongue. Babbling consists of simple 'syllables' on the general pattern of Consonant-Vowel (CV). Gradually, though, at around eight to ten months, the babbling starts to feature recognisable sounds of the mother tongue (it's hard to say whether we could really call them phonemes or allophones at this stage).

Next, at around ten to twelve months, the first word or two comes out. Of course, it can be hard to tell what is meaningless babble and what is an intentionally produced 'word', and still harder to tell what the 'words' mean at first (and parental indulgence may dull the scientific desire for accurate knowledge). Usually the first words have a very simple phonetic structure, often a bilabial ([p], [m] or [b]) followed by a low vowel such as [a]. The fact that the words for 'mother' and 'father' in many languages have a form like *ma* and *pa* is probably connected to this. At this point, then, when the babbling begins to take on meaning, we can say that the child has (somehow) acquired, and put into action, duality of patterning.

So we come to the one-word stage. The child gradually picks up a simple vocabulary and extends the repertoire of syllable types. Some time around eighteen months, the two-word stage starts. This, as the name implies, involves the apparent juxtaposition of words in order to create some kind of (compositional) meaning. Typical two-word utterances by English-speaking children are:

(1)   a. Daddy shoe.
        b. Allgone milk.
        c. Hit doggy.

The typical semantic relation between the two words seems to be generally either possession ('daddy's shoe'), predication ('the milk is all gone/finished') or verb-object with the subject not there, as in (1c). The order of verb and object (and other combinations) is usually the right one for the language, so English-acquiring children produce VO orders like (1c). It can often be very hard to tell what the semantic relations are, and of course there is always a temptation to read too much into a child's utterances.

It's important to point out that terms like 'one-word stage' and 'two-word stage' refer only to children's production. We're merely observing their performance here, not their competence. In fact, children understand longer sentences at these stages, indicating that their competence outstrips their performance. Indeed, it's quite possible that children at these stages already have a fully specified, recursive syntactic system but they can't put it to full use at this early age because of performance factors such as memory limitations, short attention span, limited vocabulary, etc.

One important feature of this period is that there are no words representing functional categories such as articles or auxiliaries and no inflections in the children's production; again, though, there is evidence that children understand these elements at this stage. This is also true of the next stage of acquisition, from roughly twenty-four to thirty months. Here we see longer utterances but still no words belonging to functional categories or inflectional morphology, as in:

(2)   a. Baby doll ride truck.
        b. Pig say oink.
        c. Want lady get chocolate.

(You can see that in (2c) the subject is missing, but probably the intended subject is 1sg here; 'missing' subjects are another striking syntactic feature of early speech). Owing to the lack of closed-class words and inflections, this stage is often referred to as 'telegraphic speech' (harking back to the days of telegrams, an obsolete means of communication where you had to pay for every word, so people tended to leave out the functional words and stick to the lexical categories).

The next stage is perhaps the most interesting. We've just seen that after the two-word stage somewhat longer sentences start to emerge. There is apparently no recognisable three-word or four-word stage. At around thirty months, what happens is a kind of grammatical explosion. The child starts producing something very close to fully grammatical, adult-like sentences, complete with closed-class elements like articles and auxiliaries, as well as inflections:

(3)   a. I'm having this little one.
        b. Mummy hasn't finished yet, has she?

It seems, then, that at this stage the syntax comes on line for real. Of course, there's more to do still: lots of vocabulary to learn and often inflections need sorting out.

One well-established result in the research literature on first-language acquisition concerns past-tense inflections in English. As we saw in Chapter 2, the regular past-tense ending is <(e)d>, phonologically conditioned as /d, t, ɪd/. Then there are the various irregular verbs such as *sing, bring,* etc. One perfectly reasonable thing to expect children might do is to overgeneralise the regular inflections, saying things like *singed* and *bringed* and so on. Children do in fact do this, but it's more interesting. The acquisition of past-tense inflections follows a U-shaped curve, in that, at first, children mostly 'get it right': they correctly produce both regular and irregular inflections. *Then* they go through a phase of overgeneralising, and *then,* finally, they distinguish the irregulars from the regulars, approximating very closely to the adult language. Psycholinguists have interpreted this to mean that, at first, children treat all verbs as irregular; they simply haven't figured out any 'rule' for the past tense and are learning the past-tense verbs one by one. Then they figure out the 'add-<(e)d>' rule and over-apply it. And finally they work out which verbs are regular and which are not. So the children go from no rule, to an over general rule, to the 'correct' rule.

Here's another one, this time involving how children acquire quantification. It has long been observed, possibly first by the Swiss psychologist Jean Piaget and his collaborator Barbara Inhelder, that children between roughly ages three and seven make interesting errors with universal quantifiers. Look at the following array of shapes:

Are all the circles black? Of course they are. But when children are asked this, they typically reply 'No: there are two black squares'. In other words, they interpret the question to mean 'Are all the black things circles?' This result has been quite consistently attained for four- and five-year-olds in a variety of different experimental settings. At a later stage of acquisition, they correctly apply the quantifier. There is much debate among psycholinguistics as to what is going on here, but two things are clear. First, the phenomenon is real; children really do this at a certain stage of language acquisition. Second, they only do it with universal quantifiers. Fascinating and mysterious stuff, I'm sure you'll agree.

So there is absolutely no question that first-language acquisition is an impressive feat. Children appear to have all of the structural mechanisms we described in Chapters 1 to 5 – fine-grained control of the organs of speech, phonological rules, duality of patterning, recursive syntax and compositional semantics – in place before they start school. In fact, in most cases, well before they can tie their shoelaces. It is a simply staggering intellectual feat, probably the most impressive such feat most of us ever manage in our whole lives.

Just to rub the point in, think of the acquisition of vocabulary alone. So forget all the fancy phonetics, phonology, morphology and syntax for a moment. How do children figure out that words mean what they mean? We don't know, but we do know that, at around three to five years old, children are learning on average *ten new words a day*. Given that they typically sleep ten to twelve hours a day at that age, they're almost learning one new word every waking hour!

Now think of learning a foreign language (which I'm sure you've tried to do at some point). Learning ten words a day (seventy a week, three hundred a month) is damn hard work. And if your French teacher tells you that *vache* means 'cow', you have the advantage of already knowing what a cow is. Children learning their first language don't have dictionaries and translations. Ok, you might say that they learn by being shown what a cow is. You can learn what a cow is if someone points at one and says 'cow'. But try figuring out whether it's the cow's colour, its shape, the space it's occupying, a future hamburger or a non-detachable cow-part that's being pointed at. This method of learning word meanings gets you nowhere. Try to work out the meaning of *three, not, give, climb, me, you, that* or *existence* on this basis.

So how *on earth* do children do it? This is where the philosophers come in . . .

∾

The great Cambridge philosopher Alfred North Whitehead (friend and collaborator with the even greater Bertrand Russell) once said 'the safest general characterisation of the European philosophical tradition is that it consists of a series of footnotes to Plato'. The issues connected to first-language acquisition make up one of the longer and, certainly for linguists, one of the more interesting footnotes. The fundamental question is this: is there such a thing as 'innate ideas', ideas – or knowledge – inborn in us and so not determined purely by experience? This question is fundamental to philosophy of mind and epistemology (the study of the nature of knowledge). Over the centuries it has also taken on political and religious connotations.

Plato believed that we do have innate ideas. He thought we remembered these from an earlier existence. His mentor Socrates demonstrated the existence of such ideas by eliciting a theorem from a boy untrained in mathematics. Under the questioning of Socrates (the 'Socratic method'), the boy had nothing other than his innate geometrical intuitions for answers on the nature of shapes, areas and related concepts: he could *just see* – with his mind's eye – how these concepts fit together (literally), just as we can know how it must be true that the square of the hypotenuse of a right-angled triangle is equal to the sum of the squares of the other two sides ($a^2 + b^2 = c^2$). Plato's solution to the problem of how we can see this kind of truth is that we were born with the relevant knowledge.

This point of view has come down through the centuries in various guises. The seventeenth-century French philosopher René Descartes (who we briefly encountered in the last chapter) held a similar view. For example, he pointed out that we never see a true triangle, as every 'actual' triangle we see in this imperfect world has wiggly bits instead of three perfectly straight sides, and the angles don't add up to precisely $180°$. But when your geometry teacher starts telling you about triangles, you can intuitively understand what a true triangle looks like because you have an innate idea of The Triangle. Descartes went on to suggest that the contents of our minds (which he held to be made of a different substance from our – or any – body, the doctrine known as metaphysical dualism) consist in part of 'clear and distinct' ideas, put there by God. On the other hand, various British philosophers, notably John Locke and David Hume, argued that the mind is a blank slate on which experience writes. According to them, knowledge comes either from experience or from 'association of ideas'.

What has first-language acquisition got to do with all this high-flown philosophising? The astonishing feat of acquiring such complex knowledge at such an early age (and seemingly without trying too hard) raises the issue of innate ideas all over again. The central question is this: what does a newborn know about language? The obvious answer is 'not much', but not much isn't the same as nothing, and first-language acquisition raises the question in an acute way. In fact, we'll see later that it may be that newborns actually know quite a bit.

The common-sense view (which many people in the English-speaking world in particular have inherited from Locke and Hume without realising it) is that newborns know nothing about anything, except perhaps nipples. They learn their first language from experience, and their parents and siblings play a role in 'teaching' it to them (for example, by pointing at a cow and saying 'cow'). Partly for reasons given earlier (point at the cow's colour, etc.), partly because of the results of psycholinguistic research and partly because it's very hard to see how notions such as duality of patterning, recursion and compositional semantics could be taught to babies or toddlers, we know that the idea that parents and siblings 'teach' little children their language is a non-starter. Children are linguistic autodidacts, although of course they need to hear a language in their environment, and which language they hear will determine which language they end up speaking.

More generally, common sense has no role in scientific or philosophical investigation. Ask a physicist what she thinks about the common-sense view of space and time and how that relates to what physicists now understand as 'physical reality'. Common sense has absolutely no logical or epistemological priority.

So: what do newborns 'know' about language? Chomsky has put forward a view which has become known as the argument from the poverty of the stimulus. It goes like this: Any form of a person's knowledge must either come from experience, i.e. from outside the person, or from within. If it comes from within, it arises either by inference – as a matter of logical deduction – or from some predetermined constraint on knowledge, i.e. as a kind of innate idea. Where does knowledge of your native language, competence in your I-language, fit into this picture?

Well, very little of that knowledge can be deduced from first principles using known forms of logical inference, so that method doesn't seem to apply. The central question then is: can linguistic knowledge be entirely learned from experience? Chomsky's answer is no: the knowledge in its final state – the I-language competence of the average five-year-old – is too complex, too structured and too rich to have been learnable on the basis of experience alone. The simple facts about vocabulary acquisition – so many words, so little time and nothing to go on – bear this out. And of course when we think of the phonetics, the phonology, the morphology and, above all, the recursive syntax and the compositional semantics, the point becomes still more forceful.

So I-language competence is neither deduced nor picked up from experience (at least not in total). Therefore, *something must be there at the start*; the blank-slate idea just won't allow us to make sense of first-language acquisition. More precisely, the 'something' must be a general schema for language which constrains the acquisition process by making certain logically possible or imaginable types of language actually *im*possible. So then all human languages must conform to certain general predetermined schemata (e.g. they must have phonemes, morphemes, PS-rules, etc). These things must be 'there', i.e. in the newborn mind, at the start, at birth or even before (depending on how much cognitive development goes on in the womb). So, linguistic innate ideas – a very nice footnote to Plato.

Where do these innate ideas come from? Probably nobody literally believes in Plato's ideas about remembering an earlier existence any more, and God is pretty much absent from modern scientific thinking (mainly because He doesn't seem to do much; most things can be explained without divine intervention). But nowadays we have genetics: the innate ideas might reside in the human genome. Given that only humans have language, the innate language faculty could be a product of our special 2 percent, which I mentioned in the Introduction.

So that's the view: the complexity of the linguistic knowledge of the usual five-year-old is such that it is implausible to think that it was all acquired from experience. Experience must be shaped and constrained by something predetermined: a set of 'innate ideas' about the structure of language, presumably somehow encoded in our special 2 percent of genome, the 2 percent that distinguishes us from chimps.

This argument is important, and has been hugely influential in linguistics, psychology and philosophy. It is also, you won't be surprised to learn, very controversial. Before getting to the controversies, let's just clarify two points.

The first is that the argument is *not* a deductive proof (although it may be possible to prove that recursion can't be learned from experience, but this would go beyond the informal version of the argument that I gave above). The crucial word in my summary of it above is 'implausible'. It's implausible, but not impossible, that all aspects of linguistic knowledge are learned from experience. The second point is that Chomsky isn't saying, and has never said, that *all* linguistic knowledge is innate; some of it comes from experience for sure. For example, which language you end up speaking is determined by your linguistic environment, so nobody is suggesting that Chinese or English are innate.

The principal criticism of Chomsky's position to emerge in recent years is that it is possible, and some developments in computer science make it plausible, that humans are much more efficient learners than has been assumed. In particular, certain kinds of statistical learning (figuring out what's most likely to follow what on the basis of exposure to examples) may be able to account for an awful lot of the mysterious-seeming aspects of first-language acquisition. It certainly can't be denied that predictive text is possible; you've probably got it in your phone. That kind of thing is based on modelling and learning statistical correlations (which your phone can do). So are children just really smart smartphones?

As I said, it's possible. But smartphones have 'innate ideas' too. They're programmed to do predictive text and programmed to learn. So really the statistical learning idea doesn't do away completely with the idea that something about language is predetermined. But this position contrasts with the Chomskyan view as I presented it in two ways. First, there's arguably less stuff predetermined, and, second, it's not specific to language. The statistical learner can learn all sorts of things. So the real questions that first-language acquisition raises are not whether something is innate, but how much, and what. These remain open and much-debated questions. Research on areas as diverse as language acquisition, how computers can simulate learning, how different we really are from chimps and – as we'll see in the next chapter – the diversity of languages contributes to trying to figure out the answers to these very important questions.

Here we've looked at just three questions in psycholinguistics. The first one was a brief look at the main kinds of aphasia that have been identified. The second was what goes on when children acquire their first language, and here we saw the stages of acquisition and some of the rather surprising things that psycholinguistic research in this area has turned up. The third related to Chomsky's argument from the poverty of the stimulus that something predetermines the form of language, which explains how children are so incredibly good at language acquisition. This 'something' predetermining the form of language revives the age-old philosophical question of innate ideas.

There's another consequence of Chomsky's argument which I've barely mentioned here. If there is some innate linguistic capacity, and if we're all the same (at least as newborns), then all languages must show signs of this capacity. There must be universal features of language. This is why Chomsky's theory is referred to as **Universal Grammar**. In the next chapter, I'll turn to the question of whether, by studying the diversity of languages, we can discern at the same time what does not vary, what is universal.

10 How to Build a Language
Language Typology and Universals

In Brazil, one can always find a five-legged cat.

(attributed to Voltaire)

Up to now, I've mostly talked about English. The reason for this is very simple: that's the one language I can be sure you know or you wouldn't be reading this book in the first place. And English is a real language, with lots of native speakers (about 400 million, in fact, making it third in the world after Mandarin and Spanish) and a fairly well-documented history. But there are plenty of other languages around, somewhere in the region of six to seven thousand according to most estimates. Of these, we now have some kind of linguistic description of about two thousand or more; most of the available information can be found on-line at the database of the World Atlas of Language Structures (www.wals.info). So now it's time to take a look at what's out there. There are two reasons for doing this. First, it's intrinsically interesting to see the world's linguistic flora and fauna. Second, as we'll see, there appear to be patterns in the variation we observe among the world's languages. We're interested in patterns, as I've mentioned a couple of times. But, picking up the thread from the end of the last chapter, these patterns might conceivably be telling us something about Universal Grammar. So looking at diversity always involves looking at the other side of the coin: trying to see what does *not* vary and may therefore be universal and so, perhaps, innate. I'm going to concentrate on syntactic diversity and universals, partly for reasons of brevity and partly because this is where most of the interesting work has been done (although there's plenty to say about phonological and morphological diversity too).

The pioneer in the field of language typology was Joseph Greenberg. In his original research during the early 1960s,

Greenberg looked at thirty languages from around the world and observed about forty-five universals of different types. One of the things he looked at was the basic order of the main elements in a simple sentence: subject (S), verb (V) and object (O). We saw in Chapter 7 that we can distinguish VO languages like English, where the verb normally precedes the object (as in *eat a mouse*) from OV languages like Japanese where the order is the opposite (*a mouse eat*). In Greenberg's early work, the subject was brought into the picture too, so we talk about SVO languages like English (*Clover ate a mouse*) as opposed to SOV languages like Japanese (*Clover a mouse ate*).

So, S, V and O give you three basic elements in the sentence. That means there are six logically possible permutations. All six are found in the world's languages, which may not come as a surprise. But what's interesting is that *the incidence of the orders is highly skewed.* Two orders are much commoner than all of the others, SVO and SOV, and two other orders, OVS and OSV, are extremely rare (in fact, they were not known to exist for sure until the 1970s). The picture is summarised by the data from the 1,377 languages analysed for word order in the World Atlas of Language Structures in (1):

(1)   SOV (*Clover a mouse ate*): 565 languages = 41 percent
         SVO (*Clover ate a mouse*): 488 languages = 35 percent
         VSO (*Ate Clover a mouse*): 95 languages = 7 percent
         VOS (*Ate a mouse Clover*): 25 languages = 2 percent
         OVS (*A mouse ate Clover*): 11 languages = 0.8 percent
         OSV (*A mouse Clover ate*): 4 langauges = 0.3 percent

You might have noticed that the percentages only add up to 86.1 percent. The other 13.9 percent (189 languages) are languages for which a single basic order can't be isolated for one reason or another. But it's absolutely clear that there is a skewing here. We ought to expect each order to show up a sixth of the time (or if we allow a category of "no dominant order", thinking of the missing 14 percent, a seventh) which would be in the region of 15 percent. But what we see is a big preference for SOV and SVO and a big aversion to OVS and OSV. Why should this be? There are basic-ally four possible answers to this question.

The first is that it isn't really true. We've only looked at around a third of the world's languages here, and so maybe the other 4,000 or so will turn up a whole lot more OVS and OSV languages. That's of course possible, but as our databases have grown over the years, the basic tendencies have remained pretty constant; the only thing which has really changed has been the discovery of the OSV and OVS languages, which are so rare (and mostly spoken in inaccessible parts of the Amazon jungle) that they were only discovered quite recently. Every survey so far has shown SVO and SOV to be the big winners.

A second answer is that it's due to history. Languages can change their orders (we saw that when we looked at syntactic reconstruction in Chapter 7), and so maybe they tend to change in the same ways and, perhaps starting from a more even distribution in the distant past (something we can never know for sure), they've moved towards SOV and SVO. But this only shifts the question: why should languages all change that way? Of course, it could be a coincidence but it's a very odd one, and we don't like coincidences anyway.

The third possibility is to appeal to psycholinguistics. Maybe we prefer to 'process' the favoured orders. Perhaps SVO and SOV orders are just, to put it very simply, easier to use, or to understand. This view is quite influential, and there is some psycholinguistic evidence to support it (we didn't go into this area of psycholinguistics in Chapter 9 so I won't say any more here).

The fourth possibility is that Universal Grammar, while obviously allowing all of the orders, prefers SOV and SVO. Perhaps the PS-rules that generate these orders are somehow more natural than others. Remember from Chapter 4 that the verb and its direct object form a constituent, the VP, in English. SOV and SVO are the two orders which need the basic PS-rule $S \rightarrow NP\ VP$ (with the expansion of VP determining whether you have OV or VO), while the others seemingly have something else. This view is also influential, but as you can see it depends on working out which syntactic rules might be favoured and why. That can be done, but it would take us far beyond what can be looked at here.

So you can see that even a set of cross-linguistic data as simple as what we have in (1) raises really interesting and tricky questions, and potentially links up with things we saw in the other chapters, notably psycholinguistics.

One of the really important innovations in Greenberg's early work was the idea of **implicational universals**. These are if-then statements about cross-linguistic variation like (2):

(2)   If a language has VSO order, it has Prepositions.

Greenberg had in mind the notion of implication from propositional logic (not the pragmatically enriched everyday notion). We saw the truth table for this in Chapter 5, and I'm repeating it here:

(3) p q $p \rightarrow q$
        t   t   t
        f   t   t
        t   f   f
        f   f   t

So let's take p to be 'this language has VSO order' and q to be 'This language has Prepositions'. (Here *Pre*positions are opposed to *Post*positions, so it's a question of whether you say *to London*, with a Preposition, or *London to*, with a Postposition). So, what (2) says is that you can find VSO languages with Prepositions, i.e. where both p and q hold; Welsh is like this, for example. It also says you can find non-VSO languages with Prepositions, i.e. where p is false and q is true. English is a language like this. But you can't find VSO languages with Postpositions (p is true and q is false). As far as we know, this is true. There are very few languages with this combination of orders in the sentence and in the PP (in fact, the World Atlas of Language Structures lists just eight languages out of a total of 1,076, so this combination of orders does exist, but it's very rare, being found in under 1 percent of the languages surveyed; see www.wals.info). On the other hand, non-VSO languages with Postpositions (p and q both false) are found, e.g. Japanese. So what an implicational universal says is that, out of the four possible combinations of two properties, one of them won't be found. If that turns out to be true, the same question as we saw in relation to the preference for SVO and SOV orders arises, with the same possible answers.

Comparing what we saw regarding the preference for SVO and SOV with the implicational universal in (2), we can see that the first deals with a statistical preference while the latter, if it really holds, is an absolute statement. That makes our question (why?) and the possible answers all the more interesting.

Greenberg used implicational universals, both statistical and absolute ones, to define **language types**. This was the second really important idea in Greenberg's early work. To see how language types can be set up, let's look at French. French is an SVO language, as you can see from (4):

(4)   Le chat (S) mange (V) la souris (O).
        'The cat eats the mouse'.

In French, we also have Prepositions rather than Postpositions, as (5) shows:

(5)   sous (P) la table (O)
        'under the table'

So we can say French is PO language. Next, in possessive constructions, the possessor (the owner) follows the possessee (the thing owned):

(6)   la plume (N) de ma tante (Poss)
        'the pen of my aunt'

Finally, adjectives usually follow nouns:

(7)   le chat (N) intelligent (A)
        'the cat intelligent (i.e. the intelligent cat)'

So we can call French an SVO, PO, NPoss, NA language. That (partially) defines its word-order type. This particular type is very common around the world. Other languages following this pattern include the other Romance languages, Albanian, Yoruba, Edo, all the Bantu languages, most of the Chadic languages of West Africa, Khmer (spoken in Cambodia), Vietnamese, Thai and many Austronesian languages of South-East Asia and the Pacific, including Malay. English almost fits this pattern, but you can put the possessor before the possessed noun (as in *my auntie's pen*), and adjectives of course precede nouns. So English is of the SVO, PO, PossN, AN type, a slightly rarer one than the French type.

Now let's look at Japanese. As I already mentioned, this is an SOV language:

(8)   Taroo-ga tegami-o kaita.
       Taroo (S) letter (O) wrote (V)
       'Taroo wrote the letter'.

It has Postpositions:

(9)   Tokyo kara
       Tokyo (O) from (P)
       'from Tokyo'

Possessors precede the possessed noun:

(10)   Taroo-no ie
       Taroo (Poss) house (N)
       'Taroo's house'

And adjectives precede nouns:

(11)   kono omosiroi hon
       this interesting(A) book(N)
       'this interesting book'

So Japanese is SOV, OP, PossN, AN, the opposite of French on every count. This is also a very common type. Other languages following this pattern include: Hindi, Bengali and the other Indic languages of Northern India, Modern Armenian, most of the Finno-Ugric languages of Northern Russia and Siberia (but not Finnish), the Altaic languages of Central Asia, the Paleo-Siberian languages, Korean, Ainu (the indigenous language of Japan), Hottentot (spoken in South Africa), Abkhaz and other Caucasian languages, the Dravidian languages of South India, the Sino-Tibetan languages of China, South-East Asia and Tibet (although Mandarin is slightly exceptional), Navaho (the most spoken surviving Native American language) and Quechua (spoken in the Andes, the ancient language of the Incas).

So we see another tendency: languages tend to favour the French type or the Japanese type. Most SVO languages are like French (but not all, of course, as we can see from English), and most SOV languages are like Japanese.

Now let's look at Welsh, a VSO language. Here we see the following pattern:

(12)   a. Lladdodd y dyn ddraig.
         Killed (V) the man(S) dragon(O)
         'The man killed a dragon'.
     b. i Fangor
         to(P) Bangor(O)
     c. car John
         (N) (Poss)
         'John's car'
     d. bws bach
         bus(N) little(A)
         'little bus'

So Welsh is VSO, PO, NPoss and AN. This is just like French on all counts except the first. But if we leave aside the position of the subject, and just look at the order of the verb (V) and the direct object (O), then we see that Welsh and French are the same. This is one reason why some typologists have suggested leaving the subject out of basic word-order typology.

Here are some examples of the other basic word-order types:

(13)   Malagasy, VOS:
        nahita ny vehivahy ny mpianatra
        saw the woman the student
        'The student saw the woman'.

(14)   Hixkaryana, OVS:
        toto yonove kamara
        man he-ate-him jaguar
        'The jaguar ate the man'.

(15)   Nadëb (OSV):
        samũũy yi qa-wùh
        howler-monkey people eat
        'People eat howler monkeys'.

Hixkaryana and Nadëb are both spoken in the Amazon jungle.
Malagasy is spoken on the island of Madagascar.

These word-order correlations, as they are known, can be
elaborated further. In a famous 1992 paper, Matthew Dryer established the following sixteen correlations:

(16)

a.	V	object	*see [the man]*
b.	P	object	*in Cambridge*
c.	V	PP	*slept [on the floor]*
d.	want	infinitive	*wants [to see Mary]*
e.	copular	predicate	*is [a teacher]*
f.	aux	VP	*has [eaten dinner]*
g.	Neg-Aux	VP	*don't know*
h.	Comp	sentence	*that [John is sick]*
i.	Q-marker	sentence	*if [John is sick]*
j.	adverb	sentence	*because [John is sick]*
k.	V	manner adverb	*ran slowly*
l.	article	noun	*the man*
m.	plural marker	noun	*PL man (= "men")*
n.	noun	relative clause	*movies [that we saw]*
o.	noun	genitive	*father [of John]*
p.	adjective	standard of comparison	*taller [than John]*

Dryer showed that the best predictor of all the other pairs was the
order of verb and direct object, again indicating that VO and OV
are the most basic typological distinctions as far as word order is
concerned. Again, our earlier question, along with its four possible
answers, comes up here, and still more forcefully.

In addition to implicational universals and language types,
there are two further kinds of possible universals: substantive
universals and formal universals (this distinction was originally
made by Chomsky). Substantive universals are grammatical categories and notions of the kind we looked at throughout Chapters 1 to 5, although I mostly illustrated them from English. This
includes things like tense, negation, interrogatives, nouns, verbs,
vowels, etc. As far as we know, all languages have these. So all

languages can talk about the time of an event in relation to the time of utterance (although by no means all languages do this with inflectional morphology), all languages have some way of denying the truth of a proposition and have some way of asking questions. Furthermore, the basic noun (thing words) vs verb (event words) distinction seems to hold universally. Finally, in the domain of phonetics and phonology, all languages seem to make a distinction between vowels and consonants. These are very interesting universals, if they really hold. Perhaps the most interesting one is the noun-verb distinction. Talking about time, denying things and asking questions could all be universal because these are obvious things to do with language, and things people are interested in doing: this would be a functional explanation for the universals. Similarly, all languages distinguish vowels and consonants because of the way the organs of speech are set up. But why distinguish nouns and verbs? The question is all more interesting in the light of type theory, as discussed in Chapter 5. If predicates and common nouns are of the same type, $<e,t>$, then there's not even a semantic reason. So this starts to look like a candidate for a feature of Universal Grammar. Maybe.

Another type of substantive universal might be a set of universally *available* categories from which languages select. This might include things like nasalised vowels (French has them, English doesn't, as we mentioned in Chapter 1), adjectives (certainly not all languages have these, 'qualities' can be expressed with verbs or nouns, i.e. instead of *the fat cat*, you can say something like *the cat fats*), auxiliaries, articles and so on. When languages have these things, they tend to behave alike, but certainly not all languages have them.

Formal universals, on the other hand, are statements about the actual rules of syntax. One might be that no language has a rule which simply reverses the order of all the words in a clause in order to form an interrogative from a declarative, as in (17):

(17) a. This is the house that Jack built.
   b. *Built Jack that house the is this?

As far as we know, this is unknown in the world's languages. But changing the order of words in a sentence for one reason or another is quite common. So the rules that permute order (to use the technical term, which we didn't get to in Chapter 4) are constrained. A much more interesting constraint than 'no reversing the order' is **structure dependency**. We can see this in operation with the English rule that swaps the position of the auxiliary and the subject to turn a declarative sentence into an interrogative (this one we did see in Chapter 4) as with the auxiliary *is* in (18):

(18)   a. The person is here.
         b. Is the person here?

At first sight it seems easier (both for us and, presumably, for a computer or a smartphone) to apply this rule to the first auxiliary in the sentence. But we can see that isn't true from the next pair:

(19)   a. The person who is here is rich.
         c. *Is the person who – here is rich?

(19b) is ungrammatical. But here we applied the dumb inversion rule of moving the first auxiliary in the sentence (going from left to right). The grammatical version of (19b) is (20):

(19)   Is the person who is here – rich?

Here we've applied the rule, correctly, to the second *is*. The reason for this is that the rule inverts *the first auxiliary after the subject NP*. In the declarative sentence (19a) the subject NP is complex, containing a relative clause: *the person who is here*. So the first *is* after the subject NP is actually the second one in the sentence. Rules like this don't just look at the linear order, but at the hierarchical structure of sentences. They're sensitive to hierarchical notions like NPs, rather than linear notions like 'first (or second) going from left to right'. If this is correct, then this kind of structure dependency is a good candidate for something in Universal Grammar, as it limits what the rules can do.

∾

So here we've seen several important aspects of diversity and universals. We've seen that the world's languages vary a lot – look at how Japanese and French differ on all the word-order features we looked at – but that the variation shows interesting patterns. The closer one looks at word order, the more of this kind of thing one observes. How to explain it is a different matter, and several general lines of explanation are available, as we saw. We also briefly looked at substantive universals, noting in particular the prevalence of the noun vs verb distinction. Finally, we briefly looked at structure dependency as a possible formal universal.

A major question, and a much-debated one, is how typological observations like those concerning word order in the world's languages that we looked at here, could be connected to something like Chomsky's notion of Universal Grammar. At first sight, it seems that there's no hope of a Universal Grammar for word order because we find so much variation. But then when you start to see patterns you might think again. One way to reconcile systematic variation with Universal Grammar has been under development since around 1980. This is the principles-and-parameters approach. The idea is that certain things are absolutely fixed and part of Universal Grammar (there might not be many of these, but the noun-verb distinction and structure dependency are quite good candidates): these are the principles. Then there are parameters of variation, governing things like whether the language is VO or OV (which might predict lots of other word-order properties, as we saw). The principles and the parameters can be thought of as innate; they make up Universal Grammar, and then the child acquiring a language has to 'fix the values' of the parameters in order to acquire I-language competence. This idea seems to be able to reconcile the idea of an innate Universal Grammar with the variation we can observe in the world's languages.

But every aspect of this is controversial. There are linguists who don't think any of the universals put forward by Greenberg, Dryer and others are universal at all; or at least that they'll all turn out to be wrong as we get more and more data about more and more languages. There are those who find the notion of innate ideas difficult and look for other explanations for first-language acquisition and any universals we might have found. There are many who recognise that probably something has to be innate, but it might be a generalised capacity to learn complicated systems, or a capacity to communicate, rather than anything specific to language (and as odd as the verb-noun distinction). And finally there are those who accept Chomsky's general position but are sceptical about the principles-and-parameters idea.

It seems there are no absolute certainties here. But there may be one: these questions, like everything else about language, are fascinating, complex and profound.

What their answers are we just don't know, but we're working on it.

Epilogue
More about Cats and Extra-terrestrials

Let's go right back to the start and talk about Clover some more. As I said, he's really very intelligent: he knows exactly how to wake me up in the morning, exactly which shelf in which cupboard his food is kept on, where his bowl is, how to get let out, and lots of other things. You won't catch the average ant, starfish or parsnip doing any of that. By the standards of nearly everything in the known universe, he *really is* smart. But of course we're much smarter. There are plenty of things in the world, especially in our mental world, that poor Clover has absolutely no inkling of: the moon, the stars, numbers and of course language. These things are every bit as much beyond Clover as waking me up to get me to feed it would be for a parsnip or starfish. Obviously the fact that we have language has a lot to do with this cognitive gulf between us and our pets, although that may not be the whole story.

But a natural question to ask is: is there a similar cognitive gulf between us and other forms of intelligence? We seem to be smartest creatures on our planet, so this is where the extra-terrestrials come in. Here I'm not interested in various forms of slime that might be around on Mars or elsewhere, but intelligent extra-terrestrials, the sort that might build spaceships. Could there be extra-terrestrials so much smarter than us that they would keep us as pets? Or (cue the creepy sci-fi music), are we already pets but we just don't know it? After all, Clover doesn't know he's my pet. Are there, in other words, concepts as impossible for us as the concepts three, noun or syllable are for Clover?

Most people would probably say yes to this question. But the answer doesn't have to be yes. It is also quite possible that we, as a species, have crossed a cognitive threshold. Our capacity to express anything, through the recursive syntax and compositional semantics of natural language, might have taken us into a cognitive realm where anything, everything, is possible. Effectively, having language has made us the equal of any extraterrestrial (who would in any case have to have something like language in order to build their spaceships). We can make this thought a little more precise: there might have been a crucial mutation in human evolution which led, in almost no time from an evolutionary perspective, from caves to spaceships. It's a plausible speculation that the mutation in question was whatever it is that makes our brains capable of computing recursive syntax, since it's the recursive syntax that really gives language – and thought – their unlimited expressive power. It's one small step from syntax to spaceships, but a great leap for humans.

Anyway, something (God, natural selection, a random mutation, an alien monolith) has given us our extraordinary minds with our extraordinary capacity for generating, storing and transmitting knowledge. Language really must be central to these abilities. So understanding language means understanding a very big part of what it is to be human, what it is to be you. And that is perhaps the greatest wonder of language of all.

Further Reading

Since this isn't a textbook, I've avoided peppering the text with references and further reading, simply mentioning the key names here and there (Chomsky, de Saussure, Grimm, Labov, Austin, Grice, Greenberg and a few others). But I do want to encourage you to go on, and so here are a few things that you might find interesting and enjoyable now you've got this far. The first set are all general references; there are of course plenty of textbooks on all of the various areas of linguistics, and I've indicated the best ones to start with if there's a particular area you want to read about in more detail. Of course, there are *lots* more textbooks on the various subareas, but you can get to those later by following the references in the readings suggested here. It's very important to start with an overview of the whole field and not to specialise too much too soon.

General Introductions

Fromkin, Victoria, ed. *Linguistics: An Introduction to Linguistic Theory*. Oxford: Blackwell, 2000.

Fromkin, Victoria, Robert Rodman and Nina Hyams. *An Introduction to Language*. 7th edn. Boston, Mass.: Thomson Heinle, 2003.

Isac, Donca and Charles Rice. *I-language*. Oxford: Oxford University Press, 2013.

Larson, Richard. *Grammar as Science*. Cambridge, Mass.: MIT Press, 2010.

Pinker, Steven. *The Language Instinct: How the Mind Creates Language*. New York: Harper Collins, 1994.

Smith, Neil. *The Twitter Machine: Reflections on Language*. Oxford: Blackwell, 1991.

Language, Bananas and Bonobos: Linguistic Problems, Puzzles and Polemics. Oxford: Blackwell, 2002.

Specific Topics

Sign Language

Sutton-Spence, Rachel and Bencie Woll. *The Linguistics of British Sign Language: An Introduction.* Cambridge: Cambridge University Press, 1999.

Phonetics

Ladefoged, P. *Vowels and Consonants.* 2nd edn. Oxford: Blackwell, 2004.

Phonology

Hayes, B. 2009. *Introductory Phonology.* Oxford: Blackwell, 2009.

Morphology

Haspelmath, M. and Andrea D. Sims. *Understanding Morphology.* London: Routledge, 2002.

Syntax

Jackendoff, Ray. *Patterns in the Mind: Language and Human Nature.* New York: Harvester Wheatsheaf, 1993.
Smith, Neil. *Chomsky: Ideas and Ideals.* Cambridge: Cambridge University Press, 1999.

Semantics

Elbourne, P. *Meaning: A Slim Guide to Semantics.* Oxford: Oxford University Press, 2011.

Pragmatics

Allott, N. *Key Terms in Pragmatics.* London: Bloomsbury Press, 2010.

Historical Linguistics

Campbell, L. *Historical Linguistics: An Introduction.* Cambridge, Mass.: MIT Press, 1998.

Sociolinguistics

Trudgill, P. *Introducing Language and Society.* London: Penguin English, 1992.

Psycholinguistics/Language acquisition

Clark, E. *First Language Acquisition.* Cambridge: Cambridge University Press, 2003.

Language Typology

Comrie, B. *Language Universals and Linguistic Typology; Syntax and Typology.* 2nd edn. Oxford: Blackwell, 1989.

Glossary

Here I give very brief definitions of the technical terms introduced in the text. Terms defined elsewhere in the Glossary are given in the definitions in **bold**. The definitions are intended for reference only, and in some cases are rather terse; in general, the relevant passages in the main text of the book contain fuller explanation and illustration. For further details on these and many other technical terms in linguistics, see P. Matthews's *Oxford Dictionary of Linguistics*, Oxford University Press, 2014.

accent   (i) a diacritic mark on a letter, as in the <é> of French *café*, accents have different phonetic or phonological values depending on the spelling conventions of the language in question; accents are often used to mark **tone** in tone languages, as in the standard transliteration of Mandarin Chinese; (ii) a regional or social phonetic/phonologically defined variety of a language, often non-standard (as in 'Northern accent', 'Cockney accent', etc.); in ordinary usage the term refers to non-standard varieties and can be slightly pejorative, hence standard speech may be described as having 'no accent', although from a linguistic point of view this is incoherent since the term refers to the variety's phonetics/phonology, and all varieties have this; non-standard varieties which show distinct **morphology**, **syntax** and **lexicon** from the standard are usually referred as dialects; (iii) a synonym for stress, referring to the most prominent syllable in a multisyllable word (where 'prominence' is a perceptual term with complex articulatory correlates involving loudness and pitch).

accusative one of the **case forms** found in Latin, Sanskrit and many other languages. It typically marks the **direct object** of a verb.

affricates a class of **consonants** with a complex articulation involving a **stop** phase and delayed release, giving rise to **fricative** noise. Since they involve two phonetically distinguishable phases, they are written as digraphs in the IPA. Received Pronunciation has two affricates: [ʧ] and [ʤ].

agent the 'doer' of an action described by a verb of the relevant type, e.g. *Mary* in *Mary ate her dinner*. If there is an Agent, it corresponds to the **subject** of an active clause.

air stream in articulatory **phonetics**, the flow of air which is modified in the articulation of **consonants** or **vowels**. English uses only the air stream emanating from the lungs in normal exhalation (known as the pulmonic egressive airstream), and this is the only one discussed here. Other languages make use, to varying degrees, of other air streams: pulmonic ingressive (inhaled air), glottalic egressive and ingressive and velaric egressive and ingressive. See Further Reading for more on these.

allomorph
a variant form of a **morpheme**; allomorphy may arise through **free variation**, be phonologically conditioned or morphologically conditioned.

allophone
a variant form of a **phoneme**; allophony may arise through **free variation** or be phonologically conditioned.

alveolar
a **natural class** of consonants whose articulation involves total or partial blockage at the **alveolar ridge**, these include English /t, d, s, n, l/; defined by the **distinctive features** [+ant, +cor].

alveolar ridge
a ridge at the front of the **hard palate** behind the upper teeth, involved in the articulation of **alveolar** consonants.

aphasia
a form of acquired (i.e. non-congenital) language impairment arising from damage to **Broca's area** or **Wernicke's area**, or both, usually caused by trauma or stroke; the two main types of aphasia are known as **Broca's aphasia** and **Wernicke's aphasia** respectively.

arbitrary
relating to the conventional nature of the sound-meaning relation for the vast majority of morphemes and words in all languages; famously

encapsulated in de Saussure's doctrine of the arbitrary nature of the linguistic sign.

argument in **predicate logic**, the name for the constant or variable associated with a **predicate**; in the usual notation, written as a lower case letter in parentheses immediately following the symbol designating the predicate.

aspiration a delay in the onset of **voicing** after the release of a **stop consonant** giving rise to a brief [h]-like articulation, IPA [ʰ].

assimilation a phonological process whereby nearby (typically adjacent) phonemes undergo phonetic modification in such a way that they become more similar; the realisation of English past-tense /d/ as /t/ following a verb ending in a voiceless **obstruent** is an example of **voicing** assimilation.

auxiliary a 'helping' verb, which supplements the meaning of the main verb in some way, often connected with **tense** or **mood**; *have* in *I have eaten lunch* is an auxiliary.

back (i) in the standard terminology of articulatory **phonetics**, a class of vowels characterised by an articulation involving backing of the tongue body towards the **velum**, as in English [uː, ʊ, ɔː, ɑː, ɒ]; in English, only back vowels are also **rounded**; (ii) in **phonology** a **distinctive feature** whose positive value designates both **vowels** and

consonants whose articulation
involves raising of the body of the
tongue towards the **velum**; thus, in
addition to the vowels mentioned
under (i), the consonants /k/ and /g/
are [+back].

bilabial   a type of articulation of **obstruents**
involving disturbance of the **air
stream** by the lips; English has two
bilabial **stops**, /p/ and /b/.

blade   area of the tongue behind the tip but
in front of the main body involved in
the articulation of typical
pronunciations of **alveolar** and
interdental consonants.

bound morpheme   a **morpheme** which cannot occur alone
but must occur attached to another
morpheme, e.g. English past-tense -*d*.

branch   in **syntax**, a line connecting two
nodes in a tree.

branching node   in **syntax**, a **node** which immediately
dominates more than one
constituent, hence two branches
emanate underneath it in the
standard format for representing
constituent structure in a **tree
diagram**; branching nodes are always
non-terminal nodes.

Broca's aphasia   also known as agrammatic aphasia or
expressive aphasia, one of the two
main kinds of **aphasia**, characterised
by highly disfluent speech with
missing functional categories and
inflections, as well as impaired stress
and intonation; involves damage to
Broca's area.

Broca's area
a region of the brain in the inferior frontal gyrus of the left hemisphere; damage to this area leads to **Broca's aphasia**. The nature of Broca's aphasia makes it tempting to conjecture that this region of the brain may form a significant part of the neural substrate for **morphology** and **syntax**.

case
a class of **bound morphemes** (typically **suffixes**) which attach to nouns in many languages to mark the syntactic role of a noun or noun phrase in the sentence.

case forms
the morphophonological forms of **case suffixes**.

category
in **syntax**, a class of morphemes sharing the same distribution, morphological markings and (roughly) semantic properties, e.g. noun, verb, etc. Roughly corresponds to the traditional notion of 'part of speech'.

centring diphthongs
a class of diphthongs found in most varieties of British English (and **non-rhotic** varieties generally) involving movement of the tongue from a peripheral part of the **vowel** space to a central area, roughly where **schwa** is articulated.

comparative reconstruction
in **historical linguistics**, the technique for postulating forms of **protolanguages** based on correspondence sets; for **morphology** and **phonology**, the technique relies on the thesis of the regularity of **sound change**.

competence	the system of linguistic knowledge underlying a normal adult's ability to produce and understand an unbounded range of sentences in the native language; as opposed to **performance**, competence need not be overtly manifested in behaviour.
complementary distribution	in **phonology**, the case where distinct **allophones** of a given **phoneme** always appear in identifiable phonologically conditioned contexts; opposed to **free variation**.
compositional semantics	the approach to **sentence meaning** which follows the principle that the meaning of a complex expression can be computed from the meanings of its parts; in many approaches to compositional semantics, some version of **type theory** is involved.
compound	in **morphology**, a complex word consisting of at least two elements which are independently able to be **free morphemes**, possibly with further **bound morphemes**, e.g. *blackbird* and *coffee-maker*.
conditioned allomorphy	in **morphology**, the case where the forms of distinct **allomorphs** of a given **morpheme** are determined by their morphological context (morphologically conditioned allomorphy) or by their phonological context (phonologically conditional allomorphy).
conjugation	generally, morphological classes of verbs; in Latin and the Romance languages, the three or four

morphological classes defined by theme vowels.

conjunction in **logic**, the **connective** which connects two **propositions** such that the resulting proposition is true only where both conjoined propositions are true; conventionally written '&'.

connective in **logic**, elements which typically connect two propositions in such a way that the truth of the resulting proposition can be computed from the truth of the connected propositions combined with the semantics of the connective in question (these are the **truth-functional** connectives); the connectives are **conjunction**, disjunction, **implication** and **equivalence**.

consonant in **phonetics**, a sound articulated such that the **air stream** is perturbed so that turbulence or blockage is produced; in **phonology**, a phoneme which cannot appear (in most languages) in the **syllable** nucleus.

constituency the fundamental syntactic relation, specified by **Phrase-Structure Rules** and indicated by **dominance** relations in **tree diagrams**.

constituent in **syntax**, a **category** A is a constituent of another category B just where a continuous set of **branches** can be traced from A to B going consistently 'upward' in the **tree diagram**; the inverse of **dominance**.

constituent structure	the core set of relations in **syntax**, **generated** by **Phrase-Structure Rules** and represented equivalently by **labelled bracketings** or **tree diagrams**.
conventional	the **arbitrary** relation between sound and meaning for the vast majority of words and **morphemes** in all languages.
conventional implicature	in Gricean **pragmatics**, the case of **implicature** where the implicature is conventionalised, perhaps as a lexical property of a given word or **morpheme**, e.g. *but* is logically synonymous with *and* but carries a conventional implicature of contrast.
Co-operative Principle	in Gricean **pragmatics**, the general principle that speakers and hearers interact rationally in order to communicate effectively; the conversational maxims (Quality, Quantity, Manner and Relevance) are cases of this principle.
covert prestige	in **sociolinguistics**, the form of prestige which arises from (sometimes conscious) use of **low prestige** forms, particularly prevalent among lower middle-class and upper working-class males.
denotation	a general term for the semantic value of a term (a **category**, word or **phrase**).
derivation	in **phonology**, a series of ordered **rules** leading from the **underlying form** to something close to the observed

phoneme sequence, in **morphology**, the process of adding **suffixes** which change a word's **category**.

design feature of
language

a seemingly fundamental aspect of language which distinguishes language from many other aspects of cognition; **duality of patterning** and discrete infinity are good candidates.

determiner

a functional category (D), which modifies or quantifies over the rest of the noun phrase it is part of; **definite** and **indefinite articles** and many **quantifiers** are examples.

direct object

a noun phrase which typically marks the 'undergoer' of an action described by a verb, and forms part of the verb phrase with the verb, e.g. *the pizza* in *Mary [VP ate the pizza].*

distinctive features

in **phonology**, the system of features which allows **phonemes** to be broken down into smaller units reflecting **natural classes; phonological rules** are formulated using distinctive features.

dominance

in **syntax**, the inverse of **constituency**: a **category** A dominates another category B just where a continuous set of **branches** can be traced from A to B going consistently 'downward' in the **tree diagram**

duality of patterning

a possible **design feature of language**: the fact that language seems to involve two distinct combinatorial systems, one combining meaningless **phonemes** to make meaningful **morphemes**, and another one combining **morphemes**, words and **phrases** to make a potentially unbounded number of higher-order units (notably sentences), whose meaning can be compositionally computed from the way in which the **constituent** elements combine.

E-language   language seen as external to the individual, in contrast to **I-language**, **competence** and **performance**.

entity   in **type theory**, one of the two fundamental logical types, typically denoted by proper names, e.g. *Clover*.

equivalence   in **logic**, a **connective** linking two **propositions** such that the resulting proposition is true just where the connected propositions are either both true or both false; also known as a biconditional; standardly written '↔'; read as 'if and only if', written 'iff'.

exclusive disjunction   in **logic**, the kind of disjunction which is true where only one of the disjuncts is true, false otherwise, roughly corresponds to ordinary English 'either . . . or', standardly written ⊕.

existential quantifier   in **predicate logic**, one of the two canonical **quantifiers**, written '∃'; the meaning of '∃x' roughly corresponds to 'for some x'.

expressive aphasia   another term for **Broca's aphasia** or agrammatic aphasia. Not preferred as there is evidence that typical Broca's aphasics have comprehension difficulties in addition to their production difficulties.

felicity conditions   in **speech-act** theory, the conditions for the successful execution of a **performative**, so that it has the desired **illocutionary force** and **perlocutionary effects**.

First Germanic Sound Shift   the series of systematic changes in the Germanic **consonants** which demonstrates the regular relationship between the Germanic languages and **Proto Indo-European**, also known as **Grimm's Law**.

free morpheme   a **morpheme** which is capable of standing alone, as opposed to a **bound morpheme**.

free variation   in **phonology**, when more than one **allophone** of a given **phoneme** alternates with another with no conditioning, in opposition to **complementary distribution**, or when two **phonemes** freely vary in given context with no contrast (as in the two possible pronunciations of the first vowel of *economics*).

fricative   an **obstruent consonant** which is not a **stop**, involving approximation of articulators in the **vocal tract** such that turbulence is produced, but without complete blockage.

generalised conversational implicature   in Gricean **pragmatics**, the case of **implicature** where the implicature is not fully conventionalised but is nonetheless quite commonly used, in opposition to particular conversational implicatures, which are *ad hoc* in nature; like the other kinds of implicature, they are computed using the conversational maxims in combination with **Theory of Mind** under the **Co-operative Principle**.

generate   in **syntax**, the operation of building **constituent structure** by means of **Phrase-Structure Rules**.

genitive   one of the **case forms** found in Latin, Sanskrit and of any other languages. It roughly translates as 'of' and so typically marks possession among other things.

glottal stop   the sound produced by closing the vocal cords and then releasing them, causing a rush of higher-pressure air from the lungs; IPA [?], found in many (particularly British) English pronunciations of intervocalic <t>.

Grimm's Law   the series of systematic changes in the Germanic **consonants** which demonstrate the regular relationship between the Germanic languages and **Proto Indo-European**, also known as the **First Germanic Sound Shift**.

hard palate   corresponds roughly to what is colloquially known as the 'roof the mouth', the area from the **alveolar ridge** to the **soft palate** or **velum**; **consonants** pronounced with the tongue raised towards the hard palate are palatalised.

head   in both **morphology** and **syntax**, the most important element of a complex

high

historical linguistics

I-language

illocutionary force

immediate constituent

category, the one responsible for determining the category of the complex, e.g. the noun in a noun phrase, the verb in a verb phrase, etc. in **phonetics**, a **vowel** pronounced with the body of the tongue raised towards either the **hard** or the **soft palate**, the main high vowels in English being /iː, ɪ, uː, ʊ/; in **phonology**, a **distinctive feature** whose positive value characterises the high vowels as well as **consonants** whose articulation involves raising the tongue in the manner just described: /ŋ, w, r, j, k, g/ in English.

the study of how languages change over time.

language seen as internal to the individual, a cognitive capacity, in contrast to **E-language**; **competence** is close to synonymous with I-language, and **performance** involves the interaction of I-language with other cognitive capacities.

in **speech-act** theory, the aspect of a **performative** which leads to an illocutionary act.

in **syntax**, a **category** A is an immediate constituent of another category B just where a continuous set of **branches** can be traced from A to B going 'upward' in the **tree diagram**, and there is no category C such that A is a constituent of C and B is not a constituent of C; the inverse of immediate dominance.

imperfect   a set of **tense** forms found in various
                                 languages (notably Latin and the
                                 Romance languages) which indicates
                                 ongoing action in the past, roughly
                                 translating 'Mary was verbing/Mary
                                 used to verb'.

implication   in **logic**, a **connective** linking two
                                 propositions p and q such that the
                                 resulting proposition is false just
                                 where p is true and q is false and true
                                 otherwise; standardly written '$\rightarrow$';
                                 read as 'if p then q'.

implicational   in **language typology**, a relation
universal   between two potentially variant
                                 features of a language p and q such
                                 that where p holds q must hold, but
                                 not necessarily vice-versa.

implicature   the core concept in Gricean
                                 pragmatics: one utterance may
                                 implicate another where one
                                 interlocutor is able to infer, using the
                                 Co-operative Principle and **Theory
                                 of Mind**, that the other interlocutor
                                 intended q by uttering p under the
                                 relevant conversational conditions;
                                 there are three types of implicature:
                                 **conventional implicature,
                                 generalised conversational
                                 implicature** and (particular)
                                 conversational implicature.

inclusive disjunction   in **logic**, a **connective** linking two
                                 propositions p and q such that the
                                 resulting proposition is true where
                                 either or both of p and q are true and
                                 false otherwise; standardly written 'v';
                                 read as 'p and/or q', to be

distinguished from **exclusive disjunction**.

indefinite article   a **determiner** whose meaning corresponds roughly to the **existential quantifier**, e.g. English *a(n)*.

infinitive   the canonical non-finite form of the verb in many languages, including English, where it is almost always preceded by *to*, as in *To sing is fun*.

inflection   one way of forming complex words, which involves adding a **bound morpheme** to a **root** without changing its category, but indicating grammatical information, such as **tense** on verbs and **case** on nouns.

interdental   a place of articulation of **fricatives**, involving placing the **blade** of the tongue either in between the upper and lower teeth or behind the upper teeth; English has the **voiced** and **voiceless** interdental fricatives written with **IPA** [ð] and [θ] respectively.

International Phonetic Alphabet (IPA)   the standard system of phonetic and phonemic transcription, endorsed by the International Phonetics Association.

isogloss   an imaginary line drawn on a map, separating areas which are linguistically distinct in some way.

labelled brackets   in **syntax**, one of the standard ways of indicating **constituent structure**, along with **tree diagrams** (which are equivalent).

labio-dental   a place of articulation of **fricatives**, involving placing the lower lip behind

the upper teeth; English has the
voiced and **voiceless** interdental
fricatives written with IPA [v] and [f]
respectively.

language types   groups of languages which share
some salient structural property
or properties, in principle
independently of any historical
relationship among them;
implicational universals can be used
to define language types.

language typology   the study and establishment of
language types and other similarities
and differences among the languages
of the world; may involve simply
cataloguing what is found where.

lateral   a class of **sonorant** formed by
blocking the central flow of the **air
stream** (in English, at the **alveolar
ridge**) and lowering the sides of the
tongue so that the air passes out that
way; English has the one lateral,
IPA [l].

lexicon   the mental dictionary, the repository
of at least all idiosyncratic
information (including the **arbitrary**
sound-meaning relation and the
morphosyntactic **category**) of the
morphemes of a competent speaker's
native language.

liquid   a class of **sonorants** including **laterals**
and **rhotics**; English has /l/ and /r/.

locutionary act   in **speech-act** theory, the actual
spoken sentence or utterance,
which carries **illocutionary
force**.

logic	the study of the laws of valid inference, relevant for **semantics** since sound inferences are truth-preserving, and truth provides a way to elucidate meaning in **truth-conditional** semantics.
logical form	the formal aspects of a sentence that are important for understanding how that sentence conveys a **proposition** with particular logical properties; **propositional logic** and **predicate logic** provide different ways of presenting aspects of logical form in coherent and well-understood notations.
long vowel	a **vowel** pronounced with extra duration; in English, a long vowel may constitute a stressed **syllable** on its own (as in *I*, pronounced /aɪ/), but a short vowel may not (there is no stressed syllable consisting only of /ɪ/).
low	in **phonetics**, a **vowel** pronounced with the tongue low in the mouth, in or close to its at-rest position, e.g. English /æ, ɑː ɔː ɒ/; in **phonology**, a distinctive feature whose positive value distinguishes low vowels from all others.
low prestige	in **sociolinguistics**, a form which lacks **social value**, except in terms of **covert prestige**.
minimal pair	the principal way of identifying distinct phonemes, as in English *pit* vs *bit* which show that /p/ and /b/ are distinct phonemes.

mood   a type of verbal **inflection** found in
                       many languages (e.g. Latin and the
                       Romance languages) which indicates
                       whether the action described by the
                       verb is assumed to really take place,
                       or whether there is some doubt about
                       this; the chief moods in European
                       languages are the **indicative** and the
                       subjunctive; in English mood is
                       indicated by **auxiliaries** rather than
                       by verbal inflection.

morpheme   the minimal unit of meaning in
                       language; morphemes may be smaller
                       than words (as in *bake* + *(e)r*), or a word
                       may be a single morpheme (as in *bake*);
                       morphemes may be **free** or **bound**.

morphology   the study of the internal structure of
                       words.

nasal   in **phonetics**, the class of sounds
                       whose articulation involves lowering
                       the **velum** so that the **air stream** can
                       pass out through the **nasal cavity**,
                       while there is a blockage to the air
                       stream in the oral cavity, the nasal
                       consonants of English are /m, n, ŋ/; in
                       phonology, the **distinctive feature**
                       whose positive value distinguishes
                       /m, n, ŋ/ from all the other English
                       phonemes.

nasal cavity   the part of the **vocal tract** through
                       which the **air stream** passes when the
                       velum is lowered, giving rise to a
                       nasal consonant if there is blockage
                       in the oral cavity, and a nasalised
                       vowel if the air stream is also allowed
                       to pass through the oral cavity.

natural class	in **phonology**, a class of sounds or **phonemes** described by a set of distinctive features, e.g. voiced phonemes (described by [+voice]) or nasals (described by [+nas]).
negation	in **logic**, a **constant** applying to a single **proposition** so as to change its **truth value** from true to false or from false to true, standardly written '¬', read as 'not'; in **morphology** and **syntax**, a **morpheme** or word expressing something approximating to logical negation, e.g. the English word *not* or the prefix *un-*, as in *unlawful*.
negative concord	the phenomenon, found in French and many other languages, whereby the co-occurrence of two negative morphemes in a sentence does not give rise to logical double negation ($\neg\neg p = p$), but rather either an intensified negation, or just normal negation; found in many varieties of non-standard English, and illogically stigmatised.
node	in **syntax**, a position in a **tree diagram** from which either at least one **branch** emanates 'downwards' (a **non-terminal node**), or a site of lexical insertion (a **terminal node**).
nominative	one of the **case forms** found in Latin, Sanskrit and many other languages. It typically marks the **subject** of a verb.
non-rhotic	a variety of English in which <r> is not pronounced after a **vowel** in the same **syllable**, hence *car* is

non-terminal node

pronounced /kɑː/. Standard British English, as well as Australian and New Zealand English, are non-rhotic. in **syntax**, a **node** in a **tree diagram** from which at least one branch emanates 'downwards', and hence which **dominates** at least one other **node**.

nucleus

the central, most 'sonorous' part of a **syllable**; in many languages, only **vowels** can be nuclei, but in English nasals and liquids can be (as in one pronunciation of *button* as /bʌtn/).

number

the inflectional category which distinguishes singular from plural, marked on nouns in many languages, and on verbs in quite a few (in English only in the present **tense**); some languages, e.g. Mandarin, have no obligatory number marking (either on nouns or verbs); others have a dual in addition to singular and plural, marking two of something, in this case, plural means 'three or more'.

obstruent

a **natural class** of **consonants** defined as involving audible turbulence in the **vocal tract**, i.e. the **stops** and **fricatives**; defined by **distinctive feature** [-son].

organs of speech

the organs of the oral cavity (tongue, lips, teeth, **velum**), pharynx and larynx which contribute to the articulation of the sounds of speech (also known as the **speech organs** or **vocal tract**).

overt prestige	positive **social value** associated with a **sociolinguistic variable**.
performance	putting **competence** into practice in production and comprehension, involves competence combined with short-term memory, attention and other non-linguistic cognitive capacities.
performative	an utterance which performs a **speech act**, opposed to a constative, which has a **truth value**.
perlocutionary effect	the result of a successful **performative**, whose **illocutionary force** has this effect.
person	the inflectional category which distinguishes among first, second and third, marked on pronouns in very many languages, and on verbs in many languages (in English only in the third person of the present **tense**).
phoneme	the basic contrastive unit of **phonology**; phonemic distinctions are established by the principle of contrast among **minimal pairs**.
phonetics	the study of the sounds of speech; there are three main branches: articulatory phonetics is the study of how the **organs of speech** produce those sounds, acoustic phonetics deals with the physical aspects of the perturbations to the ambient air caused by the articulatory movements of the **organs of speech**, and perceptual phonetics deals with how those sounds are perceived and processed in the ear and the brain.

phonology	the branch of linguistics dealing with how speech sounds are organised in linguistic systems.
phonological rule	a **rule**, standardly formulated using **distinctive features**, which applies during a **derivation** describing systematic changes in the realisation of the **underlying forms** of phonemes and other phonological material.
phrase	in **syntax**, a unit of organisation of **morphemes** and words, intermediate between the word/morpheme level (indicated by **terminal nodes**) and the sentence, indicated by **non-terminal nodes**.
Phrase-Structure Rules	the **rules** which **generate constituent structure**, whose output is indicated equivalently by **tree diagrams** or **labelled brackets**.
place of articulation	for **consonants**, the position where an obstruction to the **air stream** of some kind takes place; for **vowels**, the area(s) in the vowel space to which the body of the tongue moves during articulation.
plosive	the **natural class** of **obstruents** whose articulation involves total blockage of the **air stream** at some **place of articulation**; in **distinctive-feature** terms, plosives are characterised as [-cont], also known as **stops**.
post-alveolar	a **place of articulation** just behind that of the standard **alveolar consonants**; in **distinctive features**, this **natural class** is characterised as [+cor, -ant]; the English post-alveolar

	fricatives are /ʃ/ (voiceless) and /ʒ/ (**voiced**).
pragmatics	the branch of linguistics which deals with how interlocutors manage to convey more than what is actually said in typical interactions; the key concept is speaker meaning as opposed to **sentence meaning**.
predicate	in **predicate logic**, the class of constants associated with **arguments**, typically corresponding to adjective or verb phrases in **syntax** (although they may correspond to nouns too), standardly written in capitals, with the arguments in lowercase in parentheses following them.
predicate logic	the branch of **logic** which breaks **propositions** down into **predicates** and **arguments**; a key aspect of predicate logic is its ability to represent **quantification**.
prestige form	a linguistic form with positive **social value**.
proposition	a semantic representation of a sentence, usually in **logical form**, which bears a **truth value**.
propositional logic	the branch of **logic** dealing with logical relations among **propositions**, the key relations being realised by the **connectives**.
Proto Indo-European	a **proto-language** at the origin of almost all of the languages of Modern Europe and many of those of South-West Asia and Northern India.
protolanguage	a hypothesised language at the origin of a given language family, whose

existence is established by **comparative reconstruction**.

psycholinguistics   the branch of linguistics dealing with questions common to linguistics and psychology, primarily language acquisition and learning, language disorders and language processing/ comprehension.

quantification   in **predicate logic**, a mode of representation expressions of generality which are not predicated of individuals, which involves a relation between a **quantifier** and a **variable** functioning as the **argument** of a **predicate** inside the immediately following parenthesis; one of the principal advantages of predicate logic.

quantifier   in **predicate logic**, involved in the representation of expressions of generality which are not predicated of individuals: a quantifier binds a **variable** functioning as the **argument** of a **predicate** inside the immediately following parenthesis; there are two quantifiers, the **existential quantifier** and the **universal quantifier**; in **syntax** quantifiers are often **determiners**.

recursion   the property of **Phrase-Structure Rules** that allows them to apply to their own output and thereby create an unbounded number of well-formed sentences, underlies discrete infinity, which may be a **design feature of language**.

reference in **semantics**, the relation between a word, especially a noun or noun phrase, and the thing(s) it names; intuitively, one of the core aspects of meaning, along with **sense**.

relative clause a complex modifier of a noun or noun phrase which contains a disguised sentence, as in *The woman* [RelativeClause *who I met yesterday*]; since relative clauses contain sentences, and occur inside noun phrases inside sentences, this can be seen as one instance of **recursion**, illustrated by the nursery rhyme *The House that Jack Built*.

rhotic (i) a general term for a subclass of **liquids** involving 'r-like' articulation; (ii) a variety of English in which <r> is pronounced after a **vowel** in the same **syllable**, hence *car* is pronounced /kɑr/. Standard American English as well as most varieties of Scottish and Irish English are rhotic.

rhoticity the property of a variety of English as being **rhotic** or **non-rhotic**; rhoticity has **social value** in many parts of the English-speaking world, being an **overt prestige** form in New York, for example, but a **low prestige** form in many parts of England.

root in a complex word consisting of (in English) a potentially **free morpheme**, to which **derivational** and/or **inflectional suffixes** are added, the potentially free morpheme is the root, e.g. *bake* in *bake+r+s*.

rounded vowel   a **vowel** pronounced with the lips
                           rounded, or pursed; in English the
                           rounded vowels are /u: ʊ, ɔ:, ɒ/, all
                           rounded vowels are **back** vowels in
                           English.

rule   in **phonology**, the ordered sequence
                           of operations expressed using
                           distinctive features, which
                           constitutes the **phonological
                           derivation**; in **syntax**, an operation
                           which builds (or possibly permutes)
                           constituent structure.

scalar implicature   in Gricean **pragmatics**, an
                           implicature which involves always
                           giving the 'strongest' statement
                           compatible with the situation to be
                           described, e.g. if I have two children,
                           although the statement *I have one
                           child* is true, it carries the **scalar
                           implicature** that I have exactly one
                           child, which is false.

schwa   an **unrounded**, mid, central vowel
                           found in many unstressed syllables in
                           English (e.g. in the first syllable of
                           about), IPA [ə].

semantics   the study of meaning, particularly
                           sentence meaning.

semi-vowel   a sound which is phonetically a
                           vowel, in that it does not involve
                           obstruction of the **air stream** passing
                           through the **vocal tract**, but
                           phonologically a **consonant**, in that
                           it never appears in the **syllable
                           nucleus**; English is normally
                           described as having two semi-vowels,
                           /j/ and /w/.

sense	the aspect of the meaning of an expression that, intuitively, makes it mean what it means, that gives it the power of **reference** to whatever it refers to; expressions referring to non-existent entities may have sense but no reference, e.g. *unicorn*.
sentence meaning	the meaning of a sentence; following **compositional semantics**, the meaning of a sentence is computed from the meanings (or **denotations**) of its parts; sentence meaning can be expressed in terms of the **truth conditions** borne by the **proposition** the sentence expresses; contrasts with speaker meaning.
short vowel	a vowel which is not long; in English short vowels cannot form **syllables** on their own, but must be accompanied by preceding and following **consonants** known technically as an onset and a coda; the English short vowels are /ɪ, ɛ, æ, ɒ, ʊ, ə, ʌ/.
sign languages	languages transmitted through the visual-gestural rather than the oral-aural medium, mostly used by deaf communities; sign languages are now known to be languages in every sense of the word, having all the salient structural properties (and **design features**) of oral-aural languages.
social value	the property of a sociolinguistic variable of having high or **low prestige**.
sociolinguistics	the branch of linguistics dealing with questions common to linguistics and sociology, primarily the social

stratification of speech, language and gender, etc.

soft palate also known as the **velum**, the region of the 'roof of the mouth' behind the **hard palate**; raising the soft palate allows air to pass through the **nasal cavity**, giving rise to **nasal** or nasalised sounds; **consonants** articulated in this region are velars; English has two velar **stops**, /k/ and /g/.

sonorant a sound articulated without audible turbulence in the **air stream**; includes **vowels** and non-**obstruent consonants**, in English /m, n, ŋ, l, r, j, w, h/; defined by the **distinctive feature** [+son].

sound change a **phonetic** or **phonological** change taking place over time; on the basis of **Grimm's Law** and Verner's Law, sound change is usually thought to be regular, i.e. without exceptions.

speech act a **performative** act, with associated **illocutionary force** and **perlocutionary effects**.

speech organs the organs of the oral cavity (tongue, lips, teeth, **velum**), pharynx and larynx which contribute to the articulation of the sounds of speech (also known as the **organs of speech** or **vocal tract**).

stop consonant the **natural class** of **obstruents** whose articulation involves total blockage of the **air stream** at some **place of articulation**; in **distinctive-feature** terms, stops are characterised as [-cont], also known as **plosives**.

structure dependency	the property of certain kinds of syntactic rules (e.g. **auxiliary** inversion in English) such that they appear sensitive to the **constituent structure** of sentences, possibly a **design feature of language**.
subject	a noun phrase which typically marks the **agent** of an action described by a verb phrase, e.g. *Mary* in *Mary ate the pizza*.
subjunctive	a **mood** usually marked on verbs, signifying that the action described is not necessarily assumed to actually take place, that there is some doubt as to the reality of the action.
suffix	a **bound morpheme** (**inflectional** or **derivational**) attached to a **root** to form complex word.
syllable	a phonological unit consisting of at least a **nucleus**, usually a **vowel**, possibly flanked a sequences of **consonants** and/or **semi-vowels**; the sequence preceding the vowel is the onset, and that following the vowel is the coda; the vowel and the coda are sometimes said to form a unit known as the rime.
syntactic rules	rules that **generate constituent structure**, typically **Phrase-Structure Rules**; there are also rules that permute parts of constituent structure, e.g. **auxiliary** inversion.
syntax	the study of the structure of sentences.
synthetic compound	a **compound** formed by combining one or more **roots** and a **bound**

morpheme (usually **derivational**) as in *truck+drive+r*.

tense a type of verbal **inflection** found in many languages, including English, which indicates in the basic cases the time of the action described by the verb in relation to the time the sentence containing the verb is used; the main tenses in English and many other languages are present (or non-past) and past; other languages, e.g. Latin and the Romance languages, have a richer system of tenses including the future (in English the future is indicated by **auxiliaries** rather than by verbal inflection).

terminal node in **syntax**, a **node** in a **tree diagram** which **dominates** no other **node**; the site of lexical insertion.

Theory of Mind our intuitive theory of the contents of other people's minds, i.e. what their thoughts, beliefs and desires may be; crucial for the **Co-operative Principle** and other aspects of Gricean **pragmatics**.

tone phonemic tone distinguishes words and morphemes by the pitch with which they are pronounced; the best-known tone language is Mandarin, but there are many others in East Asia, Africa and the Americas.

tree diagram in **syntax**, one of the standard ways of indicating **constituent structure**, along with **labelled brackets** (which are equivalent).

truth conditions the standard way of understanding **sentence meaning**; the central idea is that to know the meaning of a (declarative) sentence is to understand what the world would have to be like for the sentence to be true; may run into problems with non-declarative sentences.

truth-conditional semantics the approach to **semantics** based on the idea that to know the meaning of a (declarative) sentence is to understand what the world would have to be like in order for the sentence to be true.

truth-functional a feature of the **connectives** of standard **propositional logic** and **predicate logic**; truth-functional connectives work in such a way that the truth of the complex **proposition** formed by combining two propositions can be directly computed as a function of the truth of the two constituent propositions.

truth table a way of presenting the workings of a given **truth-functional connective**, showing the precise effects of combining the constituent **propositions** using that connective.

truth value true or false, according to whether a **proposition** corresponds to the way world is (true) or not (false); in **type theory**, one of the two fundamental logical **types**, typically denoted by sentences.

type theory in **compositional semantics**, a way of assigning **denotations** to, in principle, any syntactic **category**; there are two basic types: **entity** <e> and **truth value** <t>, which may combine to form more complex types, such as <e, t> for **predicate**.

underlying form   the starting point of a **phonological derivation**, in which the 'real' forms of **morphemes** (i.e. those which are entered in the **lexicon**) appear, which may then be modified by the operation of the **phonological rules**.

Universal Grammar   the set of invariant syntactic forms, **categories** and **rules** which may be common to all languages and form part of what the child brings to first-language acquisition, given the argument from the poverty of the stimulus.

universal quantifier   in **predicate logic**, one of the two canonical **quantifiers**, written '∀'; the meaning of '∀x' roughly corresponds to 'for all/every x'.

unrounded vowel   a **vowel** pronounced with the lips unrounded, or spread; in English the unrounded vowels are /iː, ɛ, æ, ɑː ʌ, ɜː ə/, no unrounded vowel is **back** in English.

variable   in **predicate logic**, an **argument** of a **predicate** bound by a **quantifier**.

velum   also known as the **soft palate**, the region of the 'roof of the mouth' behind the **hard palate**; raising the soft palate allows air to pass through the **nasal cavity**, giving rise to **nasal** or nasalised sounds; **consonants** articulated in this region are velars; English has two velar **stops**, /k/ and /g/.

vocal folds   two pieces of cartilage inside the larynx which are kept apart in normal breathing to allow the air to pass through to and from the lungs; may be drawn together so as to close the glottis, release gives rise to the **glottal stop**; if drawn closely enough together so as to vibrate in the **air stream**, the effect is to produce **voicing**; other positions of the vocal folds may give rise to whisper and to creaky voice.

vocal tract   the organs of the oral cavity (tongue, lips, teeth, **velum**), pharynx and larynx which contribute to the articulation of the sounds of speech (also known as the **organs of speech** or **speech organs**).

voiced   in **phonetics**, a sound with the property of **voicing**; in **phonology**, a **phoneme** with the **distinctive feature** [+voice].

voicing   the result of drawing the **vocal folds** closely enough together so as to vibrate in the **air stream**.

vowels   in **phonetics**, sounds produced without obstruction or blockage of the **air stream** passing through the **vocal tract**; in **phonology**, **phonemes** which can only appear in a **syllable nucleus**.

Wernicke's aphasia   also known as receptive aphasia, one of the two main kinds of **aphasia**, characterised by poor comprehension, fluent but somewhat incoherent speech with many content words paraphrased in rather confused fashion, speech is spontaneous but not always controlled or understood by the speaker; involves damage to **Wernicke's area**.

Wernicke's area   a region of the brain in the posterior part of the superior temporal gyrus in the left hemisphere; damage to this area leads to **Wernicke's aphasia**.

Index

AAVE. *See* African American Vernacular English
accents, 49–50, 139–42, 186–7
  social class and, 143–4
accusative, 58, 187
affricates, 15–16, 187
African American Vernacular English (AAVE), 149–50
agent, 67, 187
air flow, modulation of, 7
air stream, 7, 13–14, 187–8
allomorph, 53, 188
allomorphy, conditioned, 53, 55–6, 192
allophones, 29, 188
  conditioned allophony, 28–31
  language and organisation of, 30
  of phoneme, 28–30
alveolar
  nasal, 14
  post-, 10, 208
  ridge, 8–9, 188
  stops, 13
American English, 18, 23–4, 142
anterior, 37–8
aphasia, 151–5, 188. *See also* Broca's aphasia; Wernicke's aphasia
arbitrary, 82, 188–9
arguments, 92, 189
aspiration, 28, 189
assimilation, 38–9, 189
Austin, J.L., 105–6
auxiliaries, 69–70, 189

back, 17–18, 33, 35, 189–90
bilabial, 13–14, 190
bilabial stops, 12–13
blade, tongue, 10, 190
bleeding order, 42–3
bound morpheme, 49, 190–1
brain damage, 151–5
  in Broca's aphasia, 154
  in Wernicke's aphasia, 154
branches, 72–3, 190
branching nodes, 72–3, 190
British English, 18, 23–4, 139–42
  RP, 142–3
Broca's aphasia (expressive aphasia), 152–4, 188, 190, 196–7
Broca's area, 154–5, 190

case, 191
  forms, 58, 187, 191
  markings, 57–60
categories, 191. *See also* functional categories; lexical categories
  PS-rules and, 77
  syntax, 66–70
  universal, 177
centring diphthongs, 21–4, 191
children, first-language acquisition, 155–67
Chomsky, Noam, 64–5
  argument from poverty of stimulus, 164–5
  competence and performance distinction, 156–7

221

Chomsky, Noam (cont.)
    I-language/E-language distinction,
        156
    on innate ideas, 165–7
    substantive universals, 176–8
    Universal Grammar, 167–8
comparative reconstruction, 133–7,
        191
    of inflectional morphology, 136
    Old English case paradigm, 136
    Proto Indo-European, 134–5
    of syntax, 136–7
    Uralic languages, 135
    verbal morphology, 136
competence, 63–4, 192
    I-language, 157, 164–5
    performance and, 156–7
complementary distribution, 28–30
complementisers, 77–8
complex words, 49–52
compositional semantics, 97–103, 192
compounds, 46–7, 49–51, 192
    meaning and, 50
    order and, 49
    stress or accent pattern and,
        49–50
    synthetic, 50–1, 215–16
concepts, 83
conditioned allomorphy, 53, 55–6, 192
conditioned allophony, 28–31
conjugations, 56–7, 192–3
conjunction, 88–9, 95–6
connectives, 88, 193
consonantal, 36–7
consonants, 7–16, 187–8, 193. *See also*
        stop consonants
    affricates, 15, 187
    fricatives, 9–11
    liquids, 15–16
    nasal, 13–14, 33
    natural classes of, 32–4

non-obstruent, 32, 36–7
phonemes, 32
syllable and, 24
vowels compared with, 16
constative sentences, 106
constituency, 73–7, 193
constituent, 65, 193
    immediate, 73–4, 199
constituent structure, 70–4, 194
    dominance and, 73
    labelled brackets for representing,
        71–2
    PS-rules and, 74
    tree diagrams, 72–4
continuant, 37–8
conventional, 82, 194
    implicature, 111, 194
conversational implicature, 111–13
    generalised, 111–13, 197–8
Cooperative Principle, 109–11, 194
correspondence, 120–6
    borrowing and, 121
    English-Latin, 127–8
    Latin-Greek-Sanskrit, 125
    parent languages and, 122–4
    patterning and, 120–1
    Proto Germanic, 126–8
    of Romance languages, 123–4
    systematic sound, 121–4
covert prestige, 144–6, 194

definite articles, 69, 194
denotations, 98–9, 194
derivation, 41–3, 51–2, 194
Descartes, René, 163–4
design feature of language, 44, 195
determiner, 72, 195
diphthongs, 21–4
    centring, 21–2, 191
    equilateral plotting of, 22
direct object, 58, 187, 195

disjunction, 89
  exclusive, 89
  inclusive, 89, 200
distinctive features, 34–9, 44, 188, 195
  natural classes and, 34
  of obstruents, 37–8
  of past-tense endings, 38–43
  of semi-vowels, 36–7
  of vowels, 36–7
dominance, 73, 75–7, 195
Dryer, Matthew, 176

Ebonics. *See* African American
  Vernacular English
E-language. *See* External Language
English. *See also* African American
  Vernacular English; American
  English; British English
  accent groups in, 142
  case marking on pronouns in, 57–8
  German and, 121–2
  Latin correspondence with, 127–8
  non-standard, 145–50
  Old, 131–2, 136
entities, 97–102, 196
equivalence, 90–1, 196
exclusive disjunction, 89, 196
existential quantifiers, 94–6, 196
expressive aphasia. *See* Broca's aphasia
External Language (E-language), 156, 196

false propositions, 90
felicity conditions of speech acts, 106–8,
  197
First Germanic Sound Shift, 129–32, 197
first-language acquisition, 155–67
  argument from poverty of stimulus
    and, 164–5
  common-sense view of, 164
  distinguishing mother tongue and,
    157–8

experience and, 166
  first linguistic behaviour in, 158
  first word in, 158–9
  genetics and, 165–7
  I-language competence and, 164–5
  innate ideas and, 164
  longer utterances in, 160
  past-tense inflections and, 160–1
  quantification and, 161
  sentences and, 160
  statistical learning and, 166–7
  two-word stage of, 159
  vocabulary and, 162
formal universals, 176–8
free morpheme, 49, 197
free variation, 31, 188, 197
French, 123–4, 147–8, 173–4
fricatives, 8–11, 16, 187, 197
  English, 11
  interdental, 10, 201
  labio-dental, 9–10, 201–2
  post-alveolar, 10
  velar, 11
  voiceless glottal, 11
  voiceless interdental, 10
  voiceless postalveolar, 10
front vowels, 17–18, 33
functional categories, 69–70

gender, 145–6
generate, 74, 198
genetics, 1–2, 165–7
genitive, 60, 198
gestural-visual channel of language, 5
glottal stop, 9, 13, 198
Greek, 125
Greenberg, Joseph, 169–76
  implicational universals and, 172–6
  language types and, 173–6
  subject, verb, object sentence
    elements, 169–72

Grice, H. Paul, 109–10
Grimm's Law, 129–30, 198
    exceptions to, 132–3
    in Indo-European context, 130–1

hard palate, 17, 188, 198
head, 50, 198–9
high, 36, 199
historical linguistics, 3, 118–38, 199
    asterisk in, 134
    comparative reconstruction, 133–7
    correspondence and, 120–6
    evolution of language and, 119
    systematic sound changes and,
        126–33
hypercorrection, 144

I-language. *See* Internal Language
illocutionary act, 106
illocutionary force, 106, 199
imperfect tense, 55, 200
implication, 90, 200
implicational universals, 172–6, 200
implicature, 109–15, 200. *See also*
        conversational implicature
    conventional, 111, 194
    conversational, 111–13
    Cooperative Principle and, 109–11
    reasoning and, 109–10
    scalar, 113–15
    of utterances, 115–16
inclusive disjunction, 89, 200
indefinite articles, 69, 201
indicative, 56–7
infinitive, 56–7, 201
inflection, 52–62, 201
    first-language acquisition and
        past-tense, 160–1
    in Italian, 54–7
    in Latin, 58–60
    in Mandarin, 60–2

morphemes, 52–3
    noun, 57–8
    past-tense, 52–3, 160–1
    plural ending, 53–4
inflectional morphology, 52–62, 136
innate ideas, 164, 179–80
    genetics and, 165–7
    language structure, 165–6
interdental fricatives, 10, 201
Internal Language (I-language), 156–7,
    164–5, 199
International Phonetic Alphabet (IPA),
    201
    consonants, 8–16
    phonemes in, 28
    vowels, 16–25
interrogatives, 108
IPA. *See* International Phonetic
    Alphabet
isogloss, 141–2, 201
Italian
    correspondence in Romance
        languages, 123–4
    inflection in, 54–7
    moods, 56–7
    other tenses in, 55–6
    present-tense in, 54–5

Japanese, 174–5

labelled brackets, 71–2, 201
labio-dental fricatives, 9–10, 201–2
Labov, William, 143–5, 149–50
language. *See also specific languages and
        topics*
    biological capacity for, 1–2
    building, 169–80
    definition of, 155–6
    endangerment, 138
    evolution of, 119
    extinction of, 138

knowledge and, 1–2
types, 173–6, 202
larynx, 7, 9
lateral, 15, 202
Latin, 59–60, 122–3
  case markings on nouns in,
    58–60
  correspondences of, 123–5, 127–8
  Old English and, 131–2
  Proto West Germanic and, 124–6
  Romance languages and, 123–4
lax vowel, 19–20
lexical categories, 66–7
lexicon, 64, 186–7, 202
liquids, 15–16, 202
locutionary act, 106
logic, 203. *See also* predicate logic;
    propositional logic
  semantics and, 86–97
  truth and, 86–7
logical form, 87, 203
logical inferences, 86–7
logical scales, 113–14
long vowels, 17–20, 203
low, 36, 203
low prestige, 143, 203

Mandarin, inflection in, 60–2
Maxim of Manner, 110
Maxim of Quality, 110
Maxim of Quantity, 112–13
meaning, 81, 105. *See also* sentence
    meaning
  arbitrary nature of, 82
  compounds and, 50
  conventional, 82
  noise and, 6
  reference and, 83–4
  sense and, 84
  sounds and, 45–6
  speaker, 105

truth and, 81–7
  understanding, 82–3
metaphors, 110
minimal pair, 27–8, 31, 203
monosyllabic words, 24
mood, 189, 204
morphemes, 2–3, 188, 204
  bound, 49, 190–1
  free, 49, 197
morphology, 2–3, 45–62, 186–7, 204
  compounds and, 49–51
  derivation and, 51–2
  duality of patterning and, 47–9
  functional categories and, 69
  inflectional, 52–62, 136
  lexical categories and, 67
  sociolinguistic variation in, 146–7
  verbal, comparative reconstruction,
    136

nasal, 35, 204
nasal cavity, 13–14, 204
nasals, 13–16, 33
  alveolar, 14
  bilabial, 13–14
  velar, 14
natural classes, 27, 32–4, 205
  distinctive features and, 34
  generalisations about, 43
negation, 88, 95–6, 205
  expression of, in language, 147–8
  in non-standard English,
    145–50
negative concord, 148–50, 205
nodes, 72–3, 205
nominative, 58, 205
non-obstruent consonants, 32, 36–7
non-rhotic, 148, 205–6
non-standard English, 145–50
non-terminal node, 72–3, 206
noun phrases, 68, 71

nouns
  case markings on, in Latin, 58–60
  case of, 57
  inflection of, 57–8
  modifiers, 71
  plural markings on, 61–2
Noun-Verb distinction, 176–7
nucleus, 35, 206
number, 54–5, 206

object, 169–72
  direct, 58, 187, 195
obstruents, 16, 37–8, 206
Old English, 131–2, 136
oral/aural channel, of language, 5
OV languages, 137
overt prestige, 144–6, 207

palatalised phoneme, 30–1
parent languages, 122–4
past-tense
  inflection, 52–3, 160–1
  verb endings, 38–43
patterning, 120–1
  duality of, 47–9, 195–6
patterns, 169
performance, 63–4, 156–7, 207
performative, 106, 207
perlocutionary effect, 106–8, 207
person, 54–5, 207
phoneme, 27–30, 34, 188, 207
  allophone of, 28–30
  consonant, 32
  duality of patterning and, 47–8
  free variation of, 31
  IPA representation of, 28
  minimal pairs and isolating, 27–8, 31
  natural classes, 27, 32–4
  organisation of, 30
  palatised, 30–1
  sounds compared with, 28–9

velarised, 30–1
vowel, 32
phonetics, 2–3, 6–26, 8, 187–8, 207
  consonants, 8–16
  phonology compared with, 27
  vowels, 16–25
phonological rules, 27, 44, 208, 212
  Rule One, 39–43
  Rule Two, 40–3
phonology, 2–3, 27–44, 208
  distinctive features and, 34–9
  phonetics compared with, 27
phrases, 65, 208
  noun, 68, 71
  verb, 68, 71
phrase-structure rules (PS-rules), 74–80,
  208
  complementisers and, 77–8
  constituency and, 75–7
  dominance and, 75–7
  infinite number of sentences
    generated by, 78–80
  recursion and, 79–80
Pinker, Steven, 65
place of articulation, 8–9, 208
Plato, 162–3
plosives, 12–13, 208
plural ending inflection, 53–4
plural markings, on nouns,
  61–2
post-alveolar, 10, 208
postpositions, 172–3
pragmatics, 3, 105–17, 209
  implicatures, 109–15
  speech acts, 105–9
predicate, 92, 209
predicate logic, 92–7, 189,
  209
  quantification and, 92–3
  quantifiers, 94–6
prepositions, 60, 172–3

prestige, 143
    covert, 144–6, 194
    low, 143, 203
    overt, 144–6, 207
pronouns, 57–8
pronunciation, 17, 143
proposition, 87, 90, 115–16, 209
propositional logic, 87–92, 209
    connectives and, 88
    limits of, 91–2
Proto West Germanic, 122–3
    Latin and, 124–6
    Proto Indo European and, 125–6,
        128–9
Proto Germanic
    correspondences, 126–8
    English and, 121–2
Proto Indo European, 125–6, 209
    comparative reconstruction, 134–5
    Grimm's Law and, 130–1
    numerals, 130
    Proto West Germanic and, 125–6,
        128–9
    word order in, 137
proto-language, 133–4, 209
p-sounds, 28–30
PS-rules. *See* phrase-structure rules
psycholinguistics, 3–4, 151–68, 210
    aphasia, 151–5
    first-language acquisition, 155–67
    I-language and, 156

quantification, 93, 210
    first-language acquisition and, 161
    predicate logic and, 92–3
    scalar implicature and, 114–15
quantifiers, 92–6, 210
    compositional semantics and, 102–3
    existential, 94–6, 196
    universal, 96, 218
questions, 108

racial prejudice, 149–50
reasoning, implicature and, 109–10
Received Pronunciation (RP), 142–3
recursion, 79–80, 210
reference, 83–6, 211
relative clauses, 71, 211
rhotic, 143, 211
rhoticity, 143–5, 211
Romance languages, correspondences of,
    123–4
root, 48, 211
round, 35
rounded vowels, 17–18, 33, 212
RP. *See* Received Pronunciation
rule, 212. *See also* phonological rules;
    phrase-structure rules

Sanskrit, 125, 132–3
scalar implicature, 113–15
schwa, 20, 212
Second Germanic Sound Shift,
    129–30
semantics, 2–3, 81–104, 212
    compositional, 97–103, 192
    definition of, 82
    logic and, 86–97
    meaning and truth in, 81–6
    pragmatics and, 3
    truth-conditional, 85, 217
semi-vowels, 24–5, 32, 36–7, 212
sense, 84–6, 213
sentence meaning, 84–6, 105, 213
    reference and, 85–6
    truth and, 85–6
sentences
    constative, 106
    first-language acquisition and, 160
    performative, 106
    proposition, utterance and, 115–16
    PS-rules generating infinite number
        of, 78–80

sentences (cont.)
  subject, verb, object elements of,
    169–72
  unlimited possibilities of, 64–5
short vowels, 19–20, 213
  lax, 19–20
  schwa, 20
  tense, 19–20
sign, 5
Sign Languages, 2–3, 213
social class, 145–7
social stratification of speech, 142–5
social value, 143, 213
sociolinguistics, 3–4, 139–50, 213
  accents, 139–42
  morphology and, 146–7
  negation in non-standard English
    and, 145–50
  social stratification of speech and,
    142–5
Socrates, 163
soft palate, 11, 214. *See also* velum
sonorant, 16, 36–7, 214
sound laws, 131
  Grimm's Law, 129, 132–3
  Verner's Law, 132–3
sounds, 2–3. *See also* systematic sound
    changes, 133, 145, 214
  meaning and, 45–6
  p-, 28–30
  phonemes compared with, 28–9
  systematic sound changes, 126–33
Spanish, correspondence in Romance
    languages, 123–4
spectrogram, stop consonants,
    11–12
speech acts, 105–9, 214
  felicity conditions of, 106–8, 197
  indirect, 112–13
  performatives and, 106
  perlocutionary effects of, 106–8

speech communities, 82
speech organs, 6–9, 206, 214
spelling, pronunciation compared with,
    17
statistical learning, 166–7
stop consonants, 11–16, 187, 189,
    214
  alveolar, 13
  bilateral, 12–13
  glottal, 9, 13
  spectrogram, 11–12
  velar, 13
stresses, 49–50, 132–3
structure, 44, 165–6. *See also* constituent
    structure; phrase-structure rules
  dependency, 177–8, 215
  syntactic, 99–100
  of words, 52
subject, 58, 67, 187, 215
  in sentences, 169–72
subjunctive, 56–7, 215
substantive universals, 176–8
suffix, 47–8, 215
syllabic, 35
syllable, 24, 35, 215
syntactic rules, 65, 74–80, 215
syntactic structure, 99–100
syntax, 2–3, 63–80, 186–7, 215
  Broca's aphasia and, 152–3
  categories, 66–70
  comparative reconstruction of,
    136–7
  constituent structure and,
    70–4
  functional categories, 69–70
  lexical categories, 66–7
synthetic compounds, 50–1,
    215–16
systematic sound
  changes, 126–33
  correspondence, 121–4

tense, 19–20, 189, 216. *See also specific tenses*
terminal node, 72–3, 216
Theory of Mind, 110–11, 216
tones, 60–1, 186–7, 216
tongue, 17–18, 20
    blade, 10, 190
tree diagrams, 72–4, 216
Trudgill, Peter, 145–6
truth, 86
    logic and, 86–7
    meaning and, 87
    sentence meaning and, 85–6
truth conditions, 85, 217
truth tables, 88, 217
truth values, 97–102, 217
truth-conditional semantics, 85, 217
truth-functional, 88, 217
truth-functional connectives, 88
    conjunction, 88–9
    disjunction, 89
    equivalence, 90–1
    implication, 90
    negation, 88
type theory, 97–102, 217–18
typology, language, 3–4, 169–80, 202

underlying form, 41–2, 218
universal categories, 177
Universal Grammar, 167–8, 218
    subject, object, verb sentence elements and, 171
    word order and, 179
universal quantifiers, 96, 218
universal statements, 114
universals, 169–80
    controversy about, 179–80
    formal, 176–8
    implicational, 172–6, 200
    substantive, 176–8
    word order and, 177–8

unrounded vowels, 17–18, 33, 218
unsaid, 105
Uralic languages, 135
utterance, 115–16, 160

variables, 94, 100, 218
velar fricatives, 11
velar nasal, 14
velar stops, 13
velarised phoneme, 30–1
velum, 11, 189–90, 218–19
verb, 169–72, 176–7
    phrases, 68, 71
Verner, Karl, 132–3
Verner's Law, 132–3
VO languages, 137
vocabulary, first-language acquisition and, 162
vocal folds, 9, 219
vocal tract, 7, 17, 219
voice, 35, 39–40
voiced, 219
    post-alveolar fricatives, 10
    velar fricatives, 11
voiceless
    glottal fricative, 11
    interdental fricatives, 10, 219
    obstruent, 189
    post-alveolar fricatives, 10
    velar fricatives, 11
voicing, 8–9, 189, 219
    assimilation, 38–9, 189
    vocal folds and, 9
"vowel triangle," 20
vowels, 7, 16–25, 187–8, 219
    consonants compared with, 16
    diphthongs, 21–4
    distinctive features of, 36–7
    long, 17–20, 203
    natural classes of, 32–4
    oral, 17

vowels (cont.)
  phonemes, 32
  semi-, 24–5, 32, 36–7, 212
  short, 19–20
  syllable and, 24

Welsh, 175
Wernicke's aphasia, 153–4, 188, 219–20
Wernicke's area, 154–5, 220
Whitehead, Alfred North, 162–3

word order, 137, 176
  in Indo-European languages, 137
  Universal Grammar and, 179
  universals and, 177–8
words, 45–62. *See also* complex words
  English, 46
  in first-language acquisition, 158–9
  monosyllabic, 24
  patterns and, 47
  structure of, 52

Printed in Great Britain
by Amazon

67328352R00138